Rhetorical Studies of National Political Debates

PRAEGER SERIES IN POLITICAL COMMUNICATION

Robert E. Denton, Jr., General Editor

Playing the Game: The Presidential Rhetoric of Ronald Reagan
Mary E. Stuckey

Rhetorical Studies of National Political Debates: 1960–1988
Edited by Robert V. Friedenberg

Political Communication in America: Second Edition
Robert E. Denton, Jr., and Gary C. Woodward

Television Access and Political Power: The Networks, the Presidency, and the "Loyal Opposition"
Joe S. Foote

Listening for a President: A Citizen's Campaign Methodology
Ruth M. Gonchar Brennan and Dan F. Hahn

Attack Politics: Strategy and Defense
Michael Pfau and Henry C. Kenski

Presidential Press Conferences: A Critical Approach
Carolyn Smith

Rhetorical Studies of National Political Debates

1960-1988

Edited by
Robert V. Friedenberg

Praeger Series in Political Communication

New York
Westport, Connecticut
London

Library of Congress Cataloging-in-Publication Data

Rhetorical studies of national political debates, 1960–1988 / edited
by Robert V. Friedenberg.
p. cm.—(Praeger series in political communication)
Includes bibliographical references.
ISBN 0–275–93226–5 (alk. paper)
1. Campaign debates—United States—History—20th century.
2. Communication in politics—United States—History—20th century.
3. United States—Politics and government—1945– 4. Presidents—United States—Election. 5. Rhetoric—Political aspects—United States—History—20th century. I. Friedenberg, Robert V.
II. Series.
E839.5.R46 1990
808.53'0973'09045—dc20 89–36696

Library of Congress Catalog Card Number: 89–36696
ISBN: 0–275–93226–5

First published in 1990

Praeger Publishers, One Madison Avenue, New York, NY 10010
An imprint of Greenwood Publishing Group, Inc.

Printed in the United States of America

The paper used in this book complies with the
Permanent Paper Standard issued by the National
Information Standards Organization (Z39.48–1984).

10 9 8 7 6 5 4 3 2 1

Contents

Series Foreword

Robert E. Denton, Jr.

Those of us from the discipline of communication studies have long believed that communication is prior to all other fields of inquiry. In several other forums I have argued that the essence of politics is "talk" or human interaction.[1] Such interaction may be formal or informal, verbal or nonverbal, public or private, but always persuasive forcing us consciously or subconsciously to interpret, to evaluate and to act. Communication is the vehicle for human action.

From this perspective, it is not surprising that Aristotle recognized the natural kinship of politics and communication in his writings on *Politics* and *Rhetoric*. In the former, he establishes that humans are "political beings" who "alone of the animals is furnished with the faculty of language."[2] And in the latter, he begins his systematic analysis of discourse by proclaiming that "rhetorical study, in its strict sense, is concerned with the modes of persuasion."[3] Thus, it was recognized over fifteen hundred years ago that politics and communication go hand in hand because they are essential parts of human nature.

Back in 1981, Dan Nimmo and Keith Sanders proclaimed that political communication was an emerging field.[4] Although its origin, as noted, dates back centuries, a "self-consciously cross-disciplinary" focus began in the late 1950s. Thousands of books and articles later, colleges and universities offer a variety of graduate and undergraduate coursework in the area in such diverse departments as communication, mass communication, journalism, political science, and sociology.[5] In Nimmo and Sanders' early assessment, the "key areas of inquiry" included rhetorical analysis, propaganda analysis, attitude change studies, voting studies, government and the news media, functional and systems analyses, technological changes, media technologies, campaign techniques, and research techniques.[6] In a survey of the state of the field in 1983 by the same authors and Lynda Kaid, they found additional, more specific areas of concerns such as the presidency, political polls, public opinion, debates, and advertising, to name a few.[7] Since the first study, they also noted a shift away from the rather strict behavioral approach.

Then as now, the field of political communication continues to emerge. There is no precise definition, method, or disciplinary home of the area of inquiry. Its domain, quite simply is the role, processes, and effects of communication within the context of politics.

In 1985, the editors of *Political Communication Yearbook: 1984* noted that "more things are happening in the study, teaching, and practice of political communication than can be captured within the space limitations of the relatively few publications available."[8] In addition, they argued that the backgrounds of "those involved in the field [are] so varied and plurist in outlook and approach, . . . it [is] a mistake to adhere slavishly to any set format in shaping the content."[9]

In agreement with this assessment of the area, Praeger established the series entitled "Praeger Series in Political Communication." The series is open to all qualitative and quantitative methodologies as well as contemporary and historical studies. The key to characterizing the studies in the series is the focus on communication variables or activities within a political context or dimension.

This volume on presidential debate brings together the thoughts and ideas of eleven outstanding scholars of political communication and debate. It provides a systematic analysis of the eight national political debates held between 1960 and 1988. Because contemporary presidential debate has become an institutionalized part of our campaign, the time is ripe for a new and broader investigation of its role and impact in the electoral process. Each analysis addresses the factors motivating the candidate to debate, the goals of each candidate in debating, the rhetorical strategies utilized by each candidate, and the impact of the debate. Such an approach not only increases our understanding of each debate, but also helps identify trends and patterns in the debates across time.

This book makes an important contribution to the literature on presidential debates. Unlike other treatments, the microanalyses reveal the strategic development and use of debate by challengers and incumbents. Debates are more than just campaign spectacles but complex, calculated political events with significant consequences. There are numerous image and issue goals; predebate, debate, and postdebate strategies; and an ever-evolving pattern of public perceptions and expectations as to their form, structure, and content. Presidential debates are not only part of our political history, they have also become part of the political process. This book investigates both dimensions.

I am, without shame or modesty, a fan of the series. The joy of serving as its editor is in participating in the dialogue of the field of political communication and in reading the contributors' work. I invite you to join me.

NOTES

1. See Robert E. Denton, Jr., *The Symbolic Dimensions of the American Presidency* (Prospect Heights, Ill.: Waveland Press, 1982); Robert E. Denton, Jr., and Gary Woodward, *Political Communication in America* (New York: Praeger, 1985); Robert E. Denton, Jr., and Dan Hahn, *Presidential Communication* (New York: Praeger, 1986); and Robert E. Denton, Jr., *The Primetime Presidency of Ronald Reagan* (New York: Praeger, 1988).
2. Aristotle, *The Politics of Aristotle*, trans. Ernest Barker (New York: Oxford University Press, 1970), p. 5.
3. Aristotle, *Rhetoric*, trans. Rhys Roberts (New York: The Modern Library, 1954), p. 22.
4. Dan Nimmo and Keith Sanders, "Introduction: The Emergence of Political Communication as a Field," in *Handbook of Political Communication*, ed. Dan Nimmo and Keith Sanders (Beverly Hills, Calif.: Sage, 1981), pp. 11–36.
5. Ibid., p. 15.
6. Ibid., pp. 17–27.
7. Keith Sanders, Lynda Kaid, and Dan Nimmo, eds., *Political Communication Yearbook: 1984* (Carbondale, Ill.: Southern Illinois University: 1985), pp. 283–308.
8. Ibid., p. xiv.
9. Ibid.

Introduction

Robert V. Friedenberg

Sixteen of the most widely seen and heard speakers in the history of mankind all have one thing in common. They were all seen and heard while engaged in national political debates as they sought the two highest offices Americans can bestow upon their countrymen. This book focuses on those individuals and the rhetorical centerpieces of their respective campaigns, their political campaign debates.

From ancient Greece and Rome to the present, free societies have relied upon the vigorous clash of ideas in an open and free marketplace of ideas as a means of decision making. American society reflects that clash of ideas at virtually every key point in its history. America was born in the clash between Whig and Tory primarily from 1763–1776. A sick nation was nurtured to health in the clash of the Constitutional Convention of 1787. Repeatedly, the clash of ideas has characterized American decision making. Most often, those clashes have taken place either in legislative proceedings or in political campaigns.

This book focuses on the eight national political debates which have been held in this country. Political debates, face-to-face confrontations between two candidates, were non-existent in national political elections prior to 1960, though they were relatively common in campaigns for lesser offices. Rather, most of the clash found in national political campaigns was in the form of a single or series of speeches by one candidate which generated a response from a second candidate. Often, that response generated yet another response from the first candidate and the clash continued. But, the candidates might be miles apart and the speeches separated in time by days or weeks. Audiences might have a sense of the flow of ideas, but it was often difficult to compare the candidates and their positions closely. Additionally, prior to 1960 surrogate debates were also an occasional feature of national campaigns. But surrogates are not the candidates themselves and such debates often generated little attention and did little to facilitate candidate comparisons.

In 1960 the decisions of Senator John F. Kennedy and Vice President Richard M. Nixon to participate in a series of joint appearances, combined with the growth of the still young television industry, enabled Kennedy and Nixon to be observed simultaneously by vast audiences while debating the issues of the day. Though one might question whether these appearances were in fact debates, none could question that the face of contemporary American political campaigning would never be the same.

Although it took sixteen years for two more presidential candidates to agree to debate, joint appearances similar to the Kennedy–Nixon debates were frequently utilized in races for lesser offices. By 1976, when Governor Jimmy Carter and President Gerald Ford decided to debate, it was natural that their vice presidential candidates, Senators Walter Mondale and Robert Dole, also debated.

In the thirty years since Kennedy and Nixon stood before the American public, political debates, at the national level, have become virtually institutionalized. When Kennedy and Nixon chose to debate, they in fact chose to debate. By 1988, the pressures to debate imposed by a society expecting the principle candidates for the highest offices in the nation to clash in a debate or quasi-debate format were so great that, as the chapters in this volume illustrate, the decision to debate was no longer altogether in the hands of the candidates themselves.

It was this awareness of the growing institutionalization of national political debates that gave rise to this volume. While each individual debate treated in these pages has been subject to extensive study heretofore, it has been difficult to compare the eight national political debates held between 1960–1988. This volume brings together the work of ten scholars with strong interests in political communication and debate. Each was asked to focus on (1) the factors motivating the candidates to debate, (2) the goals of each candidate in debating, (3) the rhetorical strategies utilized by each candidate, and (4) the effects of the debate.

By allowing skilled rhetorical critics to focus on similar aspects of each of the eight national political debates held since 1960, this volume should serve two purposes. First, it should add to our understanding of each of these eight debates. Second, trends and patterns in national political campaign debates might become evident. The ninth chapter represents the editor's attempt to synthesize the findings evident in each of the eight individual debate studies, fulfilling this second purpose of the volume.

At the conclusion of the final 1960 debate, moderator Quincy Howe of ABC News observed that "as members of a new political generation, Vice President Nixon and Senator Kennedy have used new means of communication to pioneer a new type of political debate. The character and courage with which these two men have spoken sets a high standard for generations to come. Surely they have set a new precedent. Perhaps they have established a new tradition."[1] Today we know that they did indeed establish a new tradition. To the extent that this volume contributes to a better understanding of that tradition, it will have served a valuable function.

NOTE

1. *The Joint Appearances of Senator John F. Kennedy and Vice President Richard M. Nixon: Presidential Campaign of 1960* (Washington, D.C.: Government Printing Office, 1961), p. 278.

Rhetorical Studies of National Political Debates

Chapter 1

The 1960 Kennedy–Nixon Presidential Debates

Theodore Otto Windt, Jr.

They were called the "Great Debates," although they were neither "great" nor "debates."[1] "They" were the four televised joint appearances of presidential candidates John F. Kennedy and Richard M. Nixon before different panels of journalists during the course of the 1960 presidential campaign. But Robert W. Sarnoff of NBC dubbed them the great debates, and the name stuck.

The exact role and importance the 1960 debates played in the election of John Kennedy are subject to dispute. However, the belief that without the debates Kennedy could not have won is firmly established. In an election that was decided by only 0.2 percent of the popular vote (a margin of about 112,000 out of almost 69 million votes cast), every major event in the campaign was significant. And the debates between Kennedy and Nixon, especially the first debate, were crucial. Theodore H. White, the wisest observer of that election, remarked: "When [the debates] began, Nixon was generally viewed as being the probable winner of the election contest and Kennedy as fighting an uphill battle; when they were over, the positions of the two contestants were reversed."[2] Gallup Poll data support that conclusion. Going into the first debate, Gallup reported Nixon with a 47 to 46 percent lead in the polls. But after that debate, Kennedy took a lead of 49 to 46 percent.[3] Little wonder that President–elect Kennedy noted on November 12, after the election, that: "It was TV more than anything else that turned the tide."[4]

But even more important than influencing the outcome of the election, the 1960 debates established both the precedent and format for subsequent debates. Although the presidential candidates in 1964, 1968, and 1972 did not debate, other debates on state and local levels became commonplace. And in 1976 President Ford's decision to debate Jimmy Carter set the precedent for an incumbent engaging in debates, a precedent that both Presidents Carter and Reagan observed. Also, the format for such debates was created through the 1960 experience. From then on, the structure of debates would feature a panel of journalists questioning candidates. Therefore, in this study, it seems appropriate to begin with a discussion of how the debates came about, both from the standpoint of the networks that televised them and from the standpoint of the candidates who participated.

THE DECISION TO HAVE PRESIDENTIAL DEBATES

The genesis for the debates originated in a most unlikely person: Lar "America First" Daly. Daly, who had the eccentric habit of campaigning in a red-white-and-blue Uncle Sam uniform, was a perennial candidate for one office or another. In his 1959 campaign for mayor of Chicago, he filed a complaint with the Federal Communications Commission (FCC) because certain television stations had denied him equal time after showing film clips of other candidates. He filed his complaint under Section 315(a), the equal time provision, of the Communications Act of 1934. The FCC ruled in Daly's favor on February 19, 1959. The ruling was potentially devastating, as Nicholas Zapple noted: "This ruling had a crippling effect on broadcast journalism. It required a broadcaster who devoted one minute to a legally qualified candidate participating in any program—whether it be a discussion of atomic energy or the need for adequate defense, a ribbon-cutting for a new road or bridge, or the opening of a charity drive—to make available a minute of time to every other legally qualified candidate for the same office."[5] Congress acted quickly to amend Section 315 to exempt news programs and documentaries from the equal time provision.

In 1960 Congress opened hearings on whether television stations and networks should be required to make free time available to qualified presidential candidates. At the suggestion of CBS President Frank Stanton, who testified in these hearings, Congress voted to suspend Section 315 temporarily for this purpose and thus set the stage of the Kennedy–Nixon debates.

In the spring and early summer of 1960, NBC and CBS offered to set aside time for joint appearances by the two candidates as well as to provide additional time on other programs. When the Republican convention nominated Richard Nixon, a week after Kennedy had been officially nominated, General Sarnoff sent a telegram to both candidates inviting them to participate in a series of what he called "great debates." Kennedy accepted immediately, and Nixon followed suit a few days later. In his autobiography, *Six Crises,* Nixon stated "that by this time [after the nomination] the question we had to decide was not whether we should have debates—but rather, how they should be conducted."[6] To this end Nixon laid down certain conditions for the debates in his acceptance telegram: "In general, it is my position that joint television appearances of the presidential candidates should be conducted as a full and free exchange of views without prepared text or notes, and without interruptions."[7]

Kennedy's decision to debate was readily understandable. He was the lesser known of the two candidates. He was behind in the polls after the Republican convention, albeit by only a point or two. And since Nixon was the incumbent vice president, Kennedy as challenger in the campaign had little to lose by debating, and much to gain. Kennedy desperately wanted to debate, whatever the circumstances. As one of his aides commented: "Every time we get those two fellows on the screen side by side . . . we're going to gain and he's going to lose."[8]

Nixon's decision was more complex. A number of advisers urged him not to participate in joint appearances. President Eisenhower was one of the most vocal in his opposition. Eisenhower had "serious doubts" about the value of such debates and thought they were more a test of "reaction time" than a "genuine exposition of the participants' philosophies or programs."[9] Above all, Nixon's advisers argued that in the practical sense there was little to be gained since he was the better known of the two candidates.

But also on the practical side were good reasons to participate. Although he was the better known of the two candidates, he had only a one- or two-point lead coming out of the Republican National Convention. The election would be close, no doubt, and the debates might be crucial to winning. Furthermore, Nixon had made a career out of successful debating experiences and skillful uses of television, not the least of which were his 1946 debates with Jerry Voorhis, his famous "Checkers" speech in 1952, and his "kitchen debate" with Khrushchev in 1959. In addition to these reasons, there were other political considerations. In 1960 46 percent of the American public identified themselves as Democrats while only 27 percent identified themselves as Republicans.[10] A nationally televised debate would allow Nixon to reach out to "weak" identification Democrats and to the extra 25 percent of the electorate who characterized themselves as independent. But above all, according to Nixon, there were potentially negative reactions if he did not agree to the debates: "Had I refused the challenge, I would have opened myself to the charge that I was afraid to defend the Administration's and my own record. Even more important, I would be declining to participate in a program which the majority of the American people . . . wanted to see."[11] Since Thurston Morton, the Republican National Chairman, had stated on a national television program prior to the Republican convention that the Republican nominee would participate in debates under the proper circumstances, Nixon's concern about refusing the challenge was even more poignant. With the prospect of a close election, Nixon could not afford to take this political risk.

Sometime after the convention, Nixon and his advisers made a critical decision. The key question before them was which of the debates would draw the largest audience? Nixon believed it would be the first debate, but a majority of his advisers "thought that the audience would build up because of increased interest in the debates and in the campaign generally."[12] They argued that the final debate would gather the largest audience. Nixon yielded to their advice. That was a serious mistake. The first debate outdrew the final debate by approximately 10 to 15 million viewers. But the Nixon campaign decided the first debate would be less important than the final debate, and they developed their strategy accordingly. Thus, they sought to have the first debate concern itself with domestic issues, not Nixon's strong suit, and have the final debate be on foreign affairs, Nixon's strength. In addition, Nixon's approach to the first debate, which will be discussed later, was conditioned in part by his belief that this debate would not be as important as subsequent ones. To put it simply, at the outset the Nixon campaign itself made just about every mistake imaginable as it prepared for the debates.

During August representatives of the two candidates met with representatives from the television networks to negotiate agreements on the debates. They eventually agreed to four televised joint appearances with a panel of journalists asking questions of the two candidates. Each debate would be one hour long and uninterrupted. The first of the four debates, as mentioned, would be restricted to domestic or internal affairs, the final debate to foreign affairs. In these two debates the candidates would give eight-minute opening statements and three-minute closing statements with questions from the panel sandwiched in between. For the other two programs, the topics were unrestricted, and there would be no opening or closing statements, only questions, answers, and rebuttals. Each journalist on the panel was to ask one question only in turn, and each candidate would be allowed to comment briefly on the answer given by the other candidate.

There were several precedent-setting agreements reached during these negotiations that deserve mention. They especially deserve mention in light of which parties demanded responsibility for these decisions. First, the networks wanted debates, with CBS recommending the Oregon plan that had been used by Harold Stassen and Thomas Dewey in 1948.[13] But representatives of both candidates insisted on a panel that would ask questions. The candidates won on this issue and thereby set a precedent for the format and structure of future debates. They would not be debates in the usual sense of the word at all, but would be joint press conferences. It is important to note that it was the candidates, not the networks, who insisted on this format. It was, in other words, the candidates themselves in this first series of debates who demanded the presence and active participation of journalists in their joint appearances and thus gave legitimacy to the inclusion of the press in this political event.

Consistent with this agreement was the second decision. The candidates wanted only broad topics to be discussed (limited in the first debate to domestic affairs and in the final debate to foreign affairs). They did not, like academic debaters, want to debate specific propositions of policy. They won on this decision also and again set a precedent for future joint appearances by candidates. They would not debate, either in format or form, but would answer questions from journalists about a wide range of topics.

Finally, the networks sought and got control over selection of the panel members. The networks also wanted an outstanding public figure to serve as moderator, but representatives of the candidates rejected this proposal and requested a professional broadcast journalist as moderator. The candidates got the networks to agree to include print and wire service journalists on some of the panels as well as representatives from the broadcast media.

In sum, the 1960 presidential debates were precedent-setting. Never before in American history had the candidates for president met jointly in a public forum to discuss issues facing the country. But in their jockeying and negotiating, they established a structure and format that was to have a more lasting effect than the results of the election. The decision not to debate but to have joint appearances for the purpose of answering questions from journalists had profound ramifications. Not the least of these ramifications was to elevate the press to a position of enormous importance in the political process. By insisting on the presence of journalists and by allowing them to select any questions they might consider important to the future of the country, the candidates conferred a legitimacy upon the press that not even the presidential press conference had previously conferred. No longer would the press see itself merely as reporter or conduit of political news. From this time forward, it would become an active participant (albeit within its own professional and sometimes unprofessional framework) in selecting issues of importance, in asking pertinent and impertinent questions in public of potential presidents and later actual presidents, and in being recognized by these political leaders as legitimate players in the great drama of American politics.

IF NOT DEBATES, WHAT ARE THEY?

Among all the controversies that surround presidential debates, there is one point upon which all seem to agree. They are not debates.

J. Jeffrey Auer called them "counterfeit debates" and presented compelling reasons why they were counterfeit.[14] If they are not debates, one must reasonably ask then why should the standards of academic debating be applied to these joint appearances? If they are not debates, then why judge them by debating standards? Answering such questions provokes a corollary question. If not debating standards, what standards should be used to analyze or to judge political debates? The remainder of this section will be devoted to attempting to answer that question. The standards I propose are based not only on a study of presidential debates, but also on more than ten years of experience in preparing various candidates for debates.

Let us begin by recognizing that the plain purpose of a political campaign for the candidate is to win. Every choice, every event, every activity is aimed at winning the election. Thus, debates are part of the overall strategy developed to help the candidate win the election. Putting debates in this context suggests the first important question to ask when analyzing and evaluating debates: Did they help or hurt candidates in their quest for victory? In certain circumstances, however, such a question may be misleading. In some campaigns debates have had minimal or no impact on the election. For better or for worse, that was not true in 1960. The question requires further elaboration for the purposes of rhetorical analysis.

A presidential contest is decided by the electoral college, that is, by winning 270 electoral college votes. Winning, therefore, requires that candidates target states and constituencies to gain enough votes in those states and among those constituencies to carry the majority in the electoral college. For a rhetorical analysis of presidential debates this targeting process suggests two pertinent questions:

1. Did the statements by candidates in the debates demonstrate they had developed effective rhetorical strategies that targeted such constituencies?
2. Did the statements made by the candidates contain appeals adapted to these constituencies to motivate them to vote for the candidate over the other?

These are central questions for any political debate.

But what about issues? Too often when we think of issues, we think of precise policy statements. Donald Stokes divides issues into two types that are pertinent for our analysis. One type he terms *position issues* that "involve advocacy of governmental action from a set of alternatives" and the other *valence issues* that "involve linking of the parties [or the candidates] with some condition that is positively or negatively valued by the electorate."[15] In other words, issues of governmental policy and issues of political value. To make these more precise, one should amend valence issues to link them more often than not to specific, targeted constituencies rather than to the electorate at large.

These are some of the questions that inform this analysis of the Kennedy–Nixon debates. But it should be remembered that in any presidential campaign the central issue is leadership. All other issues point to that central issue. People vote for a person, not a set of policy statements. Both candidates in 1960 recognized this. The theme for the Nixon–Lodge ticket was "They Understand What Peace Demands." The theme for the Kennedy–Johnson ticket was: "Leadership for the Sixties." With that in mind, let us turn to the two candidates on the eve of the first and most important debate of the four.

THE CANDIDATES

John F. Kennedy

Prior to the first television debate, John F. Kennedy had noticeable political strengths and weaknesses. He was a second term senator from Massachusetts who had gained some national standing when he had made an unsuccessful bid for the vice presidential nomination in 1956. Upon gaining the presidential nomination four years later, he had balanced the ticket by choosing Lyndon Johnson as his running mate. His Democratic party had greater numbers of people identifying themselves with it than did the Republican. Furthermore, he had a lackluster record as a senator that meant he was not identified with specific policies or constituencies.

But the very fact of his lackluster record was also a weakness. Many people did not know where he stood on some of the central issues of the time, such as civil rights, meeting the communist challenge, and the economy. For this reason (as well as the fact that he was a Catholic), many traditional Democrats—including most conspicuously southern whites and northern blacks—looked upon his candidacy with less than usual enthusiasm. In some cases, such as that of the Rev. Martin Luther King, Sr., it meant opposition to him and support for his opponent.[16]

Compounding this problem was the fact that he seemed very young, inexperienced, and even immature. He was forty-three years old, but looked younger. In contrast to his opponent, he had spent his entire political career in the legislative branch of government, and was not known for having had experience in foreign affairs. As early as 1958 Cabell Phillips had written that "Maturing . . . —that vague hallmark of virtue which a prospective president is required to exhibit—is not conspicuous among Kennedy's gifts."[17] Add to this list that he was not known for any forensic or oratorical skills. His reputation rested more on his gifts as a writer of a Pulitzer Prize winning book, *Profiles in Courage*.

With these problems, he was not expected to do well in the debates against the "experienced" and "mature" Richard Nixon.

In light of these political prospects, Kennedy decided to run hard all the way, taking nothing for granted. His strategy included concentrating his efforts in the nine large industrial states of the Northeast, using Johnson in the South, and hoping to pick up a few states in the Midwest. This strategy was developed to revive the old FDR coalition of union members, northern blacks, southern whites, the poor, and liberals. The debates would provide a platform for making appeals to all these groups as well as for beginning to establish his credentials as a candidate equal in knowledge and maturity to Nixon.[18] More important, since a variety of Democrats still viewed him with suspicion, his first order of business would be to unite the Democratic party behind the Kennedy–Johnson ticket. Thus, he would emphasize throughout the debate that he was leading the Democratic party, remind Democrats of their heritage, and persistently identify Nixon as a Republican.

Richard M. Nixon

Richard Nixon had served three full terms as a congressman, two years as senator from California, and eight years as vice president under the popular Eisenhower. During that tenure he had traveled throughout the world meeting foreign leaders, trips that had established his reputation for experience in foreign policy. Throughout the campaign he would make references to these meetings and emphasize his international experience.

But his claim to superior experience because he was vice president was seriously damaged at a mid-August press conference that Eisenhower held. Asked to provide an example of an idea of Nixon's that he had adopted, Eisenhower answered: "If you give me a week, I might think of one. I don't remember."[19] For the next month Nixon had to spend precious time attempting to explain that remark, which seemed to undermine his theme of experience.

Above all, there was the "political assassin" image of Nixon that had been created and sustained over the years. That image was summed up in the poster with Nixon's picture and asking the question "Would you buy a used car from this man?"

According to White, Nixon divided his campaign into three separate periods. The first phase would be low keyed and intended to "erase the image of pugnacity first."[20] This period extended into early October, that is until after the first debate, and may account in part for Nixon's subdued approach to that debate. The second phase would be to step up the partisan attack on Kennedy, and the final phase during the last three weeks of the campaign would be one in which he "let Kennedy have it."[21] That then was the rhetorical framework for the campaign, a framework within which the debates would be fitted.

PREPARATION FOR THE FIRST DEBATE

John F. Kennedy

Kennedy arrived in Chicago, early on Sunday, September 25, the day before the first debate. He spent the next day, except for a brief campaign speech, closeted with his aides pouring over potential questions and appropriate answers. They brought with them a Sears Roebuck foot locker filled with political research that they had boiled down into fifteen pages covering twelve or thirteen domestic topics. All morning long Kennedy's aids quizzed him, helped refine answers, and worked with him on his opening statement. Undoubtedly, one of the most important things they did was have Kennedy respond orally to questions. It has been my experience in preparing people for debates that they rarely have a sense of how long they have spoken or of the point they are making within a specific answer unless they practice orally. It is one thing to think through an answer. It is an entirely different process to put those answers into spoken language. In preparing as he did, Kennedy prepared himself well.

After an afternoon nap and a "splendid" dinner, Kennedy went to the television studio, inspected the set, decided to change from a white to a blue shirt, and retired to the room provided for him to wait for the debate to begin.

Richard M. Nixon

Nixon also arrived on Sunday, but late at night. The next morning he made a campaign speech before the same audience—the United Brotherhood of Carpenters and Joiners—that Kennedy had addressed. He spent the remainder of the day in his hotel room with only Mrs. Nixon as company. He poured over material that had been prepared for him by his staff, but he did so in political solitude and presumably without rehearsing orally. He had a long distance call from Lodge who reportedly advised him to erase the "assassin" image.[22] Nixon hardly needed that advice since his campaign strategists had already decided that was the principal objective in this first phase of the campaign. There are no reports that he rested or napped during the day, but instead spent it cramming for the evening's event.

During the ten-minute drive to the television studio, he seemed to pay little attention to the briefing his television aide, Ted Rogers, prepared for him. Instead, he remained within himself and immersed in his own thoughts. At the studio, he inspected the set and let himself be tested for the cameras. He made one request. He asked the producer not to put him on camera if he was wiping sweat from his face. After refusing make-up, he retired to his waiting room where a light coating of Lazy Shave, a pancake make-up, was applied to his heavy beard.

A few minutes before 9 P.M. the candidates took their places at lecterns provided for the occasion.

THE FIRST DEBATE: SEPTEMBER 26, 1960

John F. Kennedy's Opening Statement

Kennedy's opening statement reflected the classic stance of a challenger: he attacked. As the first speaker, he had the enviable opportunity to set the tone, tempo, and agenda. He did. The overall theme was that government was not doing enough to "maintain our independence" and start the country moving again.[23] This was consistent with his campaign theme of leadership for the 1960s and the theme of his speeches, to get this country moving again. He used four distinct strategies not only to support these themes, but to achieve larger campaign objectives.

First, Kennedy opened by linking the discussion of domestic issues to foreign affairs, the latter area being the one where his candidacy was most vulnerable in contrast to Nixon's. "In the election of 1860, Abraham Lincoln said the question was whether this Nation could exist half slave or half free. In the election of 1960, and with the world around us, the question is whether the world will exist half slave or half free, whether it will move in the direction of freedom, in the direction of the road that we are taking or whether it will move in the direction of slavery."

Thus, Kennedy raised the stakes at the very outset of his statement. It would not merely be a discussion of federal aid to this group or that or of the level of price supports for farmers. Nothing less than the survival of the American society hung in the balance. He continued to frame the debate in these terms: "If we do well here, if we meet our obligations, if we are moving ahead, then I think freedom will be secure around the world. If we fail, then freedom fails. Therefore, I think the question before the American people is: Are we doing as much as we can do?" And, of course, Kennedy announced that he did not believe government was doing enough.

This opening gambit was an adroit move to face a weakness at the outset and to emphasize his concern in this critical area. Furthermore, by increasing the importance of the discussion to world-wide dimensions, he appeared to be offering a longer and wider vision of the problems confronting the country.

The second strategy was to set the domestic agenda and make direct appeals to constituent groups. These Kennedy achieved primarily through a series of parallelisms that expressed his dissatisfaction with the current state of American domestic affairs.

For union members (especially steel workers in the critical state of Pennsylvania): "I'm not satisfied to have 50 percent of our steel mill capacity unused. I'm not satisfied when the United States had last year the lowest rate of economic growth of any major industrialized society in the world. . . ."

For the poor: "I'm not satisfied, when we have over $9 billion worth of food, some of it rotting though there is a hungry world and even though 4 million Americans wait every month for a food package . . . which averages 5 cents a day per individual."

For educators: "I'm not satisfied when many of our teachers are inadequately paid or when our children go to school part-time shifts."

For anti-union, right-to-work southern constituencies: "I'm not satisfied when I see men like Jimmy Hoffa, in charge of the largest union in the United States, still free."

By far the longest appeal was to black voters, a sure indication of the weak support he felt in that community:

I'm not satisfied until every American enjoys his full constitutional rights. If a Negro baby is born, and this is true also of Puerto Ricans and Mexicans in some of our cities, he has about one-half as much chance to get through high school as a white baby. He has one-third as much chance to get through college as a white student. He has about a third as much chance to be a professional man, and about half as much chance to own a house. He has about four times as much chance that he'll be out of work in his life as the white baby. I think we can do better.

The revealing part of this section was that Kennedy stressed enforcing the constitutional rights of black people rather than calling for legislation to redress grievances. It was revealing because that was exactly Kennedy's approach to the problem for the first two years of his administration: a legal approach rather than a legislative approach.[24]

These were direct appeals to constituent members of the old Democratic coalition calling for them to consider the frustrations and unfulfilled hopes of their lives.

The third strategy was a rebuttal strategy intended to defuse Republican charges of "big government" and to allay general fears of government intrusion into state or private affairs. Kennedy clearly stated the Republican criticism by saying, "there are those who say that we want to turn everything over to the [federal] Government."

He answered this charge in three ways. First, he flatly denied that it was true. To substantiate this statement, he divided political responsibilities among individuals, states, and the federal government and insisted that he was only concerned with federal responsibilities. Second, he noted that there were some things that individuals could not do for themselves, such as develop the Tennessee Valley or sustain themselves in their elderly years, but could do collectively through national programs, such as the Tennessee Valley Authority and social security. Third, he insisted he wanted effective government meeting its national responsibilities, not big government for big government's sake. And he linked government meeting these responsibilities at home to meeting its responsibilities in the world: "We cannot turn the job over to anyone else. If the United States fails, then the whole cause of freedom fails, and I think it depends in great measure on what we do here in this country."

The final strategy pervaded the opening statement. Inherent in most of what Kennedy said was the clarion call for vigorous presidential leadership. At the beginning of his statement he quoted Lincoln, and he concluded by quoting from and drawing on the example of Franklin Roosevelt, both presidents exemplifying such leadership. He stressed leadership by persistently using the personal pronoun "I" in terms of what he was dissatisfied with in America and in terms of what he believed ought to be done. Of course, being a challenger and a Democrat he could stress what he and the federal government should do to meet the domestic challenges he had outlined. But Kennedy went even further by placing such leadership on the world scene: "I want people in Latin America and Africa and Asia to start to look to America to see how we're doing things, to wonder what the President of the United States is doing, and not to look at Khrushchev or look at the Chinese Communists."

Kennedy's opening statement was classic. Obviously, it was well prepared. Kennedy had set the agenda. He presented a list of urgent domestic ills facing the country, each carefully targeted to some part of the Democratic constituency. He magnified the importance of the issues by relating them to international problems. He outlined his rebuttal of Republican criticism of his programs. He stressed the need for presidential leadership and indicated his enthusiasm for accepting that leadership. And he concluded his statement with a return to the theme of his campaign.: "I think it's time America started moving again."

Richard M. Nixon's Opening Statement

Nixon's opening statement revealed two major strategic concerns: (1) erasing the "assassin" image; and (2) refuting Kennedy point by point. I call them "concerns" rather than strategies because I do not believe Nixon had carefully thought through what he would say in his opening statement. Midway in his remarks Nixon even voiced criticism of his own effort by saying "I could give better examples but . . ." Much of what he said was a defensive response to Kennedy's statement.

For the first concern about his partisan image, Nixon opened by stressing where he and Kennedy agreed:

[T]he things that Senator Kennedy has said, many of us can agree with. There is no question but that we cannot discuss our internal affairs in the United States without recognizing that they have a tremendous bearing on our international position. There is no question but that this Nation cannot stand still, because we are in a deadly competition, a competition not only with the men in the Kremlin but the men in Peking. We're ahead in this competition as Senator Kennedy, I think, has implied. But when you're in a race, the only way to stay ahead is to move ahead, and I subscribe completely to the spirit that Senator Kennedy has expressed tonight, the spirit that the United States should move ahead.

The opening sentences were remarkable. Nixon not only agreed with his adversary, he accepted his adversary's theme of moving ahead. There can be no doubt that his reason for adopting this good-willed approach right at the outset was that he wanted to replace the image of Nixon the street-fighting, partisan politician with a loftier image of Nixon the good-willed statesman. His overriding concern about this image pervaded his opening remarks. This was acutely noticeable in the choice of verbs he used to describe Kennedy's attacks upon eight years of Republican governance. Nixon did not say that Kennedy "falsely charged" the Republicans with not solving problems or that he "distorted" the record. Instead, he chose to use milder verbs: "expressed," "suggested," "advocated," and once "charged." Typical of this approach was Nixon's characterization of the differences between the two: "We know the way to progress and I think first of all our own record proves we know the way. . . . Senator Kennedy has suggested that he believes he knows the way. . . . I respect the sincerity with which he makes that suggestion." In comparison with Kennedy's vigorous call for action, these words were tepid, neither softening the street fighter image among his detractors nor arousing enthusiasm among his supporters. The plastic man had become a placid man.

Nixon's second concern was to debate Kennedy point by point. He really seemed to believe he was in a debate with Kennedy, not in a political campaign to win the presidency.

Therefore, like any good debater, he first defined the basis for their conflict: "Where then do we disagree? I think we disagree on the implication of his remarks tonight and on the statements that he has made on many occasions during the campaign to the effect that the United States has been standing still." Nixon proceeded next to rebut Kennedy's charges point by point drawing a comparison between the Truman and Eisenhower administrations.

> Let's take schools. We have built more schools in these last 7 1/2 years than we built in the previous 7 1/2 years, for that matter in the previous 20 years.
> Let's take hydroelectric power. We have developed more hydroelectric power in these 7 1/2 years than we developed in any previous administration in history.
> Let's take hospitals. We find that more have been built in this administration than in the previous administration. The same is true of highways.

Nixon turned to a different rebuttal approach by pointing to how the two administrations' programs effected ordinary citizens:

> We find that the prices you pay went up five times as much in the Truman administration as they did in the Eisenhower administration.
> What is the net result of this?
> This means that the average family income went up 15 percent in the Eisenhower years as against 2 percent in the Truman years.

Near this point Nixon posed what he considered a most important question: "I would suggest that during the course of the evening [Kennedy] might indicate those areas in which his programs are new, where they will mean more progress than we had then." Notice that the question was posed as one important to the debate, not one that was important to the future of the nation.

Once the rebuttal was completed, the debater turned to his counterplan that included only vague promises to help in education ("programs that will expand educational opportunities") and medical care for the elderly (we "will see that our medical care for the aged is much better handled than it is at the present time"). He finished off this brief section by citing how much less ($9 to $14 billion a year) the Republican domestic programs would cost than the Democratic programs.

Nixon's primary charge against Kennedy's proposals was a disapproval of the values implicit in government action to solve current problems. "It isn't a question of which government does the most," claimed Nixon. Rather it's "a question of which administration does the right things, and in our case I do believe that our programs would stimulate the creative energies of 180 million free Americans. I believe the programs that Senator Kennedy advocates would have a tendency to stifle those creative energies." Given that Nixon surely believed that this was an important difference between the two candidates and the policies they advocated, his tippy-toe language ("would have a tendency") seemed unduly mild. This was a point to attack Kennedy's proposals directly, and he did not.

All in all, Nixon's opening statement was a debater's refutation, even

down to the stylistic device so common among debaters, of saying "We find. . . ." In contrast to Kennedy who never mentioned Nixon's name or even the Republicans during the entire course of his opening statement, Nixon referred to Kennedy by name *eleven times* in eight minutes. But it was not a hard-hitting rebuttal of his political opponent. Rather, it was one debater's response to a series of points raised by another debater.

Nixon's two major concerns came together in his closing words:

> The final point that I would like to make is this: Senator Kennedy has suggested in his speeches that we lack compassion for the poor, for the old, and for others that are unfortunate.
>
> Let us understand throughout this campaign that his motives and mine are sincere. I know what it means to be poor. I know what it means to see people who are unemployed.
>
> I know Senator Kennedy feels as deeply about these problems as I do, but our disagreement is not about the goals for America but only about the means to reach those goals.

This conclusion was less than stirring, especially in contrast to Kennedy's vigorous call to get the country moving again. These remarks addressed Nixon's concern about his image and set the stance he would take throughout the debate, but they were sadly inadequate for the challenge. Although Nixon was quite accurate in saying the two candidates did not disagree about goals—in fact, they were in agreement on more than goals—Nixon misjudged what people expected from a debate. Whether realistically or not, the public expected a clash on issues, not on means to achieve agreed-upon goals. The public expected sharp distinctions between the two candidates. As the second speaker, it was Nixon's responsibility to draw these distinctions, but he drew them with a fine-point pen, not a broad brushstroke. Thus the rhetorical stances each candidate would take in the debate had been established, and Kennedy clearly was in control, on the offensive, and off to a better start than expected.

The Question and Answer Period

In the thirty-four minutes devoted to questions, ten were asked. Five of the ten dealt with the issue of presidential leadership, four with policy questions, and one was a "trap" question. The candidates alternated in answering questions, and each had the opportunity to comment on the answers the other gave.

Leadership Questions. Right off the bat Bob Fleming of ABC News hit Kennedy with the Nixon charge that he was naive and immature. Kennedy concisely noted that he and the vice president had come to Congress in the same year and had served a comparable period of 14 years in government. But he went on to contrast the two parties they headed:

> I come out of the Democratic Party which in this century has produced Woodrow Wilson, and Franklin Roosevelt, and Harry Truman and which supported and sustained these programs which I've discussed tonight.
>
> Mr. Nixon comes out of the Republican Party. He was nominated by it, and it is a fact that through most of these last 25 years the Republican leadership has opposed Federal aid for education, medical care for the aged, development of the Tennessee Valley, development of our natural resources.

In stressing party identification, Kennedy sought to unite his party behind him and to remind viewers that Nixon was a Republican, something Nixon usually avoided mentioning in his campaign speeches as he attempted to reach out to independents and southern Democrats.

Nixon's comment on Kennedy's answer was concise, to the point, and incredible: "I have no comment." It was as if Nixon were willing to make these charges on the stump when Kennedy could not respond, but now face to face with Kennedy he lacked the courage—an ostensible prerequisite for presidential leadership—to repeat the charge. Furthermore, "experience" and "maturing" were two themes of the Nixon campaign. Yet, he passed when these were brought up.

Even if Nixon had wanted to avoid a personal attack, he could have responded by attacking the record of the Democratic party. Kennedy had opened the way for that line of argument in his answer, and Nixon had charged in his opening statement that Democratic programs would cost too much and would stifle individual initiative. It was an opportunity to go on the offensive, but he passed on this as well. The effect was nothing less than astonishing.

The second question addressed to the vice president concerned his claim to leadership, specifically what kinds of proposals resulting from his experience as vice president had been adopted. Nixon cited recommendations that he had made after each of his trips abroad, thereby reminding viewers of his highly publicized foreign forays, and his work as chairman of the President's Committee on Price Stability and Economic Growth. It was a straight-forward attempt to answer the question.

Kennedy's comment was as revealing as Nixon's comment on the first question had been. The senator spent the first half of his reply responding to one part of Nixon's opening statement, the comparison between the Truman and Eisenhower administrations. He preferred, Kennedy said, to compare the "overall percentage record of the last 20 years of the Democrats and the 8 years of the Republicans, to show an overall period of growth." He then attacked Nixon's response by saying he was unaware that any of his recommendations had ever come before Congress in the form of legislation.

Kennedy's response revealed his strategy for the debates. When it suited his political purposes, he would answer a question directly; when it did not, he would ignore the question and reply to another point more congenial to his political purposes. Soon, Nixon would pick up on this strategy, and both candidates would apply it over the course of the four encounters.

The third question on leadership was a repetition of the second, only more precisely worded. Sander Vanocur of NBC cited Eisenhower's press conference comment about Nixon's experience ("If you give me a week . . .") and pointedly asked Nixon to clarify it. The question was more important than the answer. It was informative to viewers who had not heard Eisenhower's remark. For those who had heard the remark, they were reminded of the damaging statement. And it once again put Nixon on the defensive.

The final two questions concerned leadership of Congress. Kennedy was asked why he thought he could effectively lead when he and Senator Johnson had been unable to get any significant legislation passed during the August "rump" session, even though the Democrats held majorities in both Houses. Nixon was asked how he could hope to guide legislation through Congress if it were controlled after the election by the Democrats. Both candidates dissembled in answering the exact questions, but assured the panel and viewers that they would be able to lead. Their answers were the only reasonable answers to this kind of question.

On the leadership questions, which comprised half the questions for the entire debate, Kennedy clearly had the advantage. He was precise, direct, and forceful. More important, he elevated the issue beyond mere questions of competence to issues of leadership. This was especially noteworthy in his comment on Nixon's reply to Vanocur's question. Kennedy recounted briskly his record but concluded by saying: "The question really is which candidate and which party can meet the problems that the United States is going to face in the '60's." It was a repetition of his campaign theme and the thrust of his opening statement.

Nixon faltered. He failed to comment on Kennedy's inexperience and immaturity, a damaging failure on his part. The other two major questions were ones that put Nixon on the defensive. Thus, on the vital issue of presidential leadership in this critical debate, Kennedy clearly had the advantage.

Policy Questions. The panel asked four questions dealing with policies, questions about: (1) farm surpluses and price supports; (2) providing domestic programs or reducing the national debt; (3) federal aid to pay teachers' salaries; (4) federal aid for building schools. The policy answers followed what the candidates had been saying on the stump and in position papers. Kennedy advocated greater federal involvement (and in the case of farm policy, greater government control). Nixon advocated shared responsibilities among federal, state, and local governments, although on the farm issue he defended Secretary of Agriculture Ezra Taft Benson's policy of lowering price supports. On federal aid to construct schools, the candidates agreed that there was a federal responsibility but disagreed on its extent.

Kennedy ignored the point of the question about paying for extensive domestic programs by repeating his commitment to the programs and at the same time his commitment to a balanced budget (except in times of national emergency). Kennedy contradicted himself in the two questions on education; first, he called for federal aid to pay teachers' salaries and then denied that the federal government should pay those salaries directly.

Nixon did not press the contradictions in Kennedy's answers. On the question of paying for domestic programs Nixon briefly charged that Kennedy would either have to raise taxes or unbalance the budget. But this charge was placed between his opening sentences that corrected the question by laying blame for cutting the national debt on the Democratic platform and not Kennedy and his closing statement that stressed his agreement with Kennedy about the federal government providing aid for school construction. Nixon ignored the contradiction on teachers' salaries to focus on the possibility that federal aid might result in federal control of what teachers teach. Thus, two opportunities for scoring effective political points were minimized.

The policy statements by the two candidates stressed valence issues more than positions. Kennedy emphasized the value of federal action and intervention in domestic affairs. Nixon generally questioned that value by pointing to the possibility of government control or the need for shared responsibilities among different levels of government. It is difficult to say which candidate "won" these issues in that different segments of the electorate would respond in quite different ways to the proposals depending on how the positions effected them and which values they agreed with.

The "Trap" Question. Charles Warren of Mutual News asked about domestic Communism: "Just how serious a threat to our national security are these Communist subversive activities in the United States today?" This was a trap for each candidate. For Kennedy, it opened the possibility that he might be "soft" on Communists, a charge frequently leveled against Democrats in the past. For Nixon, it opened the possibility that the "Old Nixon" of his Communist-chasing days might explode onto the scene.

Both candidates finessed the question. Kennedy answered first and agreed the domestic threat was serious. But he stated that the country already had laws to protect itself and the Justice Department and FBI to keep the nation alert. His brief answer concluded with his call for maintaining a strong society at home as the best bulwark against subversion.

In the spirit that characterized his strategy during much of the debate, Nixon opened by agreeing "with Senator Kennedy's appraisal generally in this respect." But in a comment that was longer than Kennedy's direct answer, Nixon stressed that America must remain alert and then went on to stress that he was just as "sincere" as Kennedy in his commitment to education and health care for the aged. He concluded by restating what he had said throughout the hour: "The question again is not one of goals. We are for those goals. It's one of means."

Both candidates finessed this question and avoided the traps inherent in it. If they did not gain any points by their answers, they assuredly avoided making a mistake.

Final Summations

The final statements followed the strategies and tones set by the candidates during the debate. Nixon presented a debater's summation of the debate. Kennedy summarized the issues facing the nation.

Nixon began by agreeing "with Senator Kennedy completely" on the need to spur economic growth to remain competitive with the Soviet Union. He then "respectfully" submitted that Kennedy's programs would rely too much on the federal government and would cost too much. These conditions would inhibit economic growth, Nixon charged, rather than encourage it. He closed his three-minute-and-twenty-second summary by asserting: "It is essential that a man who is President of this country, certainly stand for every program that will mean . . . growth, and I stand for programs that mean growth and progress. But it is also essential that he not allow a dollar to be spent that could be better spent by the people themselves." Thus, Nixon's turn in the first debate ended.

Kennedy followed his previous approach by making the presidency and the approach of a new president to world problems the issue. After briefly rebutting Nixon for minimizing the Soviet economic challenge and the Republicans for opposing medical care for the aged, Kennedy launched into the choice facing the American people. The "great issue" was whether people were satisfied with their current conditions or whether they believed the country must move ahead to meet the needs of the 1960s. It was a question of complacency versus action, as Kennedy pointed out in a vigorous conclusion to his summation:

I think that the tide could begin to run against us, and I don't want historians 10 years from now to say, these were the years when the tide ran out for the

United States. I want them to say, these were the years when the tide came in, these were the years when the United States started to move again. That's the question before the American people, and only you can decide what you want, what you want this country to be, what you want to do with the future.

I think we're ready to move. And it is to that great task, if we are successful, that we will address ourselves.

In his closing statement, Kennedy wove together an attack on Republicans, an affirmation of pride in Democratic domestic programs, his theme for the campaign, and a choice between complacency and action for the voters. While Nixon was talking about watching dollars and cents, Kennedy was calling for people to look to the future and the tasks that lay ahead in the next decade for the next president of the United States.

Effects of the First Debate

By every standard—whether quantitative or qualitative—John Kennedy fared as well or better than Richard Nixon in the first debate. The Schwerin Research Corporation reported that Kennedy outscored Nixon by 39 to 23 percent in its survey of viewers. The Gallup Poll showed Kennedy winning by 43 percent to 23 percent.[25] Significantly, those who only heard the debate on radio judged it to be much closer, a draw between the two. Yet, even this was a victory for Kennedy in that the expectations were that Nixon was the superior candidate and debater.[26] Prior to the debate, only three out of thirty Kennedy partisans thought their candidate would do better in the encounter. Two-thirds of the Nixon partisans thought he would fare better.[27] Just being perceived as Nixon's equal created an enormous boost to Kennedy's campaign.

Why did Kennedy fare better? There are three reasons.

First, Kennedy recognized, as Nixon apparently did not, that the debate was not a debate at all, but a political opportunity to boost his campaign. He, therefore, developed a strategic approach to the debate to achieve this purpose. And the choices he made turned out to be good choices. He made presidential leadership the centerpiece of his opening and closing statements. Since five of the ten questions also concerned leadership, Kennedy was already off and running by the time these questions came. He recognized that he had to unify the Democratic party behind his candidacy and national television provided the opportunity to do this. Again, this was a good choice. Ten southern governors, who were watching the debate in Hot Springs, Arkansas, wired Kennedy immediately after the debate congratulating him and pledging their support. This was critical in that it had been the southern politicians who had been most lukewarm or hostile to his candidacy in the past. And as the challenger, Kennedy took full advantage of that position to frame the question facing the people as one of movement versus stagnation, thus giving him the opportunity to paint a rosy picture of the future if he were elected versus the gray complacency of the present.

Second, Nixon made poor strategic choices. He was unprepared for the requirements of a political debate. There is no reason to believe that he was not fully prepared on issues and policies, but he apparently was not prepared on how to conduct himself or how to frame his answers orally. There was a "looseness" to Nixon's answers in comparison to the directness of Kennedy's precise approach ("First . . . Second . . . Third . . ."). In addition, Nixon's purpose for this debate was poorly chosen. He had a negative purpose: to erase the "assassin" or "Herblock" image of himself. He seemed to have no positive purpose for the debate, and thus no theme that he could rely on to tie together the disparate answers he would give. Finally, Nixon thought the joint appearance was actually a debate, and he debated. He isolated areas of agreement and congratulated his opponent on those agreements. He sought areas of disagreement (defined as "means" not "goals") and debated point by point. In so doing, he ignored or missed opportunities to score against Kennedy and the Democrats and failed to respond on the critical issue of Kennedy's experience and maturity. Again, Theodore White aptly caught the spirit of these mistakes: "For Mr. Nixon was debating with Mr. Kennedy as if a board of judges were scoring points; he rebutted and refuted, as he went, the inconsistencies or errors of his opponent. Nixon was addressing himself to Kennedy—but Kennedy was addressing himself to the audience that was the nation."[28] This strategic choice hurt Nixon throughout the debate.

Third and finally, there was the visual contrast between the two men. Much has been made of that contrast. Kennedy was young, vigorous, and sharp, wearing a dark suit against a light background. Nixon was pale, shifty-eyed, slouching due to reinjuring his knee upon arrival at the debate, perspiring with his perpetual five o'clock shadow seeping through his Lazy Shave, and indistinct wearing a light-colored suit against a light background. Like many others, I remember the shock of seeing what appeared to be a less than healthy Richard Nixon. That the visual image had an impact is unquestionable. That it was a lasting impact is questionable. During his subsequent campaign appearances and the other three debates, Nixon repaired this problem. Indeed, at times during the remainder of the campaign, he jumped ahead of Kennedy in the polls. His poor appearance had an immediate impact. But that visual image had to be taken in conjunction with the critical mistakes Nixon made in seeming to defer to Kennedy, in debating, in bending over backwards to change his image. Taken together, they spelled a serious political set-back for Nixon before the largest audience (between 75 and 80 million viewers) of any of the four debates.

THE FINAL THREE DEBATES

The final three debates drew smaller audiences than the first (approximately 61 million, 70 million, and 63 million respectively).[29] They will not be subjected to the detailed analysis of the first and most important debate, yet certain features of these debates should be highlighted.

In the second debate Nixon changed his rhetorical stance dramatically. Whereas in the first joint appearance he had sought to debate in a genteel fashion, he took a more aggressive approach in the second; and it was apparent in his first answer to a question about Kennedy's statement that the Eisenhower Administration was responsible for the "loss" of Cuba to Communism. Nixon charged right into the fray: "Well, first of all, I don't agree with Senator Kennedy that Cuba is lost and certainly China was lost when this administration came into power in 1953." He concluded his answer by saying: "No, Cuba is not lost, and I don't think this kind of defeatist talk by Senator Kennedy helps the situation one bit." He matched this pugnacious tone in his comment on Kennedy's explanation of why he believed President Eisenhower should have apologized to Khrushchev after the U–2 incident. Nixon began bluntly: "I think Senator Kennedy is wrong on three counts." He went on to describe his three reasons including a sly implication that the Democrats had been lax in gathering intelligence prior to the Japanese attack on Pearl Harbor where we "lost 3,000 American lives." This aggressive tone continued throughout the second debate and pervaded the third debate where Nixon seemed to blame the Democrats for all the wars America fought in the twentieth century: "I would remind Senator Kennedy of the past 50 years. I would ask him to name one Republican President who led this nation into war. There were three Democratic Presidents who led us into war." Of course, Nixon quickly disclaimed that he was trying to paint the Democratic party as the "war party" and the Republican party as the "peace party," but that was exactly what he was implying.

The two new issues that dominated the second and third debates were the Quemoy-Matsu issue and Cuba. The two were intertwined in that the valence issue involved was the determination of the candidate to confront Communism.

The small islands of Quemoy and Matsu, lying only a few miles off the shores of People's Republic of China, became an issue in the second and third debates. In the second debate, following a statement Kennedy had made the previous week, he was asked whether these islands were "unwise places to draw our defense line in the Far East." Kennedy replied that he thought our defense line in that area should be drawn around Formosa, not these two islands. Nixon disagreed completely, charging Kennedy with "woolly thinking." Nixon stated he supported the Nationalist Chinese claim to these islands and implied that he would draw our line of defense in the Far East to include them.

During the time between the second and third debates, Nixon hammered home that Kennedy would give up Quemoy and Matsu to the Communists. Much of that debate concerned this question. At issue were two separate statements from the president and Congress: the 1954 mutual defense treaty between the United States and Nationalist China and the 1955 congressional resolution that committed the United States to the defense of Formosa and "closely related localities." Both candidates cited the resolution (with Kennedy supporting the unadopted Lehman amendment that would have excluded Quemoy and Matsu) as the basis for their respective positions. The resolution neither committed the United States to defending Quemoy and Matsu nor did it prohibit defending them. As Stephen Ambrose concluded, "Kennedy said the doctrine excluded Quemoy and Matsu, which was incorrect; Nixon said it included Quemoy and Matsu, which was also incorrect."[30] As important as the policy decision would be to the next president, the valence issue of determination to face the Communist threat in the Far East was more important to voters. In this case, Nixon seemed to get the better of Kennedy for his strong stand.

On the day before the fourth debate (October 20), Kennedy dropped his bombshell. He issued a statement calling for American government support of the "non-Batista democratic anti-Castro forces in exile . . . who offer eventual hope of overthrowing Castro."[31] Immediately, this topic came up in the final debate. What is most interesting is Nixon's attack on Kennedy's statement. "I think that Senator Kennedy's policies and recommendations for the handling of the Castro regime are probably the most dangerously irresponsible recommendations that he's made during the course of the campaign." Nixon went on to detail other nonmilitary actions that should be taken to isolate and destabilize Castro. But Nixon's reply was a deliberate lie intended to cover up the CIA training of Cuban exiles that was already underway, a policy that in private Nixon supported. But in public on this occasion Nixon denounced Kennedy as irresponsible. He described his decision to take this tack in his first memoirs: "The covert operation had to be protected at all costs. I must not even suggest by implication that the United States was rendering aid to rebel forces in and out of Cuba. In fact, I must go to the other extreme: I must attack the Kennedy proposal to provide such aid as wrong and irresponsible because it would violate our treaty commitments."[32] Thus, Nixon declared publicly his opposition to a policy that he vigorously supported in private.

The problem that comes from this disclosure is a problem that plagues political rhetoric. Nixon deliberately lied in a public forum, but he claimed he did so to protect national security. At the time however, the public had no way of knowing that Nixon was lying. If this issue was important to people, how then could those people make a reasonable decision based on such an answer? Even more important, what if Nixon had been elected? After this direct statement, would President Nixon have cancelled the operation and thus saved the nation from a national disaster? These are intriguing speculative questions.

The importance of the Cuban issue in the campaign lay in its effect as a valence issue. Kennedy came across as stronger and tougher against Castro than Nixon. Even Nixon admitted that.[33] And it had enormous importance for policy when President Kennedy acted upon his campaign promise to arm the exiles and sent them into the disastrous Bay of Pigs Invasion. Here was a campaign promise kept that had terrible consequences.

The remainder of the fourth debate was a rehashing of positions the two candidates had already taken and of themes previously stated.

CONCLUSIONS

The 1960 presidential debates between John F. Kennedy and Richard M. Nixon were precedent-setting. The Gallup organization estimated that 85 million Americans watched one or all of the debates, while CBS estimated the figure at 120 million. The first debate alone drew between seventy and eighty million, the second largest audience gathered up to that time for a television program.[34]

Of the four debates, the first was most important. Kennedy demonstrated that he was the equal to Nixon and thereby gained support from both influential political figures and many people in the general public who previously had reservations about his candidacy and his ability to assume the presidency. In other words, that debate gave legitimacy and momentum to his campaign. Kennedy's shrewd preparations and strategy for the debate paid off, while Nixon suffered not only because of his poor visual appearance but also because he miscalculated the importance of the debate as well as his approach to the debate. But it should be remembered that the debates had significance in large part because the election was so closely contested. Had either candidate been considerably ahead of the other and had the election not been close, the debates surely would have had little influence on the final result.

The 1960 debates were important also because they set the precedent for future debates in participation and format. By insisting on a panel of journalists, the candidates gave a legitimacy to journalistic participation in the electoral process far beyond any they had enjoyed previously. And in that sense, they established a new forum for campaigning that was neither fish nor fowl, but a hybrid form of press conference and joint appearance with a little debating thrown in.

NOTES

1. Following the practice of others, I will refer to these joint appearances as "debates" even though I do not believe they are actually debates. Evron M. Kirkpatrick makes the same point, denying they were "great" or "debates," but follows the same practice. Much of my summary of events leading up to the 1960 debates is based on Kirkpatrick's essay, "Presidential Candidate 'Debates': What Can We Learn from 1960?" in *The Past and Future of Presidential Debates*, ed. by Austin Ranney (Washington, D.C.: American Enterprise Institute for Public Policy Research, 1979), pp. 1–50. The reader is referred to this essay for further elaboration. Also see Sig Michelson, *The Electric Mirror* (New York: Dodd Mead, 1972).

2. Theodore H. White, *The Making of the President 1960* (New York: Atheneum, 1961), pp. 290–291.

3. Cited in Edward W. Chester, *Radio, Television and American Politics* (New York: Sheed and Ward, 1969). The final numbers are the margin also cited by White as the difference between the two after all four debates were concluded. White, *The Making of the President 1960*, p. 295.

4. White, *The Making of the President 1960*, p. 294.

5. Nicholas Zapple, "Historical Evolution of Section 315," *The Past and Future of Presidential Debates*, p. 56.

6. Richard Nixon, *Six Crises* (Garden City: Doubleday, 1962), pp. 322–323.

7. Sig Michelson, *The Electric Mirror* (New York: Dodd Mead, 1972) pp. 197–198.

8. Quoted in White, *The Making of the President 1960*, p. 283.

9. Dwight D. Eisenhower, *Waging Peace* (Garden City: Doubleday, 1965), p. 599.

10. Richard A. Watson, *The Presidential Contest* (New York: John Wiley & Sons, 1984), p. 83.

11. Nixon, *Six Crises*, p. 323.

12. Ibid., p. 324.

13. In this debate, each candidate had an opening twenty-minute statement followed by an eight-and-a-half-minute rebuttal for each.

14. J. Jeffrey Auer, "The Counterfeit Debates," *The Great Debates*, ed. by Sidney Kraus (Bloomington: Indiana University Press, 1962), pp. 142–150.

15. Donald Stokes, "Spatial Models of Party Competition," in Angus Campbell, Philip Converse, Warren Miller, and Donald Stokes, *Elections and the Political Order* (New York: John Wiley & Sons, 1966), pp. 170–171.

16. Rev. King, who originally supported Nixon, switched to Kennedy after he and Robert Kennedy intervened to get King's son, Dr. Martin Luther King, Jr., out of a Georgia jail. But his initial opposition highlighted one of the problems that Kennedy had with the black community. It showed up in the final vote when Kennedy received only 68 percent of the nonwhite vote, the second lowest

percentage for a Democratic candidate between 1952 and 1988. Stevenson gathered 61 percent in 1956, two years after the *Brown v. Board of Education* decision.

17. Quoted in Bernard Rubin, *Political Television* (Belmont: Wadsworth, 1967), p. 47.

18. On Kennedy's strategy, see *The Making of the President 1960*, pp. 246–259.

19. Quoted in Kathleen Hall Jamieson, *Packaging the President* (New York: Oxford University Press, 1984), p. 146.

20. *The Making of the President 1960*, p. 266. White quotes Nixon as saying: "I have to erase the Herblock image first."

21. Ibid.

22. *The Making of the President 1960*, p. 285.

23. "Senator John F. Kennedy and Vice President Richard M. Nixon: First Joint Radio-Television Broadcast, Monday, September 26, 1960, Originating CBS, Chicago, Ill., All Networks Carried," *The Joint Appearances of Senator John F. Kennedy and Vice President Richard M. Nixon. Presidential Campaign of 1960* (Washington, D.C.: Government Printing Office, 1961), p. 73. All subsequent quotations from the four television debates are taken from this collection. The transcript of the first debate is on pages 73–92; the second debate, pages 146–165; the third debate, pages 204–222; the fourth debate, pages 260–278.

24. See also Theodore Otto Windt, Jr., "The Crisis Rhetoric of President John F. Kennedy," in *Presidents and Protestors: Political Rhetoric in the Nineteen Sixties*, to be published by the University of Alabama Press in 1990.

25. Cited in White, *The Making of the President 1960*, pp. 293–294. For additional poll data confirming these results, see Kurt Lang and Gladys Engel Lang, "Reactions of Viewers," in *The Great Debates*, ed. by Kraus, pp. 313–330. For an update on such research, see Kirkpatrick, "Presidential Candidate 'Debates': What Can We Learn from 1960?" *The Past and Future of Presidential Debates*, pp. 25–37.

26. See Lang and Lang's data on expectations in "Reactions of Viewers," pp. 315–322.

27. Ibid., p. 318.

28. *The Making of the President 1960*, pp. 287–288.

29. Chester, *Radio, Television and American Politics*, p. 120.

30. Stephen E. Ambrose, *Nixon: The Education of a Politician, 1913–1962* (New York: Simon and Schuster, 1987), p. 581.

31. "Following Is the Text of a Statement on Cuba by Senator John F. Kennedy, October 29, 1960," *The Speeches of Senator John F. Kennedy Presidential Campaign 1960* (Washington, D.C.: Government Printing Office, 1961), p. 681.

32. Nixon, *Six Crises*, p. 355.

33. Ibid., p. 357.

34. See White, *The Making of the President 1960*, pp. 283, 293.

SELECT BIBLIOGRAPHY

Chester, Edward W. *Radio, Television and American Politics*. New York: Sheed and Ward, 1969. An extremely useful background of the rise of radio and television's impact on politics; additional information on the 1960 debates and campaign.

Highlander, John P., and Lloyd I. Watkins. "A Closer Look at the Great Debates." *Western Speech Journal* (Winter 1962): 39–48. A debate analysis and evaluation of the debates—a good contrast to the analysis presented in this essay.

Kirkpatrick, Evron M. "Presidential Candidate 'Debates': What Can We Learn from 1960?" *The Past and Future of Presidential Debates*, ed. by Austin Ranney. Washington, D.C.: American Enterprise Institute, 1979, p. 1–50. This essay is an invaluable summary of much of the historical and empirical research on the 1960 debates.

Kraus, Sidney, ed. *The Great Debates: Background—Perspective—Effects*. Bloomington: Indiana University Press, 1962. The indispensible source of data and information about the 1960 debates. The work is especially strong in assessing the effects of the debates.

Nixon, Richard M. *Six Crises*. Garden City: Doubleday, 1962, pp. 322–349. The entire chapter on the 1960 campaign is valuable for the insights it provides to the Nixon campaign; the cited pages concern Nixon's view and evaluation of the debates.

Sorensen, Theodore C. *Kennedy*. New York: Harper & Row, 1965, pp. 195–206. The Kennedy view of the debates as seen by his close adviser and one who helped in his preparations for the debates.

White, Theodore H. *The Making of the President 1960*. New York: Atheneum, 1961. The best of his "Making of the President" books, and still the very best book on the campaign. His observations on the debates are the ones people still quote.

Zapple, Nicholas. "Historical Evolution of Section 315." *The Past and Future of Presidential Debates*, ed. by Austin Ranney. Washington, D.C.: American Enterprise Institute, 1979, 51–74. An excellent and to-the-point summary of how Section 315 has evolved from 1934 to 1976.

Debate Transcripts

Kraus, Sidney, ed. *The Great Debates*. Bloomington: Indiana University Press, 1962, pp. 348–430. This is the complete and most accurate transcript of the four debates, and they are prefaced by an excellent essay on creating textual accuracy. However, the editor decided to print the transcripts in long paragraphs that are difficult to read and do not capture the oral, rapid-fire quality of the answers given by the candidates.

The Joint Appearances of Senator John F. Kennedy and Vice President Richard M. Nixon: Presidential Campaign of 1960. Washington, D.C.: Government Printing Office, 1961. The first debate, pp. 73–92; the second debate, pp. 146–165; the third debate, pp. 204–222; the fourth debate, pp. 260–278. This version omits a few vocalized pauses and single, insignificant words. However, the format gives a good sense of the oral quality of the debates by using short paragraphs for the short quick answers of the candidates.

Film of the Debates

Film of the debates can be obtained through the John F. Kennedy Library, Cambridge, Massachusetts, 02138.

Chapter 2

The 1976 Carter–Ford Presidential Debates

Goodwin Berquist

The year was 1952. The speaker was J. Leonard Reinsch, media specialist for Presidents Roosevelt and Truman. Reinsch's audience included Frank Stanton, president of Columbia Broadcasting System, Governor Stevenson, the Democratic nominee for president, and General Eisenhower, the Republican standardbearer. The proposition was simple: why not stage a debate between the two nominees on national television?[1]

That year Reinsch's dream was not to be realized. But the prospect intrigued those most concerned with presidential politics in America. Imagine a prime-time audience of millions! Picture "our" candidate demonstrating once and for all his clear superiority over his opponent. Visualize "our man" delivering a dramatic knock-out blow on the eve of victory! Not until eight years later was Reinsch's dream to become reality.[2] The 1960 Kennedy–Nixon debates proved his point: even a single televised confrontation had the power to affect the outcome of a national election.[3]

Prior to the first debate in September of 1960, Nixon strategists assumed their man had a clear edge over his opponent: he had, after all, served in the vice-presidency for eight years. Consequently Republican campaign posters proudly proclaimed "Experience Counts." Yet after the very first debate, this slogan was out of date, for Senator Kennedy had persuaded millions of television viewers that he could handle the highest office in the land as well as could his opponent.[4]

For a variety of reasons, no presidential debates were televised for sixteen years after the Kennedy era.[5] Then in 1976, America's bicentennial year, the debates resumed and they have been a regular feature of presidential campaigning ever since.

This study is designed to provide answers to several questions. Why did President Ford and Governor Carter agree to participate in three debates on national television?[6] What agenda did each candidate bring to these confrontations? Which rhetorical strategy proved superior in the minds of most viewers? Finally, what effects, if any, did these debates have on the outcome of the national election?

THE DECISION TO DEBATE

In a 1979 essay in the *Journal of the American Forensic Association*, Robert Friedenberg identified six conditions, any five of which are essential if one or more presidential debates are to be held.[7]

Friedenberg's first two conditions are especially relevant in the context of the 1976 campaign: Is the forthcoming election likely to be close? And, are advantages likely to accrue to a candidate if he agrees to participate in a televised debate? Political self-interest lies at the heart of the matter.

One might assume that an incumbent president would have no interest in participating. Gerald Ford's predecessors, Presidents Johnson and Nixon, both refused to share a platform with their opponents. Furthermore, in 1976, Gerald Ford was unquestionably better known than Jimmy Carter.

But the Gallup Poll in late July showed Ford trailing Carter by 33 percentage points.[8] President Ford and his advisers concluded that he must seize the initiative. Here is Ford's own account of the crucial decision:

> About a week before the [Republican] convention began, I had mentioned something to Betty that I had been thinking about for quite a while. When I first ran for Congress, I'd challenged my opponent to a debate. I believed in debates and had engaged in them throughout my Congressional career. According to the polls, Carter had an overwhelming lead. I had to do something dramatic and different in order to win. Furthermore, I had a visceral feeling that if I didn't seize the initiative, Carter would—and that would put me on the defensive. So, why not take him on? Then the people could decide.
>
> Betty thought that was a good idea.[9]

With two years of experience in office, and the vast resources of the executive branch at his command, the incumbent president was assumed to have a significant advantage.[10] Consequently in his acceptance speech at the Republican convention on August 19, the president declared, "This year the issues are on our side. I am ready, I am eager to go before the American people and debate the real issues face to face with Jimmy Carter. The American people have a right to know firsthand exactly where both of us stand."[11]

Even before Ford completed his speech, Jody Powell, Carter's press secretary, advised reporters in Plains, Georgia, that the following morning the governor planned to challenge his Republican opponent to debate. The Carter press conference was scheduled for 9 A.M. August 20 and the accompanying press release read in part as follows: "A choice of this magnitude should not be made without the closest possible scrutiny of the candidates and their proposals for leading our country to solutions for our problems. For this reason, I am asking President Ford to join me in a debate, or series of debates, on the choices facing the American people."[12]

Jimmy Carter campaigned principally on the basis of being a Washington outsider. Untouched by either the Watergate scandal or the agonizing ordeal over Vietnam, Carter hoped to capitalize on the idea of "bringing a breath of fresh air" to the nation's capital. Since the decision to debate on the part of both candidates came only hours apart, neither gained any special advantage over the other.

Section 315 of the Federal Communications Act caused many to wonder earlier if there would be any televised debates at all, regardless of candidate preference in the matter. This "equal time" provision stipulated that all candidates for office should be guaranteed an equal amount of broadcast time, a condition the three commercial networks were unwilling to accept. Loss of prime-time revenue, plus the sizable number of minor party candidates, made "equal time" financially prohibitive. In 1960, Congress passed a special law to set aside the provision. In 1976 the Federal Communications Commission overturned its earlier blanket requirement by defining presidential debates as "bona fide" news events rather than public service programing.[13]

As Walter Mears facetiously noted in the *Columbia Journalism Review*, two months after the election, "All it takes [to produce a televised debate between presidential contenders] is an incumbent president who is thirty-three points behind in the polls, and an opponent who nevertheless figures he may have a recognition problem."[14]

The dilemma faced by Governor Carter and his advisers was dramatized by the widely repeated question "Jimmy Who?" throughout the presidential campaign. While Carter surprised almost everyone by the ease with which he outpaced his rivals in the primaries, he was nevertheless viewed at the time as a regional candidate blessed with incredible luck.[15] Many Americans, it seemed, had trouble visualizing Carter as a *national* contender for the presidency.

While it was true that Carter had a comfortable lead in the polls at the time of the Republican Convention, polls are necessarily time-bound; they may change from week to week or even, as President Ford was to later discover, within forty-eight hours. In Carter's case, a 33-point lead in late July dropped to 10 points only a month later.[16]

Thus though self interest motivated Ford and Carter, both men justified their willingness to debate on the grounds that America needed an educated electorate. Ever since the 1920s, the League of Women Voters had pursued the same goal. Naturally, then, the League was in the forefront of the campaign to bring about the debates. Peggy Lampl, former executive director of the League, described her organization's role thus:

> The League was unquestionably instrumental in making the candidates focus on the question of the debates. Without the preceding months of media and political contacts and pressure, it seemed unlikely that there would have been the simultaneous peaking of interest and acceptance by both candidates . . . there . . . were invitations by various groups. . . . The League's proposal, however, came early and persistent enough, so that each camp had ample opportunity to consider its value in developing campaign plans.[17]

In consequence, the League of Women Voters Educational Fund was placed in charge of arrangements for all these debates.[18]

A third criterion for the debates that Friedenberg advanced involved the candidate's perception of his own ability to debate. President Ford summed up the matter this way: "Throughout my Congressional career, whenever my opponents have challenged me, I'd always agree to debate—and I'd always prevailed."[19]

Jimmy Carter was equally self-confident. After all, he had won in the key states and fended off last-minute challenges by Governor Jerry Brown and Senator Frank Church.[20] Furthermore, Carter possessed an unshakable conviction that he would win the presidency from the moment he decided to run.[21] Any campaign event that could enhance his chances would be carefully studied and probably supported.

It should be remembered that in 1976 the credibility of both the candidate and the party were at stake. While the nation had survived the constitutional crisis of Watergate and impeachment only two years earlier, the voters had had no opportunity to make their views known. The Constitution stipulates that the vice president must serve in the absence of the president so Republican Gerald Ford occupied the nation's highest office between 1974 and 1976.

The Democrats, on the other hand, had not won a presidential election in twelve years. The chaotic televised convention of 1968, plus the lopsided defeat of George McGovern in 1972, caused many Americans to wonder whether this multifaceted party could ever again agree upon a winning presidential candidate.[22]

Remember further that before his selection as vice president, Gerald Ford had been simply a congressman from Michigan. He had never aspired to national office and had never been elected to either the vice presidency or the presidency. In fact, shortly before the Nixon appointment to the vice presidency, Ford was contemplating retirement from public office.[23]

To sum the matter up, it is clear that both candidates anticipated a close election in August of 1976.[24] Both thought televised debates would be in their best interest. Both rationalized their position by emphasizing the educational value of the debates for America's voters as they prepared to cast their votes the following November. In a sense, there was a crisis of confidence in both political parties. In 1976, a great deal rested on the outcome of the debates and there was cause for optimism as well as concern in the camps of both presidential contenders.

THE AGENDA

Nineteen hundred and seventy-six was not a year for manifold political issues. Representative David Stockman (later chosen as budget director for President Reagan) noted that the passage of the "Great Society" legislation of the 1960s had ended thirty years of ideological debate. "If the government wasn't doing anything to rescue the cities, to save the housing industry, to transform education, to change the ghettos," Stockman declared, "you could have great debates. But that debate was broken with the Eighty-ninth Congress after 1964. We started doing all those things, and I can't run now *against* Medicare, or aid to education, any more than the Democrats can run *for* those things, because they're already on the books. All I can do—or they can do—is propose better ways of doing it, more effective, less costly ways. And that's why ideology has declined."[25]

Jonathan Moore, director of the John F. Kennedy School of Government at Harvard University, and his colleague, Janet Fraser, have insightfully analyzed why issues played a minor role in the 1976 campaign:

> The relative insignificance of substantive policy issues can be attributed to several factors. The voters didn't place a high premium on them, perhaps because they don't entirely trust what they hear candidates say about them and have greater confidence in their ability to get some feeling for how generally capable and reliable a given candidate is. There are some hard core issues pursued by hard core groups, but they tend to cancel out. Voters tend normally to be confused by intricate and intransigent governmental problems, and once they get a general idea of where a candidate stands—how moderate, how extreme—that's likely to be enough. Indeed, the inherent complexity of most public issues inhibits their role in political campaigns. Candidates are very wary of getting in over their heads or getting hit over the head on complicated, controversial substance. Jimmy Carter chose "fuzziness" over "specificity" and apparently was right. Governor Jerry Brown admitted, "A little vagueness goes a long way in this business." Finally, the media, particularly television, is not equipped to handle serious issues competently. One of the great ironies of the campaign was media

response on several occasions when they had been successful in goading a candidate into detailed policy positions—they were the first to zap him, or they didn't accurately or adequately cover him.[26]

In a sense, the emergence of issues in a campaign with an incumbent candidate, is the mission of the challenger. For the official in office has a public record. His opponent enters the fray with largely a clean slate.

Let us turn our attention then to the Carter strategy. James Wooten, a careful student of Carter's life before the presidency, tells us that Carter learned a valuable lesson in his first two electoral campaigns. "The best candidate," Carter came to believe, "is the candidate who adopts himself to the interests of the voters within the specific context of the campaign movement."[27] According to Wooten, Carter "dismissed ideology as excess baggage; he brought to his presidential pursuit from its very conception the credentials of flexibility. He would not argue many issues but he would project personality. He would not espouse many specific positions but he would wholeheartedly embrace universally approved possibilities. On almost all matters of substance—just the sort of thing that could suddenly abort a presidential campaign—he would offer broadly phrased opinions, replete with disclaimers and open to broad and, if necessary, arguable interpretation."[28] In short, Governor Carter had become a specialist in issue avoidance as early as 1970. Carter, Wooten surmised, "believed that the candidate that took clear positions on every issue was not long for the political world."[29]

In a 1975 interview, Betty Glad reports, Carter argued that George McGovern's biggest mistake in 1972 was in making Vietnam the major issue of the campaign. "That's not how it works," Carter said.[30] On another occasion, Carter told a group of network executives and correspondents "the only Presidents he knew of who [had] emphasized the issues were Dewey, Goldwater, and McGovern."[31]

On yet another occasion, the Democratic candidate declared "I don't give a damn about abortion or amnesty or right-to-work laws. . . . They're impossible political issues. In fifty years people will still be arguing about them and they won't be any closer to resolving them than they are now. I can't possibly help anyone—including myself—if I'm out on the edge of such volatile things, and I don't intend to be. It would be foolish. If I'm going to lose, it's not going to be because I staked my whole candidacy on a ban on abortions or the right to have them."[32]

Carter's strategy was to become all things to all voters by adhering to "abstract statements of principles to which few could object."[33] As Glad saw it, Carter "skillfully fudged on the controversial issues. He did this by sending out complex messages that various listeners could interpret according to their own predispositions. From the multitude of signals—a word, a condition, a posture—Carter was able to send different people different signals about his positions."[34] As Carter himself explained in his campaign autobiography, "dozens of issues are considered during a political campaign, but candidates do not create the issues. They exist in the minds and hearts of our citizens." Carter's task, he felt, was to "reflect" what the people wanted.[35]

For Jimmy Carter, there really was only one issue in the 1976 campaign: candidate credibility. "I think our people have been hurt and scarred so badly by Vietnam, Cambodia, Watergate, the CIA revelations, that they're just simply looking for someone they can trust—just someone they believe they can believe."[36]

James Wooten describes Carter's solution to this crisis in his analysis of the Georgian's first campaign address, December 12, 1974: "It was a malaise that could only be cured by the election of a man in whom the country could once again believe. 'I'll never lie to you,' he promised. That was it. Tax reform and welfare reform and a strong national defense and a more open government with greater privacy for the individual—all of that was included, but it was included as a product of the basic premise, the need for a President the people could believe."[37]

As Patrick Caddell, Carter's pollster, said after the Democratic convention, "without the trust thing, he couldn't have made it."[38] Yet Carter was the only Democratic candidate in 1976 who could make credibility the central thrust of his campaign. As Caddell went on to explain, "most people would really rather trust other people than distrust them, except in politics; most people have a reason to distrust most candidates. Jimmy was a stranger in town. They had no reason to distrust him and he didn't give them one."[39]

And what of Gerald Ford? David Broder, columnist for the *Washington Post*, noted that Ford was "a much more open man" than his predecessor in office, Richard Nixon. "But only thirty days into his presidency he [Ford] shocked the nation by issuing a full pardon of Nixon—an act from which he never recovered politically."[40]

In essence, Jimmy Carter was right: There really was only one critical issue in the 1976 presidential campaign. And on this issue the three Carter–Ford televised debates were, on balance, to tip the scales in favor of the Georgia governor.

RHETORICAL STRATEGIES

There continues to exist in America a remarkable mythology about presidential candidates debating before a nationwide audience. Nostalgia about the Lincoln–Douglas senatorial debates of 1858 lingers on, despite dramatic differences in channel, audience, occasion, and the intensive role of the mass media. One of American television's legacies, which dates back to the very first commercial broadcasts in 1948, is the game-show–sporting-event mentality. Viewers are conditioned to expect a winner and a loser. As a result, millions of Americans readily assume a presidential debate is a sort of political game, which lends itself to instant analysis and the awarding of a decision.

The media themselves encourage this illusion. When a victor is not at once apparent, television commentators and analysts fill the vacuum by playing the dual role of referee and final judge. If as a viewer you are unsure of who won the debate, stay tuned for Dan, Tom, or Peter will surely tell you.[41]

Ironically in the aftermath of the second Ford–Carter debate, Ford's now famous Eastern Europe gaffe was not at once apparent to viewers. So the media assumed the responsibility for "setting the record straight." Immediately after the debate was over, the polls indicate Ford won the debate. But let Robert Teeter, Ford's pollster, tell the story: "In the polling we did starting in the last minute of the second debate, between 11:00 and 1:00 that night, the question of who did a better job in the debate came out Ford 44 percent, Carter 43. Between 9:00 in the morning and noon the next day, it was Ford 32, Carter 44. Between noon and 5:00 in the afternoon, it was Ford 21, Carter 43. Between 5:00 and midnight the day after, it was Ford 17, Carter 62. Reports of the debate had re-emphasized the president as a mistake prone, inept, bumbler, exactly what we had spent six or seven weeks trying to get away from."[42] Within a little over twenty-four hours, President Ford had gone from a winner at 44 percent of the vote to a loser at 17; and Carter had shifted from a loser at 43 to a winner at 62. The cause for the change? Media postdebate analysis and verdict.

The simple truth is that neither presidential candidate can afford the risk of an inaccurate off-the-cuff response on national television. Perceived weakness in the course of a program viewed by 100 million voters is simply devastating to contemplate.

Consequently, the managers of both candidates encourage their "players" to play it safe. Stick with the tried-and-true campaign positions. Memorize standard answers and one-line zingers likely to embarrass your opponent. Use the venerated political trick of responding to a question not with an answer but with a whole new attack. Worry not that such a tactic may make for boring television or may dismay your supporters. The lesser of two risks is the only road to follow when an entire campaign may be at stake. So goes the conventional wisdom.

It is of course possible to analyze in minute detail the argumentation of each candidate in all three debates: Lloyd Bitzer and Theodore Rueter have done so in their 1980 study, *Carter vs. Ford: The Counterfeit Debates of 1976*. Their ten conclusions may be paraphrased as follows:

1. In the face-to-face confrontation, Ford was less skilled than Carter.
2. Ford was also likely to make more verbal and factual errors than his opponent.

3. Ford was limited in his ability to express matters of principle and personal feeling.
4. Ford was given to presenting "shallow argument" as if he did not really understand "substantive issues."
5. On occasion, Ford's analyses of specific public questions were either inaccurate or questionable, raising again the question of his fitness to govern.
6. Sometimes Carter's positions were ill-conceived and lacking in depth.
7. Carter often resorted to hyperbole or overstatement.
8. Carter appeared to have an inflated idea of the powers of the presidency.
9. Carter evinced an inordinate confidence in reason rather than cooperation as a key to effective governance.
10. Carter raised public expectations to "dangerously high levels."[43]

While the Bitzer–Rueter analysis represents the results of careful argumentative analysis, it is the contention of this author that their study misses the point. The key to victory in the 1976 presidential debates was not argumentation per se, at least if one is to judge by opinion polls and voter decisions in November. Most American television viewers are not expert in argumentation, skillful in following an extended argument, or adept in judging the precise merits of a debater's case. The dramatic shift of opinion after the second debate, alluded to earlier, clearly indicates this point.

What Americans feel confident in doing, what each of us does day-in and day-out, in both face-to-face and televised encounters, is to size up the quality of a stranger. Twenty-three centuries ago, Aristotle told his students that ethos was probably the most potent form of proof in persuasion.[44] What he had in mind was the listener's collective perceptions of a speaker's character, intelligence, and good will. Cicero added to this philosophy in stressing the importance of prior reputation, the so-called antecedent ethos of a speaker.[45]

In the eighteenth century the Scottish preacher-rhetorician, George Campbell went yet one step further. Addressing a group of theological students, he declared that if a minister's words coincided with his actions, his power to influence others through speech would be tripled.[46]

Modern scholars of rhetoric and communication all agree—source credibility is crucial to those who wish to sway others in matters of belief and action.[47]

Thus, speaker image becomes central to the assessment of viewer response. So central in fact that one can say, and in 1976 should have said, the candidate image is *the* issue in the campaign, the one and only criterion every American voter feels qualified to apply.

The fact that all of us can be and sometimes are duped by "con artists" is beside the point. We think our own judgment of strangers is sound, and the miracle of television makes it possible for each of us to draw our own conclusions in the privacy of our living rooms.

To create a credible image and to tarnish Carter's image, President Ford essentially focused his attention on defense of his own record, allegations about Governor Carter's "fuzziness" on issues, and Carter's lack of familiarity with issues confronting the federal government.[48] Carter, on the other hand, focused attention on his own record as a competent governor of the State of Georgia and with one striking exception—the "ethnic purity" remark—adhered to an early game plan of high principles all reasonable Americans would readily endorse.[49]

EFFECTS OF THE DEBATES

Many scholars have undertaken statistical analyses of voter response to the debates. Those interested in this aspect of effectiveness should consult Sidney Kraus's collection of studies entitled *The Great Debates: Carter vs. Ford, 1976*. The question this essayist wished to address is which candidate did the better job of establishing *his own credibility* with the voters. Which candidate, Ford or Carter, did American viewer-voters consider to be most competent? most trustworthy? most likely to advance voter interests? Although contemporary theorists write glowingly of the charismatic impact of a John Kennedy, neither Mr. Ford nor Mr. Carter appeared to excel in this quarter, other than before their convention of supporters.[50] So charisma was not really a factor in these debates.

Let us begin then with competence. Normally an incumbent president with a public record, albeit only two years in duration, would be assumed to have an edge in this quarter. No matter how long one may have aspired to the office of the presidency, or how many lesser government posts one has held, the fact remains that the pressures of the presidency are unique. One who has experienced them, therefore, is presumed to have an edge.

The difficulty with this mode of thinking is that incumbency places a very large burden on the candidate-in-office. His views and actions, what he favors and what he disapproves of, are a matter of public record. A new contender has no such burden to shoulder. The newcomer has no record in office so there remains about him a protective ambiguity. As Jimmy Carter was later to discover in his debate with Ronald Reagan, incumbency is clearly no advantage in televised debates and may well be a disadvantage among some voters.[51]

President Ford had never won a national election. Named by Richard Nixon to replace Spiro Agnew in mid-term, Ford automatically assumed the presidency upon Nixon's resignation from office. So the American voters never really chose Ford to lead them; Nixon did. The 1976 campaign therefore constituted a public verdict of Mr. Ford's stewardship in office.

Lingering in the minds of many Americans was Ford's fateful decision to give a full pardon to Richard Nixon within a month after his assumption of the presidency. Ford stoutly maintained at the time that he simply could not govern until the Watergate nightmare was over. The decision to pardon Nixon, while readily understandable from the perspective of practical politics, was not at all popular with a considerable segment of the electorate. Some observers speculated that a deal had been made between Ford and Nixon early on. While no specific evidence has yet come to light to support this view, many voters felt Nixon got off much too easily, that he was not sufficiently punished for his sins in office. They held Ford responsible.

All of this reflected negatively upon Ford's credibility. To some Americans, he simply appeared to be untrustworthy and unreliable in carrying out what they considered to be the popular will.

Governor Carter had no such baggage to encumber him.

In the five sets of televised presidential debates America has witnessed since 1960, most observers view the first encounter as the acid test of a candidate's fitness for high office. John Kennedy met this test successfully in September of 1960. Jimmy Carter did the same sixteen years later. While postdebate opinion polls suggested President Ford "won" the debate by a narrow margin, it was by no means a knock-out punch but rather a decision on points. The two candidates appeared so closely matched at the time that Carter was ushered into the same arena with the president as a worthy contender.

Gerald Ford's blunder about the Soviet occupation of Eastern Europe—perhaps the only truly memorable passage of the three debates—raised anew the question about the President's ability to handle the wide-ranging demands of the office. Governor Carter hit hard at Ford's mistake, so hard in fact as to generate some sympathy for his harried Republican opponent.[52]

What the three debates served to do was to create the clear impression among the American public that Governor Carter was at least as qualified as his better known opponent. James Wooten maintained that "all that had emerged [from the debates] was the vague impression that both were probably fairly decent men, that Carter was probably better looking, that Ford was substantially taller than Carter, and that Carter was probably quicker on his feet than the President."[53]

The opinion polls taken after each debate were equally unexciting: Ford emerged as the winner of the first debate by a slight margin. Carter took the second by a much bigger margin and Carter was viewed as a slight winner in the third.[54]

But we should not harbor the opinion that these debates were without meaning. Sidney Kraus, a student of presidential televised debates since 1960, extrapolated from the Nielsen data and found that 64.1 million households watched the first debate, leading to the conclusion that there were more than 100 million viewer-listeners to the initial exchange in Philadelphia.[55] That single event was watched and heard by the largest political audience in history.

Patrick Caddell, Carter's pollster, later noted that "all three debates came at points in the campaign when Carter was in decline in our surveys. The first debate [September 23] helped stop the slide after the *Playboy* interview, the second debate [October 7] again held up a decline, and the third debate [October 22] did the same."[56]

Governor Carter himself said later on "if it hadn't been for the debates, I would have lost. They established me as competent on foreign and domestic affairs and gave the viewers reason to think that Jimmy Carter had something to offer."[57]

The postdebate assessment by the Harvard team of Moore and Fraser seems especially insightful: "Carter beat out Ford on perceptions of competence, intelligence, and concern for the average citizen [Aristotle's three dimensions of credibility]. He was preferred on strong ability, seen as being more colorful, interesting, and imaginative, and as having leadership qualities. He deliberately tried to contrast himself to Ford's dullness, questionable competence, and complacency with the way things were. Ford was regarded as stronger on experience, more moderate, more predictable, and 'non-waffling.' Carter was regarded by some as weird and Ford by some as boring." Moore and Fraser concluded that "these kinds of perceptions, opinions, and hunches are what a great deal of the time, energy, money, words and pictures were all about in 1976."[58]

Walter Mondale, Carter's runningmate, was assigned the role of reassuring traditional Democratic blocs—"labor, minorities, ethnics"—that Carter would do right by them.[59] Meanwhile Carter himself courted blacks and union members, "the two groups that did the most" to secure his election.[60]

In his memoirs Jimmy Carter summarized the campaign in these words: "To me . . . the most significant factors [in my election] were the disillusionment of the American people following the national defeat suffered in Vietnam, the Watergate scandals, and my success in convincing supporters that we should keep our faith in America and that I would never permit any repetition of such embarrassments."[61]

To this observer, Carter appears to have been remarkably accurate. The American voters were disillusioned. They did feel it was time for a change. And the change they voted into office was a hitherto obscure peanut farmer from Georgia.

NOTES

1. J. Leonard Reinsch, *Getting Elected: From Radio and Roosevelt to Television and Reagan* (New York: Hippocrene Books, 1988), pp. 78–80. In their text on political communication, Trent and Friedenberg identify Senator Blair Moody of Michigan as the author of the idea of televising debates in 1952. They cite Lee Mitchell's 1979 book, *With the Nation Watching*, as their source. See Judith Trent and Robert V. Friedenberg, *Political Campaign Communication: Principles and Practice* (New York: Praeger Publishers, 1983), pp. 240, 275 n.17. In the judgment of this author, Reinsch makes the better case; his involvement as a Democratic media consultant dates back to 1944, and one can well imagine him visualizing bigger and better ways to disseminate candidate views to the voting public from that point onward.

2. Reinsch was assigned to be in charge of television and radio for John Kennedy's 1960 campaign. His account of how the first televised debates came about appeared in chapter 14 of *Getting Elected*. See p. 127 and pp. 133–162.

3. The author subscribes to the view that millions of Americans who viewed the first Kennedy–Nixon debate made up their mind then and there as to the candidate of their choice.

4. Theodore White, *The Making of the President 1960* (New York: Atheneum, 1961), p. 296. At the Alfred E. Smith dinner in October, Kennedy made the following quip: "I think the worst news for the Republicans this week was that Casey Stengel has been fired [laughter]. It must show that perhaps experience does not count [laughter and applause]," p. 298 n.1.

5. For a thoughtful analysis of the 1964 and 1968 nondebate campaigns, see Robert V. Friedenberg's " 'We Are Present Today for the Purpose of Having a Joint Discussion': The Conditions Requisite for Political Debates," *Journal of American Forensic Association* 16, no.1 (Summer 1979): 4–5 (hereafter cited as Friedenberg, "Requisite Conditions").

6. The first debate took place in Philadelphia on September 23; the second occurred in San Francisco, October 6; and the third was staged in Williamsburg, Virginia, on October 22. (Senators Dole and Mondale, the vice presidential candidates, held their televised debate in Houston on October 15).

7. Friedenberg, "Requisite Conditions," pp. 1–2.

8. Jules Witcover, *Marathon: The Pursuit of the Presidency, 1972–1976* (New York: New American Library, 1977), p. 576.

9. Gerald R. Ford, *A Time to Heal: The Autobiography of Gerald R. Ford* (New York: Harper & Row, 1979), p. 125.

10. Yet because of this assumption, any contender who at least "breaks even" in a debate with the sitting president is thought to have won. See Goodwin F. Berquist and James L. Golden, "Media Rhetoric, Criticism, and the Public Perception of the 1980 Presidential Debates," *Quarterly Journal of Speech* 67 (May 1981): 134–135.

11. *The Presidential Campaign, 1976* vol. 3, *The Debates* (Washington: D.C. Government Printing Office, 1979), p. 1.

12. Ibid., pp. 1–2.

13. Ibid., p. 10. Trent and Friedenberg credit a law school paper of Stephen A. Sharp of the University of Virginia on the history and interpretation of Section 315 for playing a significant role in this division reversal, along with a recommendation of the Aspen Program for Media and Society in *Political Campaign Communication*. pp. 242–243.

14. Cited by Samuel L. Becker and Elmer W. Lower in "Broadcasting in Presidential Campaigns, 1960–1976" in Sidney Kraus, ed., *The Great Debates: Carter vs. Ford 1976* (Bloomington: Indiana University Press, 1979), p. 33.

15. Lloyd Bitzer and Theodore Rueter, *Carter vs. Ford: The Counterfeit Debates of 1976* (Madison: University of Wisconsin Press, 1980), pp. 17–18.

16. Witcover, *Marathon*, p. 576.

17. Kraus, *Great Debates*, p. 90.

18. Bitzer and Rueter, *Counterfeit Debates*, p. 253. The League originally came into existence in February, 1919, as a section of the National American Woman Suffrage Association. It became an independent organization a year later, changing its name in 1920 and again in 1946.

19. Ford, *A Time to Heal*, p. 414.

20. Bitzer and Rueter, *Counterfeit Debates*, p. 18.

21. James Wooten, *Dasher: The Roots and the Rising of Jimmy Carter* (New York: Summit Books, 1978), p. 37.

22. For a vivid analysis of the Democratic Convention in Chicago, see William R. Brown "Television and the Democratic National Convention of 1968," *Quarterly Journal of Speech* 55 (October 1969): 237–246.

23. Jerald F. terHorst, *Gerald Ford and the Future of the Presidency* (New York: The Third Press, 1974), p. 137.

24. Ford's concern about Carter's "overwhelming lead" has already been noted. But on July 22, 1976, Patrick Caddell, Carter's polling expert, sent a memo to the Carter campaign aides in which he stressed the "softness" of Carter supporters: "At this point roughly one-third of all Carter voters [in Illinois, Washington, Florida, Iowa, the South, the Deep South, and the Farm Belt] describe themselves as not very enthusiastic at all about their choice of Jimmy Carter. In fact, to emphasize the large pool of unenthusiastic Carter voters it should be pointed out that there is no state or area yet in which a majority of all registered voters (not merely Carter voters) is very enthusiastic or even somewhat enthusiastic about Jimmy Carter," Friedenberg, "Requisite Conditions," p. 6.

25. David S. Broder, *Changing of the Guard: Power and Leadership in America* (New York: Simon and Schuster, 1980), pp. 45–46.

26. Jonathan Moore and Janet Fraser, *Campaign for President: The Managers Look at '76* (Cambridge, Mass.: Ballinger, 1977), p. 10 (hereafter cited as Moore and Fraser, *Managers*).

27. Wooten, *Dasher*, p. 348.

28. Ibid.

29. Ibid., p. 36.

30. Betty Glad, *Jimmy Carter in Search of the Great White House* (New York: W. W. Norton, 1980), p. 304 (hereafter cited as Glad, *Search*).

31. Ibid.

32. Wooten, *Dasher*, pp. 349–350.

33. Glad, *Search*, p. 305.
34. Ibid., p. 306.
35. Ibid., pp. 304–305.
36. Wooten, *Dasher*, pp. 248–249. Also see p. 36.
37. Ibid., p. 347.
38. Ibid., p. 356.
39. Ibid.
40. Broder, *Changing*, pp. 48–49.
41. See, for example, Berquist and Golden's "Media Rhetoric," pp. 125–131. Although this study focused on the 1980 presidential debates, similar media practices occurred in 1976.
42. Moore and Fraser, *Managers*, 142.
43. Bitzer and Rueter, *Counter Debates*, 185–192.
44. Lane Cooper, trans., *The Rhetoric of Aristotle* (New York: D. Appleton and Co., 1932), p. 9.
45. James L. Golden, Goodwin F. Berquist, and William E. Coleman, eds. *The Rhetoric of Western Thought: Fourth Edition* (Dubuque, Iowa: Kendall/Hunt, 1988), pp. 58–59.
46. Ibid., p. 188.
47. See for example K. Andersen and T. Clevenger, Jr., "A Summary of Experimental Research in Ethos," *Speech Monographs* 30 (1963): 59–78.
48. Elizabeth Drew, *American Journal: The Events of 1976* (New York: Random House, 1977), pp. 98, 105–106, 166, 188, 224, 226, 414, 437, 451.
49. Glad, *Search*, pp. 304–305; Wooten, *Dasher*, p. 347. During a visit to Pennsylvania, Carter responded to a reporter's question by saying he saw nothing wrong with white suburbs retaining their "ethnic purity." This off-hand comment embroiled him in a controversy with white liberals and black voters.
50. One of Sidney Kraus's colleagues summed up his response to the first debate thusly: "Hitler's propaganda contained better rhetoric, at least, and was certainly less boring than Mr. Dull and Mr. Duller," *Great Debates*, p. 5.
51. See Berquist and Golden, "Media Rhetoric."
52. Witcover, *Marathon*, pp. 644–646.
53. Wooten, *Dasher*, p. 371.
54. Kraus, *Great Debates*, p. 368.
55. Ibid., pp. 6, 10 n.11.
56. Moore and Fraser, *Managers*, p. 141.
57. Witcover, *Marathon*, p. 687.
58. Moore and Fraser, *Managers*, pp. 11–12.
59. Ibid., p. 146.
60. Glad, *Search*, p. 401.
61. Jimmy Carter, *Keeping Faith: Memoirs of a President* (New York: Bantam Books, 1982), p. 125.

SELECT BIBLIOGRAPHY

Kraus, Sidney, ed. *The Great Debates: Carter vs. Ford 1976*. Bloomington: Indiana University Press, 1979. A compendium of twenty-six essays involving various aspects of the 1976 debate series. Especially strong on media and polling analyses of what the editor chooses to label "Great Debates."

Moore, Jonathan, and Janet Fraser. *Campaign for President: The Managers: Look at '76*. Cambridge, Mass.: Ballinger, 1977. A postcampaign oral history project of the Institute of Politics at the John F. Kennedy School of Government at Harvard, this work is particularly valuable for the candid views it contains of major campaign participants, and the authors' insightful analysis of the impact of the debates on the outcome of the election.

Witcover, Jules, *Marathon: The Pursuit of the Presidency, 1972–1976*. New York: New American Library, 1977. A play-by-play account of the countless fits and starts of the 1976 campaign by a prominent political correspondent. Done in the tradition of Theodore White's *Making of the President* series.

Wooten, James. *Dasher: The Roots and the Rising of Jimmy Carter*. New York: Summit Books, 1978. An extensive analysis of Carter's circuitous journey to the White House, done with sensitivity and balance. A truly outstanding example of highly readable campaign biography at its best.

Debate Transcript

Bitzer, Lloyd, and Theodore Rueter. *Carter vs. Ford: The Counterfeit Debates of 1976*. Madison: University of Wisconsin Press, 1980. This is the standard analysis of the text of the debates from the point of view of argumentation. Borrowing a phrase from Jeffery Auer's earlier analysis of the Kennedy–Nixon debates, the authors detail the shortcomings of the 1976 debates and the format followed there. The second half of this work is devoted to a carefully authenticated text of the three presidential and one vice presidential confrontations.

Chapter 3

The 1976 Mondale–Dole Vice Presidential Debate

Kevin Sauter

At 9:34 on the evening of October 15, 1976, on stage at the Alley Theater in Houston, Texas, Robert Dole made what might be considered the biggest mistake of his political career. Dole, Senator from Kansas and the vice presidential candidate on the Republican ticket with Gerald Ford, was over an hour into a 75 minute debate with Walter Mondale, the Minnesota Senator and runningmate of Democrat Jimmy Carter. The evening had been a difficult one for Dole. He had been suffering from a severe cold. He was tired from carrying the Republican banner on the campaign trail throughout the fall. Finally, he was in the midst of a debate which, although prompted by his challenge, he did not want and in which he held little chance of victory. His strategy that evening was to use his ascerbic wit and aggressive campaign style to both belittle the Democratic challengers and to demonstrate his toughness to the Republican faithful who were watching. The strategy had been less than successful, and the debate with Mondale was not going well for Dole. His humor was delivered with an unsmiling face and appeared more mean-spirited than funny, his attacks on Democratic positions were quickly rebutted, and his attempt to appear tough, perhaps accepted by conservative Republicans, was not effective with moderate Independents. Mondale, without the pressures faced by Dole, was able to remain above the mudslinging, recite the Party line, and wait for Dole to self-destruct. Dole accommodated him.

Throughout the debate, Mondale had been making thinly veiled references to Richard Nixon, Watergate, and the roles played by Ford and Dole in the scandal. When Walter Mears, special correspondent for the Associated Press and a panelist for the debate, asked Dole if Nixon's pardon by President Ford was a legitimate issue in the 1976 campaign, Dole could not restrain himself from making a counter argument. Said Dole: "Well, it is an appropriate topic, I guess, but it's not a very good issue any more than the War in Vietnam would be or World War II, or World War I, or the war in Korea, all Democrat wars, all in this century. I figured up the other day, if we added up the killed and wounded in Democrat wars in this century, it'd be about one point six million Americans—enough to fill the city of Detroit."[1] The response from Mondale was swift and on target: "I think Senator Dole has richly earned his reputation as a hatchet man tonight," said Mondale. "Does he really mean to suggest to the American people that there was a partisan difference over our involvement in the war to fight Nazi Germany? I don't think any reasonable American would accept that." Mondale's victory in the debate was ensured during this exchange.

The consequences of this debate seem fairly clear: Mondale won the debate with a low-key delivery style and a recitation of traditional Democratic platitudes; Dole lost the debate by appearing mean and often contradictory. The effect on the election is difficult to pinpoint, but in several studies conducted on the debates, Mondale was perceived to be a winner by an average of 27 points over Dole.[2] Beyond the 1976 campaign, the "hatchet man" image of Dole "clung to his neck like an albatross over the years, despite his concerted effort to soften his image."[3] Mondale, on the other hand, won a personal as well as an electoral victory that year. Sears and Chaffee conclude after examining a number of studies of the presidential and vice presidential debates, that Mondale's "popularity, competence, and trait evaluation all improved following the debate and more so among viewers than non-viewers."[4] While Dole made several failed attempts to later become the Republican nominee, Mondale was able to win the Democratic presidential nomination in 1984.

The vice presidential debate of 1976, then, had significant immediate effects on the election of Jimmy Carter and Walter Mondale, and had long-lasting effects on the political careers of the participants. To understand these effects, one need look no further than Dole's "Democrat wars" argument and Mondale's response. Eugene White, however, reminds us that "the meaning of the speech act is not in the urgency alone, nor in the message alone. It is in the contextual relation of the exigential flow to the rhetorical action and vice versa. The exigential flow provides the contextual, processual, and correlational character of a rhetorical action."[5] In what White calls the "evanescent moment" that Dole made his unfortunate claim, there was a configuration of urgencies, people, events, purposes, and so on—a history—which can be traced to discover what brought this rhetorical act into being. It is without question that Dole made a rhetorical misjudgment that Friday night in Houston, but by examining the configuration of forces that led him to adopt certain tactics we can understand more clearly that Dole's defeat by Mondale was almost assured by the inexorable pull of history.

The key components of this configuration are these: the decision to debate Mondale should have been considered more carefully in light of the aberrant conditions of the 1976 campaign; the goals, both immediate and long term, that both Dole and Mondale were attempting to achieve were such that Dole was faced with conflicting tasks while Mondale's objectives were more easily attainable; and the strategies and tactics that each candidate chose to reach those goals, including the arguments developed, the personal styles each used, and the nonverbal behaviors they exhibited, favored Mondale and led to a number of mistakes by Dole. "History is itself a becoming, a development that produces the 'realities' of the present," says White, and "all social unfolding and all human functioning are consequences of the past and antecedents of the future."[6] In 1976 Walter Mondale and Robert Dole were confronted with the greatest challenge of their still young political careers, and the results of that 75 minutes on national television followed them to election night and beyond.

THE DECISION TO DEBATE

The relative ease with which these debates were arranged seems, upon first examination, to be surprising, but the conditions of 1976 were such that conventional wisdom about the value of debates no longer would hold true. Trent and Friedenberg point to six questions that should be asked by a candidate when determining whether or not to debate.[7] These six questions serve to show the unusual conditions surrounding the 1976 campaign.

1. *Is this likely to be a close election?* The answer to this question in the summer of 1976 seemed to be no. Ford was running as many as 30 percentage points behind Carter in the polls, he was the nominee of the smaller political party, he was president during a time of economic recession, and he had seriously eroded the confidence the electorate had in him through the pardon of Richard Nixon. Although he had the illusion of incumbency on his side, Ford was an unelected president and, as a long-time member of the House of Representatives, had never been engaged in even a state-wide election.

Carter's position also demonstrated the difficulty of answering this question easily. Although he had a substantial lead in the polls in August, much of this support was based on the two-to-one advantage he held in party registration. In fact, after the Republican convention, some polls, both private and public, had Carter's lead down to as little as 8 or 9 points.[8] This "soft" lead in the polls would predictably dwindle as the campaign continued, and his status as an unknown and a newcomer to the national political scene could substantially undermine his popularity in the polls.

The effect of the Mondale–Dole debate within this scenario is significant. In order for Ford to win the election, he needed to maintain his base of support within a party that had been split decisively by the bitter primary battle with Ronald Reagan. Dole's selection to the ticket had been an attempt to mend the rift with the right, and the impact of Dole's participation in the campaign was, in large part, to alleviate the pressures on Ford from conservatives. Dole was also a popular figure in the farm belt and the Ford strategy for winning a close election relied heavily on Dole's ability to hold votes in traditionally Republican midwestern farm states, as well as to help swing votes in some border states.

Mondale's role would also be to stabilize the ticket. In a year when Eugene McCarthy was making a serious bid as a third-party candidate, Mondale needed to maintain support among the traditionally liberal, and Democratic, voter blocs: blacks, organized labor, and Jews. Mondale could also help to ward off attacks in the midwest from his Minnesota base, and would be an effective counter to Carter's southern roots in the industrial northeast. If this were to be a close election, and the advisors to both candidates foresaw this possibility, then the vice presidential candidates would play a crucial role in maintaining loyalty among members of each candidate's base of support.

2. *Are advantages likely to accrue to me if I debate?* The vice presidential debates were included in the initial invitation from the League of Women Voters, and Dole issued his challenge to Mondale immediately upon nomination, but it was unclear whether the debate would actually be a successful strategy for the Republicans. Carter and Mondale were sure to gain from the exposure that the debates would bring—they were both relatively unknown, were nominees of the larger political party, and, as challengers, would be able to attack the performance and policies of the administration. Dole was in a less defined situation and the Republican ticket might not be able to substantially increase its popularity through the debates. In the debate, Dole hoped to establish himself as "presidential," to attack Carter as vague on the issues, and to label Mondale as a liberal who supported big-spending social programs and opposed a strong military. It is important to note that only the first of these possible advantages would be "positive" to the Ford–Dole ticket, while the remaining two would be disadvantageous to the Carter–Mondale campaign. Mondale too would attempt to be seen as presidential, but he would also be able to appeal to the larger public about issues directly affecting them: unemployment, high inflation, poverty, the need for better health care, and so on. Indeed, in a close election, Mondale had

the chance to succeed with these debates, while Dole was placed in the position of having to "not lose."

In both cases, however, the need for exposure might have been the overriding potential advantage. In this strange election, where the incumbent was appointed and unelected, and where the unelected vice president was not running, the two vice presidential candidates needed to demonstrate their abilities to move into the presidency. However, this too was a "don't lose" proposition which favored Mondale. Inasmuch as his ticket was behind in the polls, Dole was supposed to be the aggressor in the debate, a role that had been outlined in the Ford campaign strategy drafted the previous summer.[9] Dole was to be on the offensive, a position that could be misconstrued as unpresidential, while Mondale had the advantage of maintaining distance from the attack. Certainly either candidate could gain advantage if he were able to make a favorable impression on the viewers, but Dole had the more difficult task of being both effective as an aggressive debater, and in control as a thoughtful, "presidential" contender.

3. *Am I a good debater?* Mondale and Dole were both effective members of the Senate, the first time in over twenty years that the vice presidential candidates were both from that body. Their ability to debate seemed unquestioned, though here again, Dole was in a more difficult position. Dole's style was aggressive and partisan, with a particularly strong, biting wit. Although he was an able debater, to be successful before a national television audience he could not use the same tactics he had been using on the campaign trail. While a scathing attack on the opposition played well to the party faithful in the farm belt, he was now to make his presentation to a more varied audience without such partisan attachments. The key voters for Dole were the soft Democrats in the industrial states of the northeast, and his debating style, while effective at maintaining Republican votes, could be a dangerous weapon when viewed by independents, undecideds, and those mildly committed to Carter.

Mondale was also a skilled and articulate debater, but his style was considerably more subdued than Dole. While Mondale's sincere, albeit unexciting, presentational style might make for a boring evening with the Democratic nominee, it was also more appropriate for the "don't lose" strategy that must be used to be successful in this kind of forum.

4. *Are there only two major candidates running for office?* There was a third party effort from Eugene McCarthy in 1976 that did have an effect on the Carter–Mondale campaign, but did not seriously affect the nature of the debate between Mondale and Dole. Although there was some pressure to include McCarthy and others in the debates, the courts ruled consistently in favor of the League and the two major party candidates

in response to several petitions, and the debates were scheduled and carried out without significant interruption from third-party candidates.[10] Also, the base of support for all third-party candidates was statistically so low that political pressure could not be brought to bear on the League in support of including McCarthy in the debates.

5. *Do I have control of all the important variables in the debate situation?* The meetings to determine the debates' format, dates, locations, and questioners were held primarily to satisfy the demands of the presidential candidates. The vice presidential debate between Dole and Mondale was publicly initiated by the Republicans, but they were "not prepared to state categorically that there would be a vice-presidential debate."[11] Extensive negotiations took place between the parties, and as Peggy Lampl, executive director for the League, and the person credited with first suggesting the vice presidential debate in League discussions, said the "veep negotiations were more difficult than those involving the top of the ticket."[12] Of major importance in the negotiations was the location for the debate. Seltz and Yoakam report that the Republicans at one point supported Atlanta as the site for the debate, and although the Democrats were leery of bringing the fight into the heart of the South, the League explored the option but was unable to locate an available theater. It was later agreed that the debate would take place in the more neutral, but vitally important state of Texas, at the Alley Theater in Houston.[13] Also in contention during negotiations were the length and format of the debate: Dole wanted a one-hour debate with short, one-minute answers; Mondale supported a ninety-minute debate with longer answer periods. Eventually, it was decided that the debate would be seventy-five minutes long with answers up to two-and-a-half minutes. There would be time for a one-minute rebuttal. The final compromise was on topic selection: equal time would be spent on domestic issues, foreign policy questions, and an open period for questions on any subject.

The candidates were very much in control of the debates, with the League acting as arbitrators, and the networks serving as mere conduits for the programs. As Seltz and Yoakam conclude, "Both sides knew that the candidates' representatives controlled the events, so when they were in agreement, there was little chance of other outcome."[14]

6. *Is the field clear of incumbents?* Once again, the case of 1976 appears to answer this questions clearly—President Ford was in office—but the aberration of 1976 continues. Ford's status as an incumbent is as much illusory as real. Although he was an unelected president, he nonetheless had the power and prestige of the White House behind him. Dole, however, was the first nonincumbent vice presidential candidate to run with a sitting president since Harry Truman was second on the ticket to Franklin Roosevelt in 1944. Dole was thus placed in the position of

defending the record of an administration not of his making and one with which he had some conflict as a member of the Senate. Without the benefit of incumbency, Dole had the burden of supporting and defending the Ford record, while also being the aggressor in the attack on Carter and Mondale. It is little wonder then that Dole, the ersatz incumbent, compelled to engage in the debate, was less enthusiastic about participating than was the challenger, Mondale.

The decision to debate, an imperative action for Ford, was less clear for Dole. The vice presidential candidate was reluctant to engage in the confrontation with Mondale, perhaps because he saw that the role he played in the campaign placed him in a vulnerable position during a nationally televised debate. In the end, the decision to participate in the debate was the first component in the historical configuration that led to Dole's poor performance in Houston.

GOALS OF THE CANDIDATES

The Republicans and the Democrats agreed that the election would be won or lost in several key states. The Ford–Dole ticket had strong support in the West and, to a lesser degree, in the midwestern farm belt, while Carter and Mondale held a substantial lead in the South, and had significant support in the industrial Northeast. The states on which the election would turn were New York, New Jersey, Pennsylvania, Ohio, Illinois, Michigan, and California. Carter's advisors added Indiana to the list, while Ford's staff included Texas.[15]

The Ford campaign advisor argued that the "target constituency for the President is the upper blue collar and white collar workers" with a particular emphasis on Catholic voters, a Democratic group the Ford camp felt was vulnerable. Republican strength in suburban counties in the Northeast would need to be stable, and the western states would have to vote overwhelmingly Republican for Ford and Dole to win the election.

The Carter–Mondale campaign would need to reclaim the South, a region lost to the Republican Party in recent elections, but heavily favored to vote for favorite son, Carter. In addition to consolidating southern support, Carter would need to stabilize the traditional base of the Democratic voters in urban areas, especially blacks and ethnics, Jews, intellectuals, and members of organized labor. The challenge for Carter would be to maintain support among registered Democrats, and make inroads on blocs of Independent voters, particularly in the major industrial states and in the southern border states.

The goals of Mondale and Dole as they entered the debate were dictated by the role they had each been assigned to play in the overall strategy of their respective campaigns.

Dole needed to accomplish three things in order for him and Ford to reap benefits from the debate. First, he needed to appeal to traditional Republican voters. This seemed to be the easiest of his tasks, and the one with which he had been most effective as he campaigned in the West and Midwest that fall. Dole initially had been selected for the second spot on the ticket to maintain support among the conservative followers of Ronald Reagan. The primary objective for him in the debate, as dictated by the campaign, was to appeal to the Party regulars. As Dole wrote in his memoirs, "I knew it would be a chance to score some points with groups crucial to Republican success. I went in with a simple strategy: to appeal to conservatives."[16]

Dole's second objective was to generate support among Independents, undecideds, and soft Democratic supporters by attacking Carter and Mondale as big-spending liberals. By the time of the vice presidential debate in October, the race was beginning to tighten up and the overwhelming lead Carter had enjoyed in August was under 10 points in the polls. The president's gaffe in the second debate about the lack of Soviet dominance of Eastern Europe had damaged the campaign, and one of Dole's tasks was to help regain momentum in the final weeks before the election. Dole, then, needed to bring a damaging attack to the debate, hopefully nudging moderates to the Republican ticket and bringing a sense of drama and urgency to the campaign.

Finally, Dole needed to act as a defender of the Ford administration's policies. An incumbent usually has the information, resources and power to deflect criticism by his or her opponent, but in the aberrant election of 1976, incumbency was as much a hindrance as a help. Ford, as an appointed vice president and later as an unelected president, had spent much of his short time in office trying to curb the unleashed power of a Democratic congress. While there were few Ford initiatives to debate there were many Nixon ghosts with which to contend. Dole was given the unenviable task of defending an administration of which he was not part, policies with which he had previously disagreed, and a disgraced President Nixon who was now two years removed from office. Combined with an economy in flux and an unfocused foreign policy, the goal of defending attacks against the Nixon and Ford Administrations was always difficult and occasionally distasteful.

In some ways, Mondale had tasks similar to those faced by Dole: he had to maintain support among voters previously loyal to the Party, he had to appeal to the uncommitted voter, and he was responsible for defending the policy statements of his runningmate. Mondale, however, had a significantly easier task in meeting these objectives than did his counterpart on the Republican ticket.

The Democratic Party had a two-to-one lead in registrations over the Republicans in 1976, but the crossover migration to Nixon in 1972 showed that the Democratic base was suspect. After Watergate, however, it seemed that Democrats were willing to return to the fold in 1976. This movement back to the Democratic Party by previously loyal voting blocs provided Mondale with the relatively simple task of appealing to traditional Democratic themes. The Carter–Mondale lead, slipping in recent weeks, was certainly a concern for Mondale as he prepared for the debate, but more importantly his responsibility was to act as the liberal side of the ticket and maintain loyalty among registered Party members. Dole's task, while similar, differed in that he was responsible for encouraging allegiance to Ford among many Party regulars who had been supporters of Ronald Reagan. In other words, Mondale was to "preach to the converted," while Dole had to persuade conservative Republicans to support the more moderate Ford.

Mondale's second goal, to garner support from among the uncommitted voters, was again easier for him to accomplish than it was for Dole. The lead in the polls, and the solid southern strategy, made it more important for the Carter–Mondale ticket to maintain support than to gather it. The dwindling lead in the polls was a concern for the Democratic nominee, but it was still more important, especially for Mondale, to concentrate on maintaining Party loyalty. Mondale also had many of the "people" issues on his side, with a voting record to support them. Issues of health care, employment, and housing would be natural appeals to the viewers targeted for Mondale: the urban, black, labor union voters. So, once again, while Dole had to fight an uphill battle for votes among moderates even as he had to argue conservative Republican ideology, Mondale's goals were to prevent slippage among voters committed to Carter, and appeal to those still undecided by arguing for decent housing, improved health care, full employment, and the like.

Finally, Mondale had to defend Carter's policy positions and public perceptions. President Ford's advisors had developed a campaign blueprint targeting Carter's weaknesses as being too liberal, too partisan, and too ambitious.[17] These charges became the basis for the attack that would occur in the vice presidential debate, but these were perceptual qualities about Carter, and not substantive policy attacks. Mondale's role was to displace the attack against Carter by simply enumerating his virtues, and he could easily ignore specific personality attacks. Dole, as discussed earlier, had to be responsible for defending Ford's record, a record of vetos and apparently ineffectual economic management. Once again, Mondale had the upper hand in the defense of his runningmate while Dole was in a defensive position even as his higher level goals demanded an aggressive posture.

In addition to these partisan goals, however, each of the candidates shared another goal central to their vice presidential race: to impress the viewers with their "presidential" potential. The office of vice president, often looked upon as ceremonial at best, and irrelevant at worst, had become a significant component of government in the previous three decades. Dole and Mondale were being evaluated for their potential to serve as president and the ability they would display during the debate, their only significant national appearance during the campaign, would be a major factor in assessing the impact of the debate on the 1976 vote. Their performance would also become a part of their permanent public image and would follow them in subsequent campaigns as well. In Dole's case, the need to appear presidential could be at odds with the necessary objectives he needed to accomplish as part of the Republican ticket and may have created a tension with which he was unable to contend. Mondale, however, was able to adopt a presidential posture that did not conflict with the other, more pragmatic, objectives of the campaign.

Carter's lead in the polls, the large Democratic Party base, the anemic economy, and Ford's pardon of Nixon put Mondale in a much better position than Dole to "not lose" the debate. In a year of images instead of issues, Mondale did have to deal effectively with some of the charges leveled at Carter—a lack of specificity on issues, a lack of experience with foreign affairs, a lack of good judgment for his *Playboy* interview—but these were charges that were difficult to prove. Mondale had the opportunity in this debate to focus on strategies that would allow him to meet the several campaign goals that were assigned to him, yet leave him free to pursue a strategy that would make him appear to be above the campaign mudslinging, and hence appear presidential. Dole was faced with the difficult tasks of culling support for Ford from among Reagan followers, asking moderate Independents to move to the Republican camp, and defending the policies of an administration of which he had just recently been critical. Given these disparate missions, Dole could not win this debate and he could only hope to "not lose" it.

STRATEGIES OF SENATOR DOLE

In order to accomplish his goals, Dole appears to have used several rhetorical strategies: (1) to praise Ford's leadership and experience and to attack Carter for lacking those same qualities; (2) to portray Mondale and Carter as big-spending liberals; (3) to defend the Republican party against attacks on Watergate; and (4) to use humor to soften his attack and belittle the Democratic candidates and their policy positions. These strategies, at first, seem to be appropriate responses to the urgencies Dole faced in the debate. Upon closer examination, however, the arguments can be seen as inconsistent attempts to appeal to divergent audiences. Moreover, they contain claims for which Dole provided little evidence, and they were delivered with a style of humor that was more mean than funny, more reactive than constructive. The Dole strategy, like the goals imposed upon him by the campaign, led almost inevitably to his poor performance in the debate.

In his opening statement, Dole set his agenda for the evening, arguing that Ford "projects that leadership that American needs," while Carter is vague on the issues of the campaign and overly ambitious. Said Dole, "Now I don't know much about Governor Carter. I've tried to find out. I know he's very ambitious. I know he wants to be president. He's been running for three years." Dole also asserts that Mondale is "probably the most liberal Senator in the United States Senate. And that's really what this debate's all about." Dole's attack on the Democrats as supporters of expensive social programs and opposed to defense spending begins with the claim that "my opponent has a record of voting for every inflationary spending program except in defense, where he votes for every cut." Finally, Dole uses humor to set a tone for the debate by commenting that "tonight may be sort of a fun evening. . . . [Mondale and I will] be friends when this debate is over and we'll be friends when the election is over and he'll still be in the Senate." The themes of leadership and competence, the attacks on Mondale and Carter's liberalism, and the use of humor worked well for Dole in his opening statement, but as the evening wore on, the demands of the situation made the use of these tactics ever more dangerous.

Dole referred to Ford's leadership with regularity during the debate, but he found himself in several awkward situations as he tried to support his runningmate and still respond to the questions from the panel and the statements made by Mondale. Dole said, for example, that he believed that "we're going forward in America under the leadership of President Ford," but shortly after this remark he responded to a Mondale allusion to Watergate by saying, "I think many Americans are sort of turned off, and they were turned off by the war in Southeast Asia. They were turned off by Watergate—I'll say that word first—they were turned off by Watergate. . . . They've been turned off by a lot of things they've seen in politics." Though Mondale's reference to Watergate was not a direct indictment of Ford, Dole was placed in the awkward position of having to argue that the Republican president was the best leader for America even while granting that Nixon's administration was anathema to political leadership. Later in the debate, Dole was faced with an inconsistency about his relationship with the Ford Administration. In one of the questions from the panel, Dole was quoted as saying "We're in the unfortunate position of having a president vetoing bills and getting on the wrong side of people issues." When asked if he still thought the president had used the veto too often, Dole responded that he hadn't "always agreed with President Ford and I've voted to override on occasion." He added that "hindsight's very good, particularly when you're on the ticket." The implied inconsistency was between Dole's opposition to the Ford Administration's policies as a senator and his support for them as the vice presidential candidate. Dole went on to say, "I don't suggest that every veto I must agree with. But I also suggest that I'm a Republican. I'm proud to be a Republican. We're sometimes perceived, as I've said before, as the antipeople party because we're not for spending. We're not for more government; we're for a strong defense." The appeal to Party loyalty, perhaps aimed at those who had previously supported Ronald Reagan, was certainly not the straightforward endorsement Mondale was able to give Carter, nor was it a strong argument for the moderate Independent who may have been wavering between the two parties.

Dole's difficulties continued during the first foreign policy question of the evening. When asked whether he supported Ford's secretary of state, Henry Kissinger, or the Republican platform, which could be interpreted to be a repudiation of the Kissinger foreign policy, Dole responded that he would "go with both and stay with Henry." He continued, "Henry Kissinger is a powerful man. And I haven't always agreed with Henry Kissinger but when I start disagreeing with Henry I start looking at what he's done for America—what he's done for the free world." Dole went on to list some of Kissinger's accomplishments and then reiterated his support of the Kissinger foreign policy initiatives, but the inconsistency remained between his support for Ford's policies and the positions he had taken before his nomination for vice president. Because Dole was not a member of the Ford Administration and was not part of its policy-making team, he was constantly forced to defend people and programs with which he had past disagreements. Although not as dramatic as his "Democrat wars" comment, the inconsistencies in Dole's positions contrast with the stability of support exhibited by Mondale. Dole struggled throughout the debate to remain on the offensive in his attack on the Democratic nominees, but in almost every question had to return to a defense of the Ford Administration. Each time he ran the risk of exposing yet another inconsistency between himself and his runningmate.

Finally, Dole had to deflect criticism of Ford's remark about the lack of Soviet domination over Eastern Europe. Mondale charged that the Ford remark was "probably one of the most outrageous statements made by a president in recent political history." Dole responded, "I think if we take a hard look at President Ford's record rather than all the rhetoric that followed a mistake in the last debate about Poland, we'd know very clearly where President Ford not only stands but has stood for twenty some years." Dole's defense of Ford continued with references to the favorable balance of trade with Eastern European countries, the lack of a clear foreign policy of Jimmy Carter, and ended with a commitment to "those same hopes and aspirations of the Eastern Europeans. And that's what it's all about: freedom, peace, no bloodshed." Dole's confusing defense of an indefensible position demonstrates again the problem he faced in meeting his goals during the debate.

Dole seems to have done better in his attempts to label Carter and Mondale as liberals and supporters of expensive social programs. Rarely did he provide evidence to support his claims, but he used repetition to make the charges appear to stick. On several occasions Dole charged that Mondale was "the most liberal Senator in the United States Senate, and that's his right. He wants to be liberal and spend your money and tax and tax and spend and spend." Dole also attacked Carter's lack of specificity on the issues with such statements as, "The only mystery to me is how do you know what Governor Carter stands for? I've been trying to find out for six weeks. He has three positions on everything—that's why they're having three TV debates." In both cases, Dole may have been successful in pinning the labels of "liberal" and "hazy" on Carter, but he also set up Mondale for an easy response. When Dole challenged Mondale to use the time that remained in the debate to "tell us what his running mate stands for," Mondale was afforded the opportunity to respond with a recitation of standard Democratic themes. "My candidate stands for jobs for all Americans," said Mondale. "He stands for a government which fights inflation. He stands for tax reform. . . . He stands for a program at long last to solve the high health crisis in America. He stands for, at long last, to get the housing industry back on its feet," and so on. The Dole strategy, while effective in its own right, was compromised by the ability of Mondale to argue without conflict in support of his candidate for president, and to appeal to a group of supporters who would respond to exactly those arguments: liberal Democrats.

In spite of the difficulties Dole faced in his attempt to differentiate the Democratic and Republican candidates on leadership and economic policy, the debate would probably have remained fairly innocuous if Dole had not employed his "Democrat wars" tactic to deflect criticism of Watergate. There was no question that Mondale would use Watergate and the subsequent Nixon pardon in the debate, but it also seems clear that Dole was unprepared to deal with the issue in any substantive way. Dole's wife, Elizabeth, in writing about her husband's preparation for the debate, said that he "had originally planned to prepare one afternoon a week, but that went by the boards because of increasingly heavy travel schedules. Bob was inundated with briefing books detailing Mondale's Senate voting record. I doubted whether anyone could master a foot and a half of paper while campaigning all day and half the night."[18]

This lack of preparation might have been exacerbated by the apparent frustration Dole felt as the debate developed and Mondale made repeated references, direct and implied, to Watergate and the pardon. In answer to the second round of questions, Mondale asserted that "We went through the worst political scandal in American history, with the highest officers in the country being found guilty or at least charged with guilt in very serious crimes." Dole responded that people were "turned off by Watergate. But we're looking ahead." The issue was mentioned again during the last half hour of the debate when Mondale, responding to a panelist's question about compatibility between runningmates, said, "I think the whole issue of public trust and public faith is bound up very closely with that question. . . . Americans have lost faith in public leadership." Mondale continued to press on Watergate and the "Saturday Night Massacre," calling the latter "perhaps the most treacherous moment in the history of American liberty," and claimed that "Mr. Ford and Mr. Dole stood up and defended Mr. Nixon." Dole attempted to ward off the Watergate connection by joking that "the night Watergate happened was my night off, so [you] can't hook me for that," but his rising frustration seemed evident when he said, "I don't want any rub-off from Senator Mondale's statements . . . that he might be suggesting that somehow President Ford or Senator Dole was in any way involved in Watergate; we were not." Dole continued, "He brings it up all the time, he brings up the pardon all the time. . . . But Watergate's our burden. We're going forward. It's behind us."

The momentum for Dole's gaffe was building and in the next question he was asked whether the Nixon pardon was an appropriate topic for the campaign. Dole responded with his famous reference to the Democrat wars, and Mondale reacted by calling Dole a "hatchet man." Surprisingly, Mondale claimed later that one of his advisors anticipated the Dole remark, and that the "hatchet man" phrase was a proper response. "When he went into that routine I assumed it was fatal," said Mondale, "and I assumed it was bad enough that I could be permitted to use a word that otherwise might seem a little too tough."[19]

Whatever the reason, a lack of adequate preparation, fatigue from campaigning, a bad cold, or frustration with the line of questioning, Dole made a major political blunder that he still regrets. "Win, lose, or draw," wrote Dole, "the 1976 vice-presidential debate taught me to think twice before saying something that might appear insensitive or call into question the patriotism of any American."[20]

The tactical error of defending Watergate as he did might actually be overshadowed by Dole's use of humor to attack the Democrats. In a campaign where, as Eric Severeid commented, "the issue is not issues,"[21] Dole needed to bring his case to the viewers with an image that would be positive and presidential. Dole was successful in bringing a light tone to the beginning of the debate, but as the night wore on his sarcasm and ascerbic comments became less effective. The pattern of Dole's humor might also help explain the lack of success he had with this strategy. Dole began the debate with a self-deprecatory remark, saying he was interested in the vice presidency because "it's indoor work and no heavy lifting," and later joked that "hindsight's very good, particularly when you're on the ticket."

Dole's more caustic side began to show, however, when he said, "Well I think Senator Mondale is a little nervous, but every time I think of loophole, I think of Governor Carter. I don't know why it comes to me." Dole then charged that Carter took an unnecessarily large tax write-off to buy what Dole characterized as "some peanut machinery—gonna use it next year." In the same answer Dole also made the reference to George Meany as "Mondale's makeup man." The tone continued to get more personal when Dole, in the midst of a discussion on foreign policy issues, said, "I couldn't understand what Governor Carter meant in *Playboy* magazine. I couldn't understand frankly why he was in *Playboy* magazine. But he was and we'll give him the bunny vote."

These remarks, said without a smile, may still have been within the bounds of political confrontation, but Dole next turned his attention to neutral third parties. First, the League of Women Voters. Mondale had claimed that the League's rating of voting records had listed Dole as being "wrong half the time," and that Ford was "right only 35 percent of the time." In his response, Dole quipped that "as far as the League of Women Voter's was concerned, you can look at that two ways—either I was wrong half the time or they were wrong half the time. And I think, knowing the League of Women Voters, I think I'll take my interpretation." This mean-spirited attack on the League was unnecessary. After several more pointed comments aimed at the Democrats, Dole made an implicit attack on the most important third party, the television audience, by referring to the viewers as "those who may be still tuned in" and as "those who may still be with us." The implication that those watching the debate should probably have tuned out earlier may not have been a direct affront to the viewer, but after an evening of Dole's sharp attacks on the Democrats, to make an unflattering remark about the audience was not an astute rhetorical move.

Dole's humor was a strong point in his appearances on the campaign trail, and might have been successful during the debate as well, except for two significant differences in the occasions. First, reaction shots of the audience at the debate were not allowed to be seen on television, a decision made by the advisors to Dole and Mondale. Without shots of audience members laughing, Dole's sharp remarks may have appeared less funny than if the viewer had someone with whom to laugh. Audience reaction might have served Dole much like a "laugh track" on a situation comedy. Dole's nonverbal behavior may also have been a factor in the negative reaction to his humor. Because a war injury had rendered his left arm useless, Dole spent the evening leaning on the podium in a posture that might have made him appear cocky and flippant. Dole also maintained a straight face throughout his verbal assaults, and later admitted that he "should have smiled more."[22] In contrast, after Dole's reference to the League of Women Voters, Mondale was seen in the background of a two-shot of the candidates, sitting, relaxed, and smiling in response to the first line in Dole's comment. Dole remained unsmiling and serious. Perhaps Mondale was correct when he observed later that, "I had known Dole for a long time, and I thought I knew what he was going to do, and it was going to be this kind of 'scat' talk, and that's exactly what he did, and I figured it'd get tiresome, and it did."[23]

Dole's strategies, then, were a product of his goals to placate Republican regulars by defending the Ford Administration, by attacking the liberalism of Carter and Mondale, and by attempting to deflect Watergate as a campaign issue. In addition, his personal style as a slashing campaigner led to the use of humor as an ill-advised tactic to belittle the Democratic ticket. Finally, he apparently became too involved in the immediate objectives of the campaign and was unable to accommodate the larger goal of appearing presidential during the debate. Stanley Hilton, a Dole biographer, said of his subject, he "appeared most unpresidential and graceless. He seemed uncomfortable, irritable, flippant, and particularly harsh tempered."[24] The remaining component of the configuration, the rhetorical strategy of Mondale, was the final element that sealed Dole's loss in the debate, and perhaps in the election as well.

STRATEGIES OF SENATOR MONDALE

Mondale developed three strategies to meet his goals in the debate: attack Ford on leadership and competence issues and praise Carter; recite a litany of Democratic themes; and maintain a low-key, presidential delivery style. These strategies, while similar to Dole's, were nonetheless more clear of encumbrances than were those of the Republican candidate. As the challenger, Mondale was able to attack the Republicans' record, while his defense of Carter's policy positions was a simple recitation of traditional Democratic themes. In each case, the voters to whom Mondale was appealing consisted primarily of registered Democrats, thereby reducing the pressure on him to appeal to listeners at odds with these standard Democratic appeals. The most radical difference in the approach taken by the two candidates was in their personal style. As Dole was witty and sarcastic, Mondale was low-key and sincere. This difference in delivery might have been the key factor in determining the perceived outcome of the debate.

In a fashion similar to that of Dole, Mondale used his opening statement to set forth his agenda for the evening. "I believe that most Americans would agree on the problems that this country faces," Mondale began, and "they include the need once again for an economy that works. . . . We need a government that works, and we need a government that cares, and once again we have to get back to work on education, on health, on housing, on the environment, on energy; and we need a foreign policy that once again reflects the values and beliefs of the American people." Mondale finished by saying that "this nation desperately needs new leadership. The Carter–Mondale ticket would offer a new generation of leadership dedicated to solving the problems which I have listed, and that is our appeal."

As the debate unfolded, Mondale's tactics remained consistent with his strategies. Mondale appealed to the "people issues" in nearly all of his answers and, when pulled from the context of the seventy-five minute debate, the following four examples demonstrate this repetitious pattern: (1) "We [have] got to get people back to work, attacking inflation and finally getting a policy to keep the dollar worth a dollar." "People need jobs. It's a tragedy every time an able-bodied American is denied the opportunity to work. . . . It's a tragedy when children can't get educated, when health care wipes them out, when senior citizens find that . . . Social Security and Medicaid is being taken from them." (2) "I am unashamed of my support for programs to put people back to work. I am unashamed of my support for programs to build housing . . . of supporting education programs such as Medicare." (3) "One of the key problems would be to try to finally get a health insurance program to deal with the health crisis in America. . . . We have to do something about housing. . . . We need to continue to build support . . . for education. We need to get back to work on the problems of senior citizens." (4) "What would we do to deal with the human problems in America? The first thing we would do is put people back to work." In Mondale's closing statement these themes resonated again: "We've cared too little for people in this country that have gotten sick. . . . that cannot get or afford decent housing. This administration has fought time and time again to cut back support for our senior citizens. They have no energy policy. They have no environmental policy. These things must change."

Mondale's relentless attack on the policies of the Republicans was augmented by his constant references, direct and implied, to Watergate and to leadership. In answer to the first question, Mondale said, "We need to have a new look at official lawlessness at the federal level, because we've seen too many instances where people in high public office violate the law itself." In the second answer Mondale continued the thinly veiled references to Watergate, "We went through the worst political scandal in American history, with the highest officers in government being found guilty or at least charged with guilt in very serious crimes." Mondale became more aggressive later in the debate, "We have had so much politics-as-usual, so much political trimming, that Americans have lost faith in public leadership. For example, in Watergate . . . my opponent introduced a resolution to slam the door shut on the Ervin Committee so that people could not see and hear what was going on," and "Even today this administration is fighting all the Watergate reforms." Mondale used the Watergate issue effectively to put Dole on the defensive. He did not, however, appear to have gone beyond the bounds of propriety. He also linked the issue to a general call for new leadership.

Mondale's references to Watergate were followed by these appeals to leadership: (1) "If there's one hope that Governor Carter and I have . . . it is that we can restore faith in the American people by simply telling the truth, obeying the law . . . and then I think we will see a restoration of public trust." (2) "What we're basically talking about is presidential leadership. We need leadership in the presidency." (3) "You have to bring everybody together and have a united country. . . . And that's another reason we need Governor Carter." (4) "With all of the abuse of public faith and trust that we've been through, surely that, too, is another reason for a new generation of leadership." Finally, in his closing statement, Mondale restated his leadership theme: "This country cries out for new leadership. We need a fresh start. And the Carter–Mondale ticket promises that start."

These two primary strategies employed by Mondale, to recite standard Democratic themes and to attack Ford and Dole on leadership issues, were supplemented by a delivery style that was in sharp contrast to Dole's. Although Mondale was considered to have been "just the slightest bit nervous" at the outset of the debate, he was able to remain serious without appearing mean.[25] His delivery style was fluent and in control, and he appeared to relax as the evening wore on. Mondale also was able to direct his remarks to the camera, and the television audience, more than was Dole. Dole tended to speak to the panelists when answering their questions, which gave him an off-camera focus rather than creating a sense of eye contact with the viewer. As Jules Whitcover wrote in his analysis of the campaign, Mondale "had shaken off his early nervousness and was crisp and aggressive."[26]

Mondale's strategies in the debate served his purposes well. He was able to appeal to Democratic voters through repeated references to the domestic issues most likely to affect them, to link these issues to a lack of leadership and competence in the Nixon and Ford Administrations, and he was able to present these arguments while appearing reserved and thoughtful. But more to the point, Mondale was able to contrast, in content and in style, with Dole, and the comparison was favorable for the Minnesota senator.

EFFECTS OF THE DEBATE

Robert Dole and Walter Mondale shook hands on stage after the debate and retreated to their respective dressing rooms to receive calls from their runningmates. Ford told Dole that he had "hit hard but hit fairly," while Carter told Mondale, "Fritz, you did great, man. . . . You didn't get small, you didn't get mean, you didn't get twisted in your approach."[27] For Dole and Mondale, however, the effects of the debate would be discovered during the remaining two weeks of the campaign, at the election, and for each man individually, for a long time to come.

The most immediate effect of the debate was the exposure each candidate received. It is estimated that 35 percent of American households tuned into the debate, accounting for a viewing audience of around 75 million people.[28] Inasmuch as the two vice presidential nominees were relatively unknown at the beginning of the campaign, this national television appearance would allow the viewers to see the style each brought to the debate, and perhaps, learn something about their stand on the issues as well. Lee Becker and his colleagues conclude that people watching the debates were "better able to provide concrete information on the vice-presidential candidates" than were nonviewers,[29] while another study claims that the vice presidential debate "did not, by itself, increase familiarity with the positions held by Dole and Mondale."[30] Although it might be difficult to assess the cognitive learning that took place by people watching the debate, the image of the two candidates was certainly affected during this major campaign event.

Patrick Caddell, Carter's pollster in 1976, wrote in a campaign memo that "Walter Mondale has a positive/negative rating of 44 percent to 27 percent while Dole's rating is 36 percent/35 percent."[31] This analysis, internal to the campaign, was corroborated by several studies that were being conducted at the time. A study concerned with the candidates' images as a result of the debate revealed a strong positive reaction to Mondale's "personal qualities and record of public service while minimizing his partisanship." Dole was characterized as more partisan but a better television performer than Mondale.[32] Sears and Chaffee cite a study of media influence on candidate images, and conclude that "there was also significant attitude change as a consequence of the vice presidential debate, where Mondale scored a personal triumph."[33] Finally, several studies indicate the Mondale was considered the "winner" in the debate with Dole.[34] The evidence seems sufficient to conclude that Mondale succeeded in the debate to effect a positive image among viewers, while Dole was less successful in presenting himself.

A second immediate effect of the debate was on the candidates themselves, particularly on Mondale. "The next ten days were about the best I've ever had in my political career," said Mondale. The day following the debate, for example, Mondale went to Kansas and had "five thousand people going crazy. It was unmistakable that we had won—[Dole] had crowds of four or five hundred."[35] The Democrats also began to feature Mondale in their campaign advertisements and Carter started using the vice presidential choice as a campaign issue.[36] By contrast, Jamieson claims that "if the Republicans considered Dole an advantage nationally, their advertising did not reflect it. Dole is a nonperson in the national Republican advertising."[37] The comparison of vice presidential candidates by voters is also seen in the analysis of the general election results.

By the end of the campaign, the Democratic lead in the polls had evaporated from its high point in July to a dead heat by the last weekend in October. In its postelection coverage, *Time* magazine quoted Hamilton Jordon as saying that the vice presidential debate "gave us two or three extra points . . . it was a big plus for us."[38] The same issue of *Time* reported the results of a Lou Harris poll showing that 51 percent of respondents thought favorably of Mondale as vice president, while only 33 percent considered Dole to have been helpful to his ticket.[39] *Newsweek* stated that "Mondale's across-the-board popularity with Democratic voters was a distinct help to the ticket. . . . By most accounts, he won his debate with Robert Dole."[40]

The actual impact of the vice presidential debate on voting totals is difficult to assess. It seems clear that Mondale's presence on the ticket and his performance in the debate were positive aspects of the Carter campaign and certainly contributed something to the Democratic victory. A Gallup survey, cited by Jamieson, claims that "one of twenty who switched from Ford to Carter during the campaign gave as a reason their dislike of Dole; by contrast only one in a hundred of those who switched from Carter to Ford cited Mondale's candidacy as a reason."[41] It is perhaps in this survey that the true effect of the debate becomes apparent: Mondale was able to succeed by presenting a positive, though innocuous, public image, and "not losing" the debate.

The long-term effects of the Mondale–Dole debate may have been even more striking than their effect on the election of 1976. Mondale was able to establish himself as a "presidential" political persona and to use that image to help him seek and win the Democratic nomination for president in 1984. Although he was run over by the Reagan juggernaut that year, Mondale was able to rise to the top of the Party hierarchy based in large part on the positive public image that followed him from the debate in Houston. Dole, on the other hand, had to carry the weight of his performance throughout his political career. Dole biographer Stanley Hilton cites a George Bush leaflet used in the 1988 presidential primary campaign that blamed Dole for "single-handedly" bringing down the Ford–Dole ticket,[42] and Dole himself later joked that "I went for the jugular all right—my own."[43]

The final effect of the Mondale–Dole debate was to establish the vice presidential debate as an important campaign ritual. Although Bush and Mondale did not debate in 1980, in the following two elections, the Democrat and Republican candidates for vice president did meet in nationally televised debates. This precedent, begun in 1976, will most likely continue in those years where debates are deemed necessary by the two major party nominees.

CONCLUSION

The rhetorical configuration faced by Mondale and Dole in 1976 led to a debate that favored the Democratic candidate. Perhaps Dole could have changed his strategy to be more effective, or, more likely, used tactics that could have helped him "not lose" the debate, but given the forces that were at play that year, it seems safe to conclude that it would have been nearly impossible for Dole to have won. Mondale was able to read the situation effectively and selected the appropriate strategies and tactics that allowed him to benefit from the debate and contribute to his election and that of Jimmy Carter.

NOTES

1. "The Vice Presidential Debate" in *The Great Debates: Carter vs. Ford, 1976,* ed. Sidney Kraus (Bloomington: Indiana University Press, 1979), pp. 498–518. All subsequent quotes from the debate can be found in this debate transcript.

2. David O. Sears and Stephen H. Chaffee, "Uses and Effects of the 1976 Debates: An Overview of Empirical Studies," in Kraus, *The Great Debates,* p. 238.

3. Stanley G. Hilton, *Bob Dole: An American Political Phoenix* (Chicago: Contemporary Books, 1988), pp. 3–4.

4. Sears, in Kraus, *The Great Debates,* p. 247.

5. Eugene E. White, *Rhetoric in Transition: Studies in the Nature and Uses of Rhetoric* (University Park, Penn.: Pennsylvania State University Press, 1980), p. 15.

6. Ibid., p. 18.

7. Judith S. Trent and Robert V. Friedenberg, *Political Campaign Communication: Principles and Practices* (New York: Praeger Publishers, 1983), pp. 244–246.

8. Martin Schram, *Running for President: The Carter Campaign* (New York: Stein and Day, 1977), p. 238.

9. Ibid., p. 254.

10. Herbert A. Terry and Sidney Kraus, "Legal and Political Aspects: Was Section 315 Circumvented?" in Kraus, *The Great Debates,* pp. 47–48.

11. Peggy Lampl, "The Sponsor: The League of Women Voters Education Fund," in Kraus, *The Great Debates,* p. 93.

12. Herbert A. Seltz and Richard D. Yoakam, "Production Diary of the Debates," in Kraus, *The Great Debates*, pp. 142–143.
13. Ibid.
14. Ibid., p. 152.
15. Schram, *Running for President*, p. 268.
16. Robert Dole and Elizabeth Dole, *The Doles: Unlimited Partners* (New York: Simon and Schuster, 1988), p. 174.
17. Schram, *Running for President*, p. 267.
18. Dole and Dole, *The Doles*, pp. 173–174.
19. Interview with Walter Mondale conducted by Kevin Sauter, March 31, 1989, Minneapolis, Minnesota, audiotape in personal collection of the author. (Hereafter cited as Interview with Mondale.)
20. Dole and Dole, *The Doles*, p. 175.
21. *Campaign '76*, with Walter Cronkite, CBS New Special, WTVF, Nashville, Tennessee, 15 October 1976. A copy of this program may be obtained from the Vanderbilt Television News Archive, Vanderbilt University Library, Nashville, Tennessee, 37240.
22. Dole and Dole, *The Doles*, p. 176.
23. Interview with Mondale.
24. Hilton, *Bob Dole*, p. 132.
25. "Slugfest in a Houston Alley," *Time*, October 25, 1976, p. 24.
26. Jules Whitcover, *Marathon: The Pursuit of the Presidency, 1972–1976* (New York: Viking, 1977), p. 614.
27. Ibid.
28. Herbert E. Alexander and Joel Margolis, "The Making of the Debates," in *The Presidential Debates: Media, Electoral, and Policy Perspectives*, eds. George Bishop et al. (New York: Praeger Publishers, 1978), p. 29.
29. Lee B. Becker et al., "Debates' Effects on Voters' Understanding of Candidates and Issues," in Bishop et al., *The Presidential Debates*, p. 134.
30. Sears and Chaffee, in Kraus, *The Great Debates*, p. 235.
31. Schram, *Running for President*, p. 330.
32. Dan Nimmo et al., "Persistence and Change in Candidate Images," in Bishop et al., *The Presidential Debates*, p. 154.
33. Sears and Chaffee, in Kraus, *The Great Debates*, p. 247.
34. Dennis K. Davis, "Influence on Vote Decisions," in Kraus, *The Great Debates*, p. 317. Also, Becker et al. "Debates' Effects," p. 126.
35. Interview with Mondale.
36. Finlay Lewis, *Mondale: Portrait of an American Politician* (New York: Harper & Row, 1980), p. 28.
37. Kathleen Hall Jamieson, *Packaging the Presidency: A History and Criticism of Presidential Campaign Advertising* (New York: Oxford Press, 1984), p. 368.
38. "No. 2 Made His Point," *Time*, November 15, 1976, p. 35.
39. Ibid.
40. "The Veep-Elect," *Newsweek*, November 15, 1976, p. 30.
41. Jamieson, *Packaging the Presidency*, p. 367.
42. Hilton, *Bob Dole*, p. 135.
43. Ibid., p. 133.

SELECT BIBLIOGRAPHY

Bishop, George, F., Robert G. Meadow, and Marilyn Jackson-Beeck, eds. *The Presidential Debates: Media, Electoral, and Policy Perspectives*. New York: Praeger Publishers, 1978. This collection of essays and empirical studies about the 1976 presidential and vice presidential debates provides a discussion of theoretical and methodological issues involved in conducting debate studies with historical information on the evolution of the debates and with data from studies examining the effect of the debates on viewers and nonviewers. Although the emphasis is clearly on the presidential debates, several of the studies have included the Mondale–Dole debate in their data collection.

Dole, Robert, and Elizabeth Dole. *The Doles: Unlimited Partners*. New York: Simon and Schuster, 1988. Robert Dole and his wife Elizabeth have combined to write an intriguing memoir of their respective careers in public service. The authors alternate writing their individual accounts of events. Although only several pages are devoted to the 1976 vice presidential debate, this volume represents the Doles's explanation of the choices made throughout their respective careers.

Lewis, Finlay. *Mondale: Portrait of an American Politician*. New York: Harper & Row, 1980. An authorized biography of Mondale written by a Minneapolis newspaper reporter. Because of its author's background, this assessment of Mondale's career tends to be more reportorial than analytical. Nonetheless, it is the most significant treatment of Mondale currently available.

Interview with Walter Mondale. Conducted by Kevin Sauter. March 31, 1989. Minneapolis. I conducted an interview with Mondale during which he discussed his recollections and assessments of the 1976 campaign and the debate with Dole. Mondale also commented on the role of debates in presidential campaigns, his participation in the 1984 debate with Ronald Reagan, and the possible impact of debates in future campaigns. An audiotape of the interview is available from Professor Kevin Sauter, College of St. Thomas, St. Paul, Minnesota, 55105.

Schram, Martin. *Running for President 1976: The Carter Campaign*. New York: Stein and Day, 1977. A fairly complete review of the 1976 campaign, this book uses a number of campaign documents as evidence. Particularly useful were memos sent to the presidential candidates outlining strategy and responding to campaign events.

Debate Transcript

Kraus, Sidney, ed. *The Great Debates: Carter vs. Ford, 1976*. Bloomington: Indiana University Press, 1979. An outstanding collection of essays and studies about the 1976 debates. The first section of this book provides a historical review of presidential debates, strategies of the participants, and excellent presentations of the legal and logistical constraints surrounding the debates. The second section is a compilation of reports on studies that attempted to assess the effects of the debates. Finally, the third section of the book contains transcripts of each of the presidential and vice presidential debates.

Videotape of the Debate

A videotape of the Mondale–Dole debate is available from the Vanderbilt Television News Archive, Vanderbilt University Library, Nashville, Tennessee, 37240.

Chapter 4

The 1980 Reagan–Carter Presidential Debate

Kurt Ritter and David Henry

The presidential debate between Ronald Reagan and Jimmy Carter came at the climax of the 1980 presidential campaign. It was fitting that a major media event such as the debate should cap the campaign, for the campaign marked the end of a turbulent decade of American politics in which the news media had played a central role. Both Reagan and Carter were products of the media politics of the 1970s. In 1970 Reagan was winning reelection as governor of California and was still regarded as a curiosity in national politics: an actor in public office. In the same year, Jimmy Carter was winning an upset election for governor of Georgia. A new figure on the political scene, Carter would storm into presidential politics with a media blitz in 1976.

As their political careers progressed, Reagan and Carter watched the Watergate scandal and its attendant media coverage drive Richard Nixon out of the White House. The two men came close to running against each other in 1976 when Carter was the Democratic candidate for president and Reagan lost the Republican nomination by the closest of margins. Carter won election as president, in part, on the strength of his performance in television debates with President Gerald Ford. But the television medium that had been an asset to Carter in 1976 became a liability during his term as president. Television news dramatized the energy crisis, the nation's weak economy, and above all, the Iran hostage crisis.

Television was no less important in the 1980 presidential campaign. Jimmy Carter secured renomination as the Democratic candidate in no small part because his rival, Senator Edward Kennedy of Massachusetts, had self-destructed in November 1979 during a television interview with

Roger Mudd. Reagan had entered the Republican primary campaign as the front-runner, a position he put at risk by declining to join a televised Iowa Republican debate in January. He lost the Iowa caucuses but later won the Republican nomination after participating in every subsequent television debate during the primary campaign. As the major party candidates for president of the United States, both Carter and Reagan could be regarded as veterans of television debates. Yet, it was not at all clear that they would debate each other. The risk of a debate made both cautious. When asked about the prospects of a presidential debate, one campaign aide replied: "That would be rolling the dice in one big crap shoot that could blow it all."[1]

Ultimately, but by no means inevitably, Reagan and Carter did debate. One week after the debate, Reagan won an overwhelming victory—although experts had predicted a close vote. The conventional wisdom of journalists and political operatives was that Carter had done the best debating, but that Reagan had won the audience through his superior television presentation. The present study rejects that conclusion. Instead, this study demonstrates that Reagan won the debate on both substance and style. Reagan's success—and Carter's failure—can be traced to their respective debating strategies.

THE DECISION TO DEBATE

Although political analysts frequently ground their judgments of election campaign events in the trappings of logical analysis, perhaps just as frequently major decisions may be traced to the raw political instincts of candidates and their advisers. Such is arguably the case with Governor Ronald Reagan's decision to debate President Jimmy Carter in 1980, and with Carter's decision that he could not avoid the challenge.

Indicative of the logic-centered approach, for example, is Robert Friedenberg's analysis of the 1980 presidential debates. Critics of campaign discourse ought to attend at the outset, Friedenberg contended, to questions which motivate the participants to debate in the first place. Such an analysis can be cast in terms of the questions that the presidential candidates must ask themselves: Is the election close? Will I gain an advantage by debating? Am I a good debater? Can my campaign organization influence the decisions pertinent to time, place, rules of debate, and so on? The answers rendered by Reagan and Carter in October of 1980, Friedenberg contended, made the decision to debate a logical necessity.[2]

For the record, of course, both candidates had stated for many months that they wanted to debate—as soon as a fair debate could be arranged. As early as May 1980 Ronald Reagan had declared himself "very happy to debate" Jimmy Carter, and Carter had accepted the League of Women

Voters' debate invitation. When Carter telephoned Reagan in July to congratulate him on receiving the Republican nomination, Carter added that he "would welcome a chance for several debates in different regions of the country."[3] Despite these high-minded declarations in favor of public discussion, the two candidates would not agree to debate. Ronald Reagan insisted that "fairness" required that independent candidate John Anderson be included in the debates; Reagan also demanded a small number of debates scheduled late in the campaign. Carter recognized that both those stipulations would put him at a disadvantage. He insisted that Anderson not be included. Publicly, the Carter campaign argued that Anderson lacked the status of a major party candidate, but privately Carter and his advisors shared Reagan's conviction that Anderson's candidacy was drawing support from Carter, so any political event that included Anderson would hurt Carter. Carter's advisors dismissed Reagan as an actor with a shallow grasp of public policy. Hence, they reasoned, Reagan would falter if engaged in a long series of debates that forced him to go beyond his initial statements on various campaign issues.[4]

Both candidates played out their roles as advocates of debates. Carter regularly accepted debate invitations that excluded Anderson, secure in his conviction that Reagan would refuse to debate without the Illinois congressman in the forum. Carter refused to join Reagan and Anderson in their nationally televised debate on September 21, 1980. Instead, he called a news conference to insist on a "man-to-man" debate with Reagan, whom he offered to meet "any time, any place." Reagan responded with his own news conference, where he accused Carter of being unwilling to debate with Anderson and Reagan because he wanted to "hide his record and his performance from the American people." Following the Reagan–Anderson debate, a poll of 1,500 voters conducted by the Associated Press and NBC News revealed that 55 percent disapproved of Carter's refusal to join the debate and only 24 percent approved.[5]

Myles Martel documents the careful calculations involved in the Reagan camp's decision to debate. Based largely on his role as part of a Debate Task Force established in August and headed by James Baker, Martel recalls a decision-making process rooted in the dialectical tradition. On one side, pollster Richard Wirthlin argued against the debate, seeing nothing to be gained. According to Wirthlin's surveys, the grand strategy from the Republicans' summer convention through election day was on target and should not be disrupted by a debate. William Timmons, another public opinion specialist in the Reagan campaign, echoed Wirthlin's sentiments that a debate with Carter offered little benefit. For Timmons, the compelling factor was his perception that Reagan's superior campaign organization meant that the Republicans could win the election without a debate.[6] Because of the risk inherent in a televised debate, one campaign operative advised the press: "Don't expect to see us in a debate unless the polls change and the race gets too close for comfort."[7]

Equally pragmatic, however, were Reagan advisors on the other side of the issue, who favored a televised encounter. Contrary to Wirthlin's poll results, other national surveys reflected a downward trend in Reagan's earlier lead, with some showing almost weekly changes in the front-runner. Perhaps more important, debate proponents noted, press reports of the fluctuating polls often inferred that Jimmy Carter had moved ahead of Reagan. A direct clash with Carter was thus deemed essential both to suppress the negative press coverage and to ensure balanced, or at least equal, coverage as election day neared. Nor would refusal to debate Carter likely enhance Reagan's stature as a presidential prospect, given his own earlier chastisement of Carter for rejecting the opportunity to engage Reagan and Anderson in the September debate.[8]

Finally, the Republican campaign recognized that Ronald Reagan was an exceptionally effective speaker on television. Reagan's press secretary, Lyn Nofziger, maintained that "the most effective thing we can do is put him on television whenever we can." Even though Wirthlin opposed a debate with Carter, in one of his early campaign strategy memos, he credited Reagan's television speeches and debates during the 1980 presidential primary campaign with improving his image with the voters.[9]

Logical, well reasoned arguments for debating, then, clearly influenced the campaign's thinking.[10] It was perhaps Ronald Reagan's own political instincts, however, which determined the outcome of the decision-making process. On October 16, Reagan and Carter shared the podium in New York City at the annual Al Smith dinner. Reagan's performance not only demonstrated his oratorical superiority over Carter,[11] but convinced him that he could match his opponent in a nationally televised exchange. Reagan appeared relaxed at the dinner, adhered to the "no partisan politics" rule, and engaged in self-deprecating humor during his brief speech, dismissing "the rumor that I am the only one here who was at the original Al Smith dinner." Carter, in contrast, appeared ill at ease as his own efforts at humor fell flat.[12] Reagan emerged a "clear winner," according to *Time*, "a relaxed Type B to Carter's forced Type A."[13] Reagan listened the next day as his aides argued the reasons for and against debating Carter, then decided: "Well, everything considered, I feel I should debate. If I'm going to fill the shoes of Carter, I should be willing to meet him face-to-face."[14]

Reagan's decision to debate Carter trapped the president. His pollster, Patrick Caddell had advised: "Don't debate Reagan if there is any honorable way to avoid it."[15] Caddell viewed debates as vehicles for promoting challengers. He believed that a debate late in the campaign would interfere with the "surge" that incumbent president candidates had traditionally gained just before election day. He also feared that a debate would give Reagan an opportunity to respond to the attacks being launched by the Carter campaign.[16] Moreover, in his painfully candid campaign strategy documents, Patrick Caddell cited factors that would make a debate dangerous for Carter and helpful to Reagan. He noted that in both 1960 and in 1976, the initial presidential debates had allowed the challengers to cross what he called "the acceptability threshold" of the American voters. In each of those elections, Caddell believed, the first debate caused a majority of voters to decide that the challenging candidate (even if he was "not their choice") was "qualified and able to be President." A basic tenet of Caddell's campaign strategy was to "deny Reagan the Acceptability Threshold."

In contrast, Carter's liabilities as a candidate included his "inability to communicate a vision of what America should be," and his "inability to articulate goals and programs effectively"—hardly a political profile well suited for a television debate against Ronald Reagan.[17] On October 14, apparently in an effort to sabotage negotiations for a Reagan–Carter debate, the Carter campaign considered giving Reagan an ultimatum to debate Carter by the end of the week or there would be no debate—a deadline so short that the Carter aides believed Reagan would have to reject the debate. Before the Democrats made this offer, however, events overtook them. The League of Women Voters dropped its requirement that John Anderson be included in the next debate. Reagan reversed his position on Anderson's participation and accepted the debate invitation.[18] The sudden turn of events caught the Carter campaign by surprise. Hamilton Jordan at first saw Reagan's decision as an act of desperation: "He must think he's going to lose. His people would never let him debate if they were ahead." Patrick Caddell placed a frantic telephone call to Jordan to ask: "Is there any way we can avoid debating him?" Jordan thought not.[19] After all, Carter had been publicly challenging Reagan to a one-on-one debate for weeks. As one Carter aide remarked to political journalist Elizabeth Drew, "There's no way out of it now."[20]

Ronald Reagan's sense that he was equal to the task not only influenced his decision to debate, but would bear directly on the goals, strategies, and tactics that would emanate from that decision. On the other hand, the Carter campaign's ill-placed conviction that Reagan lacked the knowledge and intellect to carry off a substantive debate influenced its approach to the debate—especially the particular strategies and tactics that Jimmy Carter would employ.

GOALS

Each campaign had developed detailed campaign strategies for the general election.[21] When the Reagan–Carter debate was actually scheduled, both candidates sought to use the debate to achieve their overall campaign objectives. The debate goals of each campaign were strikingly similar: (1) to manage "expectations" about the debate performances of the candidates in order to favor their candidate; (2) to appeal to specific "target" blocs of voters; (3) to focus on the weakness of their opponent; and (4) to stress the strengths of their candidate.

The Reagan Campaign

Reagan's campaign managers cast Reagan as the underdog against the experienced Carter, whose victory in 1976 they attributed to Carter's skill in the debates with President Gerald Ford. The Reagan campaign hoped that if the public perceived Reagan as debating as well as Carter, the debate would be translated as a moral victory for the challenger. Indeed, by the morning of the debate, veteran campaign commentators were claiming that a tie would be a victory for Reagan. Columnists David Broder and Jack Germond joined NBC's Tom Pettit on the "Today" program to assess the candidates' prospects on the morning of the October 28 debate. Broder warned Carter against attacking his opponent, noting that "everything we've seen of Governor Reagan in the past shows that he is a master at protecting himself." Germond and Pettit agreed that Reagan would gain simply by holding his own. Said Germond, "For a great many voters this is going to be essentially a first impression of Ronald Reagan, and if he does well, if he doesn't start talking about killer trees or whatever, he is going to profit from that.[22]

In addition to lowering expectations so that a draw in the debate with Carter might be interpreted as a victory, the Reagan team selected "target voters." In line with pollster Wirthlin's objective of retaining the support of the governor's core backers, Reagan advisers hoped to intensify the commitment of their candidate's conservative base. At the same time, in what might require a delicate balancing act, the campaign wanted to attract the significant numbers of voters still undecided. Writing less than three weeks before the debate, Richard Wirthlin predicted an election victory if Reagan could appeal to Independents, Anderson voters, and disaffected Democrats. Such appeal, he warned, had to be accomplished "without alienating our [Republican]base."[23] In an exceptionally volatile election year, millions of votes fit the category of "undecided." Particularly vulnerable were voters aligned at various times in the year with John Anderson's third-party effort.

The debate allowed Reagan to continue to implement his campaign's goals of focusing on Carter's record—both by stressing economic issues (inflation, jobs, economic growth, and government waste) and by pointing to Carter's performance ("ineffective," "mean-spirited," "vacillating"). The debate also served Reagan's general goal of projecting the image of a competent, decisive, and above all a "safe" world leader.[24] As Germond noted, for many voters the televised debate would be a first full look at the Republican nominee. In particular, Reagan needed to dispel fears that his election would increase the likelihood of increased militarism on the part of the United States.

The Carter Campaign

Carter's debate goals were the mirror image of Reagan's. He wanted to raise expectations for Reagan's television performance, while downgrading his own reputation as a debater. He, too, had identified his own "target voters." Finally, he sought to draw attention to Reagan's inexperience (especially in foreign affairs), while portraying himself as an experienced leader—one who had learned how to be a better president.

In an extensive memo on strategy for the debate, Patrick Caddell declared that "setting expectations is a critical game in debates particularly with the press."[25] The Carter aides took Caddell's instructions to heart and soon sounded as though it was a point of honor that Carter was less skilled on television than Reagan. One of Carter's political operatives lavished malevolent praise on Reagan, calling him "a very polished performer" in televised debates and noting that "he's got it down to a very finely honed skill." White House Press Secretary Jody Powell was anxious to concede that "the President isn't as good at it as Reagan is."[26] Lest anyone in the press miss the point, Jimmy Carter himself began to declare: "A lot of people say he's better at making speeches than I am, and I guess they're right."[27]

As a basic election strategy, the Carter campaign had targeted "weakly affiliated Democrats."[28] In discussing the debate, Carter's campaign manager Robert Strauss expressed the hope that his candidate could shepherd this voting bloc back to his party on election day.[29] One week before the debate, Caddell expanded the target audience to include three primary groups and two "minor" groups. The first primary group, which could be broadly labeled "undecided," subsumed the "weak" Democrats as well as other undecided voters, voters currently for Reagan who were not very certain to vote for him, and uncertain Anderson voters. The two other major groups were those Caddell believed were most likely to be influenced by a presidential debate: college-educated voters and women. He regarded those types of voters as Carter's "first and paramount target groups." Less prominent, but still important were two "spread groups": Jewish voters and southern voters. Caddell instructed Carter to address each of those two groups at least once in the debate.[30]

While the Reagan campaign wanted to keep the focus of the debate on Carter's record, the Carter campaign aides tried to do just the reverse. They wanted to keep the focus of the debate on the choice between two candidates—a "dangerous" Reagan and a "safe" Carter. Caddell believed that by late October, they had succeeded in "turning the electoral focus on Reagan," by which he meant "Reagan's riskiness, hip-shooting, and impulsiveness in foreign policy."[31] An important objective of the debate would be to intensify that focus. Jody Powell told news reporters that the debate would show that Reagan had not moderated, but was still devoted to right-wing politics: "How much stock can you put in a fella who reverses 20 years of political positions in the space of a few weeks of campaigning?[32] At the same time, Carter wanted to portray himself as a "man of peace," as a "moderate man," as a "man of compassion," and as a president who had learned from his difficulties in his first term. In short, the debate should portray Carter as a man who would be a better president in his second term.[33]

As each candidate prepared for the debate, the four general goals of each camp were translated into specific strategies. Ultimate success, however, would not come to both candidates. The winner would be the candidate who both had effective strategies and had the ability to implement those strategies during the debate. When the debate unfolded, that candidate proved to be Ronald Reagan.

RONALD REAGAN'S DEBATE STRATEGY

On October 21, Reagan's Debate Task Force submitted a debate strategy memorandum to the inner circle of Reagan's staff. "If the Governor succeeds Tuesday in making Jimmy Carter's record the major issue of the debate and the campaign," the authors asserted, "we will succeed in the debate and win the general election. If, however, Carter makes Ronald Reagan the issue of the debate and the campaign, we will lose both."[34] In line with that general theme, his aides offered two-fold advice on the importance of controlling the tone or tenor of the exchanges. Reagan would do best, they contended, if (1) Carter assumed the mantle of the aggressor; and if (2) Reagan responded to the incumbent's attacks with a combination of righteous indignation, restraint, and good humor.[35]

Four days before the debate, Reagan met with three members of the Debate Task Force—Jim Baker, Richard Wirthlin, and Myles Martel. Baker and Wirthlin were major figures in the Reagan campaign: Baker had managed George Bush's presidential primary bid in 1980 and had joined the Reagan team when Bush became the Republican vice presidential candidate. Wirthlin's firm, Decision Making Information (DMI), conducted politicals polls for the Reagan campaign. In contrast, Martel was a debate specialist brought into the campaign specifically for Reagan's two general election debates (Reagan vs. Anderson, and Reagan vs. Carter). A professor of speech communication at West Chester State

University in Pennsylvania, Martel had a Ph.D. in speech communication from Temple University. A former college debate coach, he was an active political debate consultant. Martel observed the practice sessions prior to the Reagan–Anderson debate, when Congressman David Stockman played the role of Anderson (as he would stand in for Jimmy Carter in subsequent practice sessions). Campaign aides viewed Martel's role as minor, because he did not take a leading role in critiquing Reagan at the end of each practice session. Instead, Martel concentrated on preparing Reagan for Carter's debating style.[36]

When Martel, Baker, and Wirthlin met privately with Reagan, Martel presented a forty-minute videotape on Carter's debating techniques, based primarily on the 1976 encounters with Ford. Martel hoped both to educate Reagan in what to expect from his opponent, and to motivate him to prepare thoroughly and well. Baker, Wirthlin, and Martel then stressed seven points in their summary of the strategy and tactics they viewed essential to success:

1. Keep the debate focused as much as possible on Carter's record . . .
2. Show righteous indignation in responding to Carter's attacks or innuendos that you are dangerous and attacks directed at your California credentials.
3. Humor or a confident smile can disarm Carter . . .
4. When Carter is speaking—especially when he is attacking you—look at him or take notes.
5. Whenever possible, weave your major theme into your responses: "Jimmy Carter has had his chance and has blown it . . . I offer promise—hope."
6. Conclude your responses with an attack line against Carter or a people-oriented line based on your proposals.
7. Show compassion by drawing from experiences on the campaign trail.[37]

Reagan proved a quick study. On the night of the debate, the challenger deftly deflected Carter's strategy of portraying Reagan as a potentially dangerous president. Reagan contrasted images of his own kindness with implications of Carter's flaws, shifted attention from his own record to Carter's alleged misinterpretations of that record, and made Carter's performance in the White House the focal point of a memorable closing statement.

Following a brief introduction to the debate's ground rules, moderator Howard K. Smith turned to panelist Marvin Stone, editor of *U.S. News and World Report*, to ask the first question. Stone moved immediately to the topic of military preparedness and defense policy. In the lengthy preamble to his question, Stone recalled Reagan's charges that Carter had been too late in responding to Soviet aggression, insufficiently attentive to the necessary build-up of American defense strength, and unable to resolve effectively crises in Afghanistan and Iran. In light of those criticisms, Stone asked, "what are the differences between the two of you on the uses of American military power?"

Reagan's opening line declared ignorance of the Carter policy, a potential blunder given that he had built substantial momentum based on consistent criticism of the president's governance. But Reagan recovered quickly, seizing the opportunity to dispel the Carter campaign's characterization of him as a potentially irresponsible, dangerous occupant of the Oval Office. "I don't know what the differences might be," Reagan began, "because I don't know what Mr. Carter's policies are. I do know what he has said about mine. And I'm only here to tell you that I believe with all my heart that our first priority must be world peace, and that use of force is always and only a last resort, when everything else has failed, and then only with regard to our national security." Following assertions that international events had "gotten out of hand in the last 3 1/2 years," Reagan concluded his first response of the debate with a declaration of his abhorrence for war: "But I have seen four wars in my lifetime. I'm a father of sons; I have a grandson. I don't ever want to see another generation of young Americans bleed their lives into sandy beachheads in the Pacific, or rice paddies and jungles in Asia, or the muddy, bloody battlefields of Europe."[38] The answer reflected two key elements of Reagan's strategy: shift the focus of the debate to Carter and demonstrate compassion in the face of charges that a Reagan victory could lead to war.

The same tactic undergirded Reagan's response a short while later to a question about the emerging underclass in America. "What, specifically," asked William Hilliard of the *Portland Oregonian*, "would you do in the next four years to reverse this trend? Reagan pointed to a program based in a combination of tax incentives, private industry's support, and a modest role for government. Noting Carter's emphasis on federal assistance and expansive government, Reagan recalled a visit he had made recently to the South Bronx, to the same spot the president had visited in 1977. Where Carter had "promised to bring a vast program to rebuild" the area, Reagan instead found what "looks like a bombed-out city—great, gaunt skeletons of buildings, windows smashed out; painted on one of them, 'Unkept promises,' on another, 'Despair.' . . . There are whole blocks . . . that are bulldozed down flat, and nothing has been done. And they are now charging to take tourists through there to see this terrible desolation." While big government was failing to resolve the inner cities' problems, Ronald Reagan was personally taking the pulse of this city's less fortunate: "I talked to a man just briefly there who asked me one simple question: 'Do I have reason to hope that I can someday take care of my family again? Nothing has been done.' " Lest the viewer miss his point, Reagan made clear that the culprit was his opponent, whose misguided dependence on government programs was doomed to failure.

Reagan subsequently shifted attention from the president's policies to his alleged penchant to distort Reagan's position and record. At the midpoint of the debate,[39] Reagan at once focused attention on Carter's personal shortcomings and initiated a pattern of commentary destined to eventuate in the evening's most memorable line. ABC's Barbara Walters had asked first Carter and then Reagan to articulate their policies for preventing or controlling terrorism. Charging that "neither candidate answered specifically the question of a specific policy for dealing with terrorism," Walters altered her follow-up question, asking whether the United States "has the power or the right to try to determine what form of government any country will have." Following a rather evasive response by Reagan, Carter redefined the question to allow an attack on his opponent's past pronunciations on nuclear arms. Reagan moved at once to dispute Carter's claim. "While I have the last word here, I would like to correct a misstatement of fact by the President. I have never made the statement that he suggested about nuclear proliferation, or the trying to halt it, would be a major part of a foreign policy of mine." This answer set the tone for the second half of the debate, in which Reagan successfully shifted the agenda of the debate from Carter's inferences about the dangers of a Reagan presidency to the incumbent's own apparent unfairness.

Even as Reagan attacked Carter's record, he disarmed his opponent and presented an appealing image to his audience by leavening his arguments with humor. The juxtaposition of Carter's aggressiveness to Reagan's personable demeanor, so evident at the Al Smith dinner slightly over a week before, became increasingly prominent as the debate moved toward its climax. Consider the exchange on the Strategic Arms Limitation Treaty (SALT). President Carter warned of his opponent's deceptively pleasant manner when, in concluding a comparison of the two candidates' positions on "the SALT treaty," he contended that Reagan's "attitude [toward SALT] is extremely dangerous and belligerent in its tone, although it's said with a quiet voice." Reagan blunted this attempt to portray him as an irresponsible president, by observing, "I know the President's supposed to be replying to me, but sometimes, I have a hard time in connecting what he's saying with what I have said or what my positions are." With a gentle smile, Reagan concluded: "I sometimes think he's like the witch doctor that gets mad when a good doctor comes along with a cure that'll work."

Unable to adjust to the new tone of the debate and to convey his own warmth and compassion effectively, Carter continued to attack. In a series of exchanges on energy policy, social security, and medical care, Reagan returned in varying degrees to the theme that he was being treated unfairly by his opponent. The culmination of the animus, arguably the climax of the debate, emerged with the penultimate question, which concerned medicare and national health insurance. After reciting the litany of public programs he advocated to ensure adequate, affordable medical care for all Americans, Carter concluded, "These are the kind of elements of a national health insurance, important to the American people. Governor Reagan, again, typically, is against such a proposal." Moderator Smith turned to Reagan: "Governor." With adroit timing, Reagan followed with the four words that would encapsulate the debate: "There you go again." Spontaneous laughter briefly prevented Reagan from completing the remainder of his answer, as the evening's drama moved to its denouement.

Following their answers to the final question—Barbara Walters's request that each candidate assess the harm to the nation that would ensue with the election of his opponent—each candidate received three minutes for a closing statement. Reagan spoke last. In a memorable speech he pulled together multiple strands of his debate strategy. He focused attention on the Carter record, conveyed sincerity and compassion for the problems yet unsolved, and intimated a personal warmth that belied the "warmonger" image with which the Carter campaign had attempted to saddle him. At the center of the response was a series of five questions, the first of which became a rallying point in the campaign's final days. Reagan faced the camera confidently, and began: "Next Tuesday is election day. Next Tuesday all of you will go to the polls; you'll stand there in the polling place and make a decision. I think when you make that decision, it might be well if you would ask yourself, are you better off than you were 4 years ago? Is it easier for you to go and buy things in the stores than it was 4 years ago? Is there more or less unemployment in the country than there was 4 years ago? Is America as respected throughout the world as it was? Do you feel that our security is as safe, that we're as strong as we were 4 years ago?"

To those who could answer "yes" to all five questions, he noted his assumption that they would vote for his opponent. To those who answered "no," however, he offered himself as a humble but worthy alternative. Reagan closed the debate by asking Americans to join him in a crusade "to take the government off the backs of the great people of this country"—a people who had "made this country great."

JIMMY CARTER'S DEBATE STRATEGY

From its inception, the Carter campaign had attempted to define the election "as a choice between two men and not as a referendum on the incumbent administration."[40] In an effort to use the debate to further that fundamental campaign goal, Patrick Caddell prepared a lengthy memo on "debate strategy," which he completed one week before the debate itself. This disjointed and rambling document, which runs almost thirty pages in published form, was complex and confusing. It guided Carter's debate preparation. From it we can glean three specific debate strategies:

1. Carter should attack Reagan, but not debate him.[41] In shorthand, this was a strategy of *attack, but don't debate*.
2. Carter should use the debate to enumerate his themes and to speak directly to his target voters.[42] Since this strategy produced a long list of issues and voting blocs, it became the *list* strategy.
3. Carter should capitalize on Reagan's mistakes in the debate, thereby revealing Reagan to be dangerously superficial, ill-informed, and simplistic.[43] Because this approach required Carter to wait for Reagan to make mistakes and then respond to his errors, this became the *mistake* strategy.

Faithful to his general campaign goal of defining the election as a choice, Carter spoke in the debate of the "sharp differences" and the "stark differences" between himself and Reagan as they looked to "the future of our nation" and to the prospects for "war and peace." Carter repeatedly contrasted the known (if not greatly admired) quality of his leadership with his fears about the nation's future under the untried leadership of Ronald Reagan. However, he was hampered in promoting that general theme by internal conflicts among his three specific strategies.

When Carter attacked Reagan in the debate, he was mindful of Caddell's injunction that he should not pursue Reagan. When counseling Carter to attack Reagan, Caddell added that "the President's role is not to debate Ronald Reagan," but merely to let the voters compare the two candidates' remarks. Caddell further warned, "It is impossible—both to look presidential and to chase Reagan. No one looks dignified chasing butterflies and no one looks in command when their punches are missing."[44] As a result of this approach, Carter employed a "hit and run" style of debate: Carter launched an attack, Reagan replied, and Carter ignored Reagan's rebuttal. When answering William Hilliard's question on social security, for example, Carter attacked Reagan's policies and simply asserted that the social security system was sound. In his rebuttal speech, Carter restated his attacks, but did not reply to Reagan's intervening speech. Moreover, in the same short "rebuttal" speech (one and a half minutes), Carter quickly shifted away from the topic of social security and attacked Reagan's policies on health care. In his third and final speech in reply to Hilliard's question, Carter ignored Reagan's intervening defense of his health care record, and instead shifted to a general appeal to the principles of the Democratic Party versus those of the Republican Party.

According to one study of the debate, Carter's debating style produced twenty-one attacks against Reagan, but only one reply to attacks made by Reagan. In contrast, Reagan attacked Carter sixteen times and replied to Carter's attacks fifteen times.[45] Another study revealed the same trend, reporting that Carter responded to only about 25 percent of the charges made by Reagan, while Reagan responded to over 50 percent of Carter's allegations.[46] To use Patrick Caddell's pugilistic metaphor, Carter jabbed and backed away, while Reagan pursued him around the ring. Rather than debate with Reagan, Carter tried to use his office to distance himself from Reagan. During the ninety-minute debate Carter invoked "the presidency" twenty-seven times. He mentioned the "Oval Office" ten times. He spoke of "lonely, life and death decisions" seven times.[47]

Carter's failure to use his twelve rebuttal speeches to reply to Reagan is peculiar because Reagan presented no "surprise" arguments. He used his standard claims and repeated familiar evidence—just as the Carter campaign expected him to do. In his memo on debate strategy, Caddell had predicted that they were "very likely to get the same Reagan that has always appeared in debates," noting that "he always tends to use the *same* answer!" Caddell recommended that the campaign "wargame the debate," especially "as it relates to the rebuttals."[48] This was done, in part, through practice debates in which Samuel Popkin, a political science professor from the University of California at San Diego, played the role of Reagan. An associate of Caddell's, Popkin had an uncanny ability to mouth Reagan's arguments. Hamilton Jordan reported that the political scientist "delighted in playing back precisely what Reagan would say in answer to a question or rebuttal."[49]

Caddell proved correct in his prediction, as Reagan used many of his standard arguments in the debate. One computer-assisted analysis of debate transcripts revealed eight different instances where Reagan not only used the same argument as he had in his debate with John Anderson, but used almost identical language as well.[50] Why did Carter not take advantage of Reagan's predictable answers? Apparently, he was too busy following one of Caddell's other directives—advice that Carter should speak to his own agenda, rather than trying to " 'nail Reagan down' on specifics."[51]

In addition to failing to present rebuttals to Reagan's arguments, Carter further weakened the impact of his attacks on Reagan by neglecting the visual dimension of a televised debate. His aide Hamilton Jordan reported that he found Carter in a "foul mood" on the day of the debate, recalling "I could see the tension written on his face." As Hamilton watched the television, his fears were confirmed. "Reagan looked relaxed, smiling; the President erect, lips tight, looking like a coiled spring, ready to pounce, an overtrained boxer, too ready for the bout."[52] During the debate, Carter failed to coordinate his nonverbal behavior with his verbal messages. Carter looked at Reagan only twice while making a statement to or about Reagan. In contrast, Reagan looked at Carter thirty-two times. There were only three instances in the debate when the two candidates were looking at each other at the same time. In each instance Reagan was speaking and Carter was listening. The image of a president listening to a lecture from his opponent was hardly inspiring, but it was worse when Carter turned away. As Reagan replied to Carter's charges, the camera followed Reagan looking at Carter as he spoke. When he turned to Carter a second time during his speech, the camera showed that "Carter's eye gaze fell to the floor avoiding direct contact with Reagan."[53]

Carter's *list* strategy dictated that he speak to specific themes, issues, and constituencies. Caddell had identified ten "positive themes" on Carter's virtues, ten "negative themes" on Reagan's vices, three major audience targets and two minor audience targets, as well as dozens of issues.[54] Caddell also devised a standard pattern for answering debate questions, which he dubbed a "symmetry of answers." The first step in that procedure was for Carter to determine which particular voting bloc he would address in that speech. Caddell had warned Carter to "avoid a crucial mistake—you cannot talk to all [target audiences] at once." Instead, Carter was instructed to "go in-depth for one group on one issue and another [voting bloc] segment on another question."[55] Carter's debate speeches sometimes began with a preamble announcing his target audience. In separate speeches, he noted that "ours is a nation of refugees, a nation of immigrants." He deplored acts of violence and terrorism against Jews "and those who live in Israel." He declared himself in favor of "guaranteeing women equal rights." And he reminded his viewers, "I'm a southerner." Carter earnestly tried to squeeze every theme and every target audience and every issue into his debate speeches. As he reflected upon the debate the next night, Carter observed: "Apparently [Reagan] made a better impression on the TV audience than I did. But I had a list of things [to say], which we believe . . . will become preeminent in the public's mind."[56]

As Carter attended to his *list* strategy, he was necessarily less attentive to the debate topics being raised by Reagan and by the panel of journalists posing the debate questions. Given the debate format, Carter presented sixteen short speeches in response to questions. His speeches provided complete answers to only 16 percent of the questions, while Reagan provided complete answers to 50 percent of his questions. On the other hand, Carter evaded any answer to 42 percent of his questions and Reagan evaded only 8 percent of his questions.[57]

Carter's concern with covering all the topics on his list might also account for his failure to develop his arguments. While Carter frequently asserted claims about his successes and Reagan's liabilities, he typically did not provide evidence and reasoning. During the first half of the debate, for instance, Carter responded to a question on inflation with a series of ringing assertions: "So, our proposals are very sound and very carefully considered to stimulate jobs, to improve the industrial complex of this country, to create tools for American workers, and at the same time would be anti-inflationary in nature." In the second half of the debate, he flatly declared: "As long as there is a Democratic president in the White House, we will have a strong viable Social Security system, free of the threat of bankruptcy." A content analysis of the debate reveals that almost 75 percent of Carter's statements were "declarative statements" (assertions without evidence or analysis), while only about 20 percent of his remarks were "evidence statements," and only about 6 percent were "analytic [reasoning] statements." Reagan used declarative statements less frequently than Carter (60 percent), while providing more evidence statements (30 percent) and more analytic statements (11 percent).[58]

Perhaps the most curious aspect of the Carter campaign's debate strategy was its conviction that Jimmy Carter could simply wait for Reagan to make fatal errors in the debate and then pounce upon them. At four different points in his memo on debate strategy, Caddell assumed that Reagan would make serious mistakes. He counseled Carter to "give Reagan enough rope to hang himself with foolish, simplistic answers." Carter was advised to capitalize upon "the simplistic and rambling nature of the responses Reagan happens to give." Carter would win, Caddell advised, by "letting Reagan wander and then calling attention to it."[59] The Carter campaign negotiated for a debate format with multiple rebuttal speeches, in part, because it believed that such a format would "increase the possibility that he'll say something dumb or screw up."[60] When Reagan declined to oblige Carter with gaffes during the debate, Carter found himself with an empty strategy.

Because he had won the flip of a coin, Carter had the option of speaking first in the debate, or having Reagan speak first. In the belief that Reagan would be more likely to make an error under the pressure of speaking first, Carter chose to speak second. As one of Carter's aides expressed it: "Let the other guy feel the heat."[61] What Carter apparently had not considered was that the rules of the debate stipulated that the candidate who spoke first would also have the final closing statement. If Reagan performed well at the beginning and the end of the debate, he could benefit from both primacy and recency in the debate. If he performed poorly, of course, his errors would be magnified. While Reagan's initial statement in the debate was unremarkable, his closing statement was powerful. Carter's decision to let Reagan have the last word was, in the words of political commentator Jeff Greenfield, "a disastrous miscalculation."[62] To make matters worse, Carter preceded Reagan's forceful final statement with undistinguished closing remarks. He seemed almost to apologize for his presidency. "I've been President now for almost 4 years. I've had to make thousands of decisions, and each one of those decisions has been a learning process. I've seen the strength of my Nation, and I've seen the crises that it approached in a tentative way." With a tone of resignation, Carter added: "And I've had to deal with those crises as best I could."

EFFECTS

Reagan's own words best captured the results of the encounter with Carter: "I've examined myself, and I can't find any wounds." James Baker, who headed the Debate Task Force, translated: "We only needed to draw to win."[63] Privately, Reagan attributed considerable significance to the debate. Shortly after his election victory over Carter, for example, the president-elect wrote to debate adviser Martel that the "debate with President Carter was, in my view, a critical element in our success in the election."[64] Though measuring the effects of such events is invariably fraught with potential pitfalls, data from two different types of measures suggest that Reagan won the debate decisively. This conclusion is supported by a *New York Times* panel study during and immediately after the debate, and a variety of public opinion polls.

The *New York Times* gathered a varied group of area residents at a midtown hotel to watch the debate and to assess its impact. Viewers included strong supporters of both candidates, as well as a number of individuals who were "undecided" or "leaning." The members of the panel had occupations ranging from being a lawyer to driving a truck. They shared their impressions immediately after the debate. Their comments indicate that Reagan achieved his goals and executed his strategy with near perfection.

The assessments by lawyer Fran Morris, for example, intimated Reagan's success both in making Carter the issue and in stimulating thought among undecided voters. "I'll probably be undecided until Election Day," she said. "I'm undecided, but I'm leaning away from Carter. My problem has been that I haven't found anyplace to lean to. Carter's been running on an incumbency and, frankly, I haven't been impressed with the last four years. I don't think he's had the record to run on."[65] Loretta Fox, who attended the session with her husband, Robert, a marketing consultant, not only concurred with Morris, but was also troubled by Carter's demeanor in the debate itself. "In philosophy a Democrat," Fox found "in Carter a great failure to produce what I consider Democratic philosophy. I think his attack on jobs has really been inadequate. [During the debate] I found that I was becoming very annoyed with him." Note that of the particular Carter policies that troubled Fox, she pointed specifically to jobs, one of few policy areas Reagan enumerated in the questions which began his closing statement.

Stockbroker Peter Schwartz captured in one observation two of Reagan's debate tactics: He viewed the attacks on Reagan as petty rather than as constructing an image of a potentially dangerous president, and he found Reagan's one-liners effective. "I thought President Carter attempted to attack Reagan and some of his policies, and the manner of his attack seemed to be on a picky type of level, going against some of the minor issues." He lauded Reagan's presence in the face of such tactics: "One of the best lines . . . was Reagan saying, 'Here we go again' [*sic*]." In Schwartz's opinion, "Reagan came out much stronger" in defending his own positions and refuting Carter's representations of his record. Reagan won, Schwartz concluded, because Carter failed in his effort to portray Reagan as a dangerous extremist. Schwartz felt that "Reagan did not come off being way off the center of the political spectrum as Carter wanted everybody to believe; that Reagan was going to push the button, that Reagan is going to eliminate Social Security and all the old people are going to starve."

While Schwartz found his commitment to Reagan was intensified by the debate, another panelist's reaction spoke to Reagan's appeal to an equally important target, undecided voters. Identified before the debate as "totally undecided," one person declared afterward that he was "more inclined after listening to the debate to vote for Reagan than to vote for Carter for the simple reason that the Federal Government is too big and is growing more and more and more, especially under Carter. . . . All my taxes go to the Federal Government. Me, I'm a registered Democrat, and it's very hard for me to vote Republican." But as of the close of the debate, such was his avowed intention.

Public opinion polling data over the following week reinforced the comments of panel study participants. The polls varied, but generally favored Reagan. *Newsweek*'s poll, taken over two nights following the debate, reported 34 percent for Reagan, 26 percent for Carter, and 31 percent undecided. An ABC News–Harris Survey found Reagan the heavy winner, 44 percent to 26 percent.[66] The CBS News–*New York Times* Election Survey of 1,062 respondents also yielded a 44 percent rating for the challenger, but gave Carter a closer 36 percent. But perhaps the more noteworthy finding of the CBS poll was that 6 percent of the respondents reported a change in their vote because of the debate. Among those voters, Reagan gained approximately two votes for every one attracted by Carter.[67] Typically, political debates reinforce the opinions of the viewers. Data from this CBS poll showed that this tendency continued in the 1980 debate.[68] Hence, the shifts of opinion reported in various polls reflect undecided voters who were won over by Ronald Reagan. Postdebate posturing by both campaigns required declarations of success in the debate. Nevertheless, the private sentiment of Carter's pollster Patrick Caddell was revealing: "I just wish we hadn't debated."[69]

Why did Reagan win more support from the debate than did Carter? Journalists had several answers: First, the press viewed the debate as "a contest of content against style," with Carter's supposedly stronger content losing to Reagan's superior style.[70] Since the journalists also wrote the first books on the 1980 presidential campaign, the judgment that Reagan's style triumphed over Carter's substance has continued.[71] Second, in explaining Carter's loss in the debate, news commentators pointed to Jimmy Carter's remark that his young daughter, Amy, had advised him that the limitation of nuclear weapons was the most important issue facing the world. Perceived by many as a contrived emotional appeal—and a bit silly for a presidential debate—that remark drew groans from Carter's own advisors, from the audience attending the debate, and from television viewers.[72] Third, investigative reporters subsequently discovered that Reagan's aides had acquired copies of debate briefing materials prepared by the Carter campaign. This raised the possibility that Reagan won the debate because he could anticipate Carter's arguments.[73]

More recent studies of the debate have cast doubt on all three of the journalistic hypotheses. Scholarly studies have demonstrated that Reagan's debating was superior in substance, as well as in style.[74] No evidence has been reported to support the notion that Carter's "Amy remark" was fatal to his campaign. And Reagan policy advisor Martin Anderson has made a reasonable case that Carter's purloined debate briefs were not used by Reagan himself. Those materials were used by Reagan's advisors, but David Stockman has maintained that the Carter material was insignificant: "You could have gotten it from campaign brochures. It wasn't anything sensitive."[75]

The present analysis indicates that Reagan won the debate because he executed an effective debating strategy that combined sustained argumentation with an appealing style of presentation. Carter lost the debate because his debate strategy was fatally flawed. It required Carter to attack without arguing, to list points without developing them fully, and to hope that Ronald Reagan would defeat himself. Jeff Greenfield, a news commentator and former political speechwriter, has remarked that what the campaign strategists and the news media both ignored in their analyses of the Reagan–Carter debate was the possibility that "large numbers of undecided Americans" would actually listen "to the arguments the candidates were making." For both Greenfield and the present authors, the real significance of the Reagan–Carter debate was that it made public advocacy both "powerful and influential in the outcome of the 1980 campaign."[76]

NOTES

1. Hedrick Smith, "Lead Slipping, a New Reagan Suits up for the Big Event," *New York Times*, October 19, 1980, p. 1E.

2. Robert V. Friedenberg, " 'Selfish Interests,' Or The Prerequisites for Political Debate: An Analysis of the 1980 Presidential Debate and Its Implications for Future Campaigns," *Journal of the American Forensic Association* 18 (1981): 91–94.

3. "Interview with Ronald Reagan: An Extremist? 'I'll Run on My Record,' " *U.S. News & World Report*, May 5, 1980, p. 34; Jimmy Carter, *Keeping Faith: Memoirs of a President* (New York: Bantam Books, 1982), p. 543.

4. "A Debate Over the Debates," *Newsweek*, September 8, 1980, pp. 18–21.

5. "Political Math: One Plus One Equals Minus One," *New York Times* September 21, 1980, p. 1E; "Poll Finds Domestic Issues Most Important," *Kansas City Times*, September 27, 1980, p. A13.

6. Myles Martel, *Political Campaign Debates: Images, Strategies and Tactics* (New York: Longman, 1983), pp. 12 and 17–18; and Myles Martel, "Debate Preparations in the Reagan Camp: An Insider's View," in *The 1980 Presidential Debates*, ed. Kurt Ritter (Lawrence, Kan.: Allen Press, 1981) [special issue of *Speaker & Gavel* 18, no. 2], pp. 34–35. For Wirthlin's review of the Reagan campaign strategy, see Richard Wirthlin, "Memorandum V" (to Ronald Reagan et al., October 9, 1980) in Elizabeth Drew, *Portrait of an Election: The 1980 Presidential Campaign* (New York: Simon and Schuster, 1981), pp. 384–385.

7. Smith, "Lead Slipping, a New Reagan Suits up for the Big Debate," p. 1E.

8. Additional poll data corroborating the concerns of the prodebate faction are cited in Friedenberg, " 'Selfish Interests,' " pp. 94–95. See also, "Battling Down the Stretch," *Time*, November 3, 1980, p. 18.

9. Nofsinger quoted in Howell Raines, "Reporter's Notebook: Ghost in Reagan Camp," *New York Times*, October 5 1980, p. 11; Richard Wirthlin, "Memorandum I: Some Initial Strategic and Tactical Considerations for the 1980 Presidential Campaign" (March 28, 1980), in Drew, *Portrait of an Election*, p. 356.

10. An alternative version of the players involved in the decision-making process and the deliberations among them is provided in "Building to a Climax," *Time*, October 27, 1980, p. 13.

11. Jack W. Germond and Jules Witcover, *Blue Smoke and Mirrors: How Reagan Won and Why Carter Lost the Election of 1980* (New York: Viking Press, 1981), p. 269.

12. "Building to a Climax," p. 13.

13. "Battling Down the Stretch," p. 20.

14. Quoted in Martel, *Political Campaign Debates*, p. 18.

15. Quoted in Hamilton Jordan, "The Campaign Carter Couldn't Win," *Life*, January 1981, p. 96.

16. Patrick H. Caddell, "The Democratic Strategy and Its Electoral Conse-

quences," in *Party Coalitions in the 1980s*, ed. Seymour Martin Lipset (San Francisco: Institute for Contemporary Studies, 1981), p. 283.

17. Patrick Caddell, "Memorandum I: General Election Strategy" (June 25, 1980), in Drew, *Portrait of an Election*, pp. 398, 403, 391.

18. Germond and Witcover, *Blue Smoke and Mirrors*, p. 275; Martel, "Debate Preparations," pp. 35, 40.

19. Hamilton Jordan, *Crisis: The Last Year of the Carter Presidency* (New York: G. P. Putnam's Sons, 1982), pp. 352–353.

20. Elizabeth Drew, "A Reporter at Large—1980: The Election," *New Yorker* 1 (December 1980), p. 159. For an analysis of the campaign "debate about debates" in 1980 and an assessment of how that controversy influenced perceptions of Reagan and Carter when they finally did debate each other, see Robert L. Scott, "You Cannot Not Debate: The Debate Over the 1980 Presidential Debates," in Ritter, *The 1980 Presidential Debates*, pp. 28–33.

21. See the memos by Wirthlin and Caddell which form a ninety-page appendix in Drew, *Portrait of an Election*, pp. 349–439.

22. Jeff Greenfield, *The Real Campaign: How the Media Missed the Story of the 1980 Campaign* (New York: Summit Brooks, 1982), p. 233.

23. Wirthlin, "Memorandum V," pp. 385–386.

24. Ibid., pp. 386–387.

25. Patrick Caddell, "Memorandum II: Debate Strategy" (October 21, 1989), in Drew, *Portrait of an Election*, p. 436.

26. Rich Jaroslovsky, "Carter, Reagan Teams Sketch Game Plan for Face-Off Tentatively Set for Oct. 28," *Wall Street Journal*, October 20, 1980, p. 4.

27. Quoted in Drew, "A Reporter at Large," p. 170.

28. Caddell, "The Democratic Strategy," p. 274.

29. Drew, "A Reporter at Large," p. 176.

30. Caddell, "Memorandum II," pp. 419–421.

31. Caddell, "The Democratic Strategy," p. 282.

32. Quoted in Jaroslovsky, "Carter, Reagan Teams Sketch Game Plan," p. 4.

33. Caddell, "Memorandum II," pp. 422–423.

34. Cited in Martel, *Political Campaign Debates*, p. 19.

35. Martel, *Political Campaign Debates*, p. 21.

36. Interview with Martin Anderson conducted by Kurt Ritter, May 25, 1989, Hoover Institution, Stanford University. An audio tape of this interview is available from Professor Kurt Ritter, Department of Communication and Theatre, Texas A and M University, College Station, Texas, 77843. For a description of Martel's role in the debate preparations, see "The Man Behind Reagan's Debate Performances," *Broadcasting*, February 2, 1981, pp. 58–59.

37. Martel, *Political Campaign Debates*, p. 21.

38. "Remarks at the 1980 Presidential Campaign Debates," October 28, 1980, *Public Papers of the Presidents of the United States: Jimmy Carter, 1980–81* (Washington, D.C.: Government Printing Office, 1982), Book III, pp. 2476–2502. All debate citations are from this text.

39. Negotiations between the Carter and Reagan staffs had resulted in a compromise format, calling for a ninety-minute debate divided equally between two phases. The length of the questions and answers effectively yielded sufficient time for only eight principal questions, with four follow-up questions. In a

departure from previous presidential debates, the format included numerous rebuttal speeches—especially during the second half of the debate. The format is explained and presented in Table 1.2 of Martel's *Political Campaign Debates*, pp. 23–24.

40. Caddell, "The Democratic Strategy," p. 271.

41. See Caddell, "Memorandum II," pp. 423, 425–427.

42. Ibid., pp. 420–423.

43. Ibid., pp. 426–427. The "mistake" strategy had been a general tenet of Carter's entire campaign strategy against Reagan; see Caddell, "Memorandum I," p. 404.

44. Caddell, "Memorandum II," pp. 426–427.

45. Robert K. Tiemens, Susan A. Hellweg, Philip Kipper, and Steven L. Phillips, "An Integrative and Visual Analysis of the Carter–Reagan Debate," *Communication Quarterly* 33 (1985): 36.

46. Robert Rowland, "The Substance of the 1980 Carter–Reagan Debate," *Southern Speech Communication Journal* 51 (1986), p. 160. The numerical reports in the Rowland study differ from those in the study by Tiemens, et al., because the two studies used different methods of content analysis; despite the different methodologies, both studies revealed the same trends when comparing Reagan and Carter.

47. Steven R. Brydon, "The Two Faces of Jimmy Carter: The Transformation of a Presidential Debater, 1976 and 1980," *Central States Speech Journal* 36 (1985): 145.

48. Caddell, "Memorandum II," pp. 435, 438.

49. Jordan, "The Campaign Carter Couldn't Win," p. 96.

50. Robert G. Meadow, "Televised Campaign Debates as Whistle-Stop Speeches," in *Television Coverage of the 1980 Presidential Campaign*, ed. by William C. Adams (Norwood, N.J.: ABLEX Publishing, 1983), pp. 95–97.

51. Caddell, "Memorandum II," p. 427.

52. Jordan, *Crisis*, pp. 354–355.

53. Tiemens, et al., "An Integrative Verbal and Visual Analysis," pp. 38, 40. In contrast to Carter, Reagan was a careful student of the visual dimension of political rhetoric, particularly televised debates. See Martin Anderson, *Revolution* (New York: Harcourt Brace Jovanovich, 1988), p. 54.

54. Ibid., pp. 419–424.

55. Ibid., pp. 421, 425.

56. Carter, *Keeping Faith*, p. 565.

57. Rowland, "The Substance of the 1980 Carter–Reagan Debate," p. 154.

58. Patricia Riley and Thomas A. Hollihan, "The 1980 Presidential Debates: A Content Analysis of the Issues and Arguments," *The 1980 Presidential Debates*, p. 54.

59. Caddell, "Memorandum II," pp. 426–427.

60. Jordan, *Crisis*, p. 353.

61. "Homestretch Debate," *Newsweek*, November 10, 1980, p. 35.

62. Greenfield, *The Real Campaign*, p. 241.

63. "Now, a Few Words in Closing," *Time*, November 10, 1980, p. 18.

64. Martel, *Political Campaign Debates*, p. 29.

65. "Excerpts from Area Panel's Remarks on the Debate," *New York Times*,

October 30, 1980, p. B20. All quotations from panelists are from this article. Bernard Weinraub summarized the panel's collective sentiments in "Area Panel's Scorecard on the Debate: Reagan Won It by a Wide Margin," *New York Times*, October 30, 1980, p. B20.

66. Both polls are reported in "The Great Homestretch Debate," p. 34.

67. Hedrick Smith, "Carter and Reagan Express Confidence on Debate Showing," *New York Times*, October 30, 1980, p. A1.

68. Lee Sigelman and Carol K. Sigelman, "Judgments of the Carter–Reagan Debate: The Eyes of the Beholders," *Public Opinion Quarterly* 48 (1984): 624–628; this research report is based upon data from the CBS poll. It should be noted that public opinion polls asking "who won" a campaign debate are problematic, because different respondents mean different things when they say one candidate "won." Nevertheless, candidates prefer to be seen as the "winner" no matter what the reason. See David L. Vancil and Sue D. Pendell, "Winning Presidential Debates: An Analysis of Criteria influencing Audience Response," *Western Journal of Speech Communication* 48 (1984): 62–74.

69. Quoted in Drew, "A Reporter at Large," p. 183.

70. Hedrick Smith, "No Clear Winner Apparent," and Adam Clymer, "Carter and Reagan Dispute Views," both in *New York Times*, October 29, 1980, p. A1.

71. Adam Clymer, "The Final Campaign," in Hedrick Smith, Adam Clymer, Leonard Silk, Robert Lindsey, and Richard Burt, *Reagan the Man, the President* (New York: Macmillan, 1980), p. 144.

72. Jordan, *Crisis*, pp. 355–356; "Carter Post-Mortem: Debate Hurt, But It Wasn't Only Cause of Defeat," *New York Times*, November 9, 1980, p. 1; Weinraub, "Area Panel's Scorecard on the Debate," p. 20B.

73. *Time* magazine White House correspondent Laurence I. Barrett broke this story in June 1983 with the release of his book, *Gambling with History: Ronald Reagan in the White House* (Garden City: Doubleday, 1983), pp. 382–383. Also see Francis X. Clines, "Casey Says He 'Wouldn't Touch' Papers from Carter Campaign," *New York Times*, July 6, 1983, pp. A1, B6; Robert J. McCloskey, "The Briefing Papers Frenzy," and Rowland Evans and Robert Novak, "A Baker–Casey Showdown," both in *The Washington Post*, July 11, 1983, pp. A10–A11; and Don Campbell, "Ethical Ghosts Likely Will Linger," *USA Today*, July 15, 1983, p. 7A.

74. See Brydon, "The Two Faces of Jimmy Carter"; Tiemens, et al., "An Integrative Verbal and Visual Analysis"; Rowland, "The Substance of the 1980 Carter–Reagan Debate"; and Riley and Hollihan, "The 1980 Presidential Debates."

75. Anderson, *Revolution*, pp. 338–342. Stockman quoted in Elizabeth Bumiller, "Ferreting Out the Mole," *The Washington Post*, June 23, 1983, p. D2.

76. Greenfield, *The Real Campaign*, pp. 246–247.

SELECT BIBLIOGRAPHY

Berquist, Goodwin F., and James L. Golden. "Media Rhetoric, Criticism, and the Public Perception of the 1980 Presidential Debates." *Quarterly Journal of Speech* 67 (1981): 125–137. Sets forth six propositions about the role the news media played in creating public expectations for the 1980 debates, in influencing the content of the debates, and in shaping public reactions to the debates.

Brydon, Steven R. "The Two Faces of Jimmy Carter: The Transformation of a Presidential Debater, 1976 and 1980." *Central States Speech Journal* 36 (1985): 138–151. In a rhetorical analysis and evaluation of Jimmy Carter's debating, the author illustrates how Carter reversed his debating strategies between 1976 and 1980 in order to rely upon the power of the incumbency. The study indicates that presidential debates are ill-suited to strategies that rely on the symbols of incumbency.

Friedenberg, Robert V. " 'Selfish Interests,' or the Prerequisites for Political Debate: An Analysis of the 1980 Presidential Debate and Its Implications for Future Campaigns." *Journal of the American Forensic Association* 18 (1981): 91–98. The author presents an analysis of the candidates' decision to debate in 1980, demonstrating that five conditions—each rooted in the candidates' perceptions of their political self-interest—made the debate likely to occur. 1980 marked the second consecutive presidential election featuring an incumbent in a debate, suggesting that the presence of an incumbent no longer seriously reduces the prospects for presidential debates.

Martel, Myles. *Political Campaign Debates: Images, Strategies, and Tactics*. New York: Longmans, 1983. The first chapter (pp. 7–30) provides the most thorough and authoritative account of Reagan's preparations for the 1980 Reagan–Carter debate. Carter's debate preparations are less fully treated, but the chapter does include information from a Carter aide that is not available in other published sources. The author was a member of Reagan's Debate Task Force.

McCall, Jeffrey M. "The Panelists as Pseudo-Debaters: An Evaluation of the Questions and the Questioners in the Major Debates of 1980." *Journal of the American Forensic Association* 21 (1984): 97–104. Based upon analyses of the 1980 Reagan–Carter and Reagan–Anderson debates, the author recommends specific guidelines and questioning techniques to improve the effectiveness of journalists serving as debate panelists.

Meadows, Robert G. "Television Presidential Debates as Whistle-Stop Speeches." *Television Coverage of the 1980 Presidential Election*. William C. Adams, ed. Norwood, N.J.: ABLEX Publishing, 1983, pp. 89–112. Reports a computer-assisted content analysis which reveals that Reagan's statements in the major 1980 presidential debates were often stock campaign responses rather than being spontaneous and original remarks.

Ritter, Kurt, ed. *The 1980 Presidential Debates*. Lawrence, Kan.: Allen Press, 1981 [special issue of *Speaker & Gavel*, vol. 18, no. 2]. The only compilation of studies exclusively on the 1980 debates. Presents eight studies; greatest attention is given to debate content and format.

Rowland, Robert. "The Substance of the 1980 Carter–Reagan Debate." *Southern Speech Communication Journal* 51 (1986): 142–165. This textual and argumentative analysis reveals that journalistic commentators were inaccurate in reporting that Carter was superior on the "substance" or "issues" in the 1980 debate, while Reagan won the television audience due to his style. Rowland concludes that Reagan was the superior debater in terms of substantive arguments.

Tiemens, Robert K., Susan A. Hellweg, Philip Kipper, and Steven L. Phillips. "An Integrative Verbal and Visual Analysis of the Carter–Reagan Debate." *Communication Quarterly* 33 (1985): 39–42. Combines verbal and visual content analyses of the 1980 debate, focusing upon points of confrontation. Demonstrates that Reagan both attacked and refuted Carter, but that Carter only attacked Reagan. Reveals that Reagan was successful in combining the visual and verbal dimensions of the debate.

Debate Transcript

"Remarks at the 1980 Presidential Campaign Debate." October 28, 1980. *Public Papers of the Presidents of the United States: Jimmy Carter, 1980–81*. Washington, DC: Government Printing Office, 1982. Book III, pp. 2476–2502.

Chapter 5

The 1984 Reagan–Mondale Presidential Debates

Craig Allen Smith and Kathy B. Smith

THE DECISION TO DEBATE

The most remarkable feature of the 1984 debates is that they occurred at all. Friedenberg suggests that political debates are likely to occur only if five of six situational preconditions can be satisfied: (1) a close election is likely; (2) each candidate perceives the likelihood of advantages; (3) the candidates perceive themselves to be good debaters; (4) there are only two major candidates running for the office; (5) both candidates are comfortable with their control over the important variables in the debate situation; and (6) the field is clear of incumbents.[1] There were but two major candidates in 1984, but none of Friedenberg's other strategic criteria were met unequivocally.

President Reagan was an incumbent in a race that showed no hint of closeness. Even with the benefit of hindsight it is possible to underestimate the enormity of Mondale's September disadvantage. The September 25, 1984, Gallup poll showed that 53.88 percent of the American public approved, and only 35.2 percent disapproved, of President Reagan's performance as president, and that was the good news for Democrats. Reagan had the approval of the majority of males (57.6 percent), females (50 percent despite Ferraro), southerners (61.9 percent), nonsoutherners (57.1 percent), everyone earning more than $5,000 (54.55 percent), whites (58.85 percent), people with at least a high school education (57.1 percent), and, of course, Republicans (92.54 percent).[2] Clearly, President Reagan had no need to debate. He had little to gain and much to lose.

In the race for a majority of the 538 votes in the electoral college, Mondale held a safe lead only for the District of Columbia's three votes.[3] In short, Ronald Reagan was standing tall in late September of 1984, and it would have taken an extraordinary campaign and considerable luck for any Democrat to have unseated him.

But a curious combination of perceptions changed the formula. If Reagan had little to gain and much to lose by debating, the actor-turned-popular-president must have thought it safe to gamble on a televised debate with a less telegenic opponent like Walter Mondale. Conversely, Mondale doubted his own television skills despite an impressive record in his 1976 debate, in the 1984 primary debates, and in his convention address. But he certainly perceived the necessity for a dramatic and highly visible moment that could turn the tide.[4] Gallup reports that 68 percent of the voters had "made up their minds" by September, preferring Reagan-Bush over Mondale-Ferraro by a 57 percent–39 percent margin.[5] To reach the 50 percent level, then, Mondale needed to persuade 23.5 percent of the voters amenable to influence, while Reagan needed to persuade only 10.7 percent. In short, Mondale doubted his television debating skills, but perceived no real strategic choice; whereas Reagan had no strategic reason to debate but was confident of his skills and perceived no serious risks.[6]

Like Jimmy Carter before him and Michael Dukakis to follow, Walter Mondale sorely needed an October foothold from which to sprint toward election day. Previous debates had attracted large audiences, and Mondale's supporters were no doubt buoyed by remembrances of Nixon's five o'clock shadow and Ford's remark about Eastern Europe. The debates were Mondale's best remaining chance to close the gap.

The two campaigns' agendas were evident in their initial demands. In desperation the Mondale forces sought six two-hour presidential and three vice presidential debates; the Reagan forces countered with a one-hour, one-issue debate.[7] Mondale wanted the debates to be strung through the campaign with the final debate just before the election; Reagan wanted time between the final debate and the election for damage control. They settled upon two ninety-minute debates (and a vice presidential debate) in mid-October.

The decision to hold two debates—in Louisville and Kansas City—as well as a vice presidential debate in mid-October was more than Mondale could have dared to expect, given the guidelines identified by Friedenberg. The compromise was closer to President Reagan's terms than it was to Mondale's, but the president need not have agreed to debate at all.

Two additional reasons help to explain the decision to debate in 1984. The first of these was public pressure in the form of voter expectations, journalistic attention to the debate issue, and an organized initiative by a legitimate sponsor. The debates in 1976, 1980, and in the Democratic primary campaigns had nurtured the public expectation that found expression in the convention addresses of Edward Kennedy and Walter

Mondale. The journalistic community found in the debate issue a glimmer of hope for interesting news. And the League of Women Voters had begun to see presidential debates as their private mission. The cold strategic calculations could not withstand this public pressure, especially when the incumbent was a former actor, popular with the public, who liked the stage and felt that he could outshine Mondale.[8] Whether public pressure transcends the factors suggested by Friedenberg or simply merits inclusion in his list is a matter for future research.

The second explanation for debates in 1984 was each campaign's determination to control the process. To induce the candidates to debate, the League reluctantly allowed the campaigns to approve the journalist-questioners. The League used the questioner-review policy it had used in 1980, but the situation had changed. Where 1980 was expected to be close, 1984 was not. In 1980 both campaigns saw advantages, in 1984 both took risks. In 1980 an unpopular incumbent needed a forum, in 1984 a popular incumbent needed no forum. So whereas the 1980 campaigners had been willing to negotiate for the chance to debate, the 1984 campaigners dealt with the League of Women Voters from a much stronger position.

It was announced publicly the day before the first debate that the campaigns had, between them, rejected all but four of the eighty-three names submitted for consideration, and one of the four had removed himself from consideration.[9] League President Dorothy S. Ridings criticized both campaigns for abusing the process to which the League had agreed, perhaps forgetting momentarily that the candidates were engaged in a struggle for dominance in which they were entitled to use whatever rules had been agreed upon.

The Ridings press conference was the beginning of the end for League of Women Voters' sponsorship of presidential debates. Since 1976 the League had held firmly to the principle that fairness requires candidate approval of the questioners, although the journalistic community is suspicious of such clearance.[10] By making private negotiations public the day before the debate, Ridings undermined public confidence in the fairness of the debate enterprise. This was unwarranted, since there was no hint that either campaign had violated its agreement with the League. Indeed, she might well have announced to the campaigns after thirty, forty, or fifty disapprovals that the principle of fairness had been served and that there would be no further lists. But she waited until the rejections neared 100, until the debate was one day away, until the public was primed, and until the League's frustration had reached adversarial proportions.

Bluntly, the League of Women Voters lost its credibility as a legitimate broker of public interests by (1) adhering rigidly to a controversial standard; (2) failing to limit either the number of disapprovals or the grounds for disapproval necessary to insure fairness to the candidates, (3) failing to fully appreciate the political risks already undertaken by the candidates; and (4) transforming these mistakes into a public condemnation of those who sought responsibly to win election to the presidency. A Commission on Presidential Debates was later formed to sponsor the 1988 debates, over the League of Women Voters' objections.

Conditions in 1984 were not conducive to presidential debates. But the incumbent's confidence in his speaking ability, the challenger's desperation, public pressure for debates, and the campaigns' exploitation of loosely defined rules combined to produce debates nonetheless. Whether that was cause for celebration, or not, is another question.

THE GOALS OF THE CANDIDATES

The Goals of the Reagan Campaign

The goals of the Reagan campaign are too easily oversimplified because, to be properly understood, they must be approached as primary, secondary, and tertiary goals. Their goals followed the basic rules of campaigning; protect your base, persuade swing voters, and undermine your opponent's base of support.

Clearly, President Reagan's primary goal was to do nothing wrong lest he jeopardize his advantage over Mondale. Lee Atwater had summarized this strategy in a memorandum written a year before the election:

> The West is very strong Republican territory indeed. Of the 13 states in the region, 12 are solidly in our corner. We can count on 107 of the West's electoral votes; this is almost 40 percent of the 270 electoral votes required to win the Presidency. To this Western stronghold, Ronald Reagan can add the South. . . . The payoff: 155 electoral votes from the South, to add to our 107 solid votes from the West. . . . With a Southern and Western base, we enter the 1984 contest with 262 secure electoral votes, just 8 shy of a majority.[11]

The strategy was right on target by October, 1984, thanks in part to Mondale's choice of New York's Geraldine Ferraro as his runningmate and his mishandling of Georgian Bert Lance—two moves that solidified Reagan's edge in the South and West. Reagan could afford to slip in the polls and still cruise to victory because of his solid lead in states able to provide 270 votes in the electoral college.

Reagan's secondary goals were to clarify, to protect, and to build upon public perceptions of his image and record. The *National Review* realized this objective and summarized it after the debates: "This year, with a much smaller percentage having described themselves as on the fence,

President Reagan must reassure voters that what they already know is true. He can afford to let up on the counterpunching. He has a record, and so does his opponent. Let him slow down and pick his own shots. Mondale can collect all the debating trophies he wants. They will be his only memories of the campaign."[12] In short, Reagan needed only to reassure voters, not to convert them; but such reassurance did not require presidential risktaking.

The tertiary goal of the Reagan campaign was to use the debate to make inroads into Mondale's Democratic base. This was an important goal for Reagan. If effective, it would force Mondale to expend his dwindling resources on rhetorical fence-mending while Reagan and Bush worked with the swing voters. Moreover, this goal had the potential, short of converting voters, to depress turnout by keeping confused and uncertain Mondale supporters at home on election day.

The Goals of the Mondale Campaign

The Democrat's rhetorical goal was less complex than Reagan's, but more difficult: Mondale needed to induce Americans to prefer him to the popular president they knew so well. This overarching goal dictated several subsidiary goals.

First, Mondale needed to create dissonance about the Reagan presidency by showing that Reagan and his record were not what people thought them to be. Trailing by 23 points on the day of the first debate, with more than two-thirds of the electorate firmly decided, Mondale had few prospective converts.[13] He needed to evoke cognitive and affective dissonance among those who approved of Reagan's presidency in order to open them to his own message.

Second, Mondale needed to enhance his own image among those not yet committed to his candidacy. According to the Gallup Poll, a majority perceived him as intelligent, moral, and likable, but Reagan rated higher still on each of these attributes and as a "strong leader" to boot (64 percent –42 percent).[14] Voters perceived Mondale as the candidate better able to handle the problems of women, the poor, and minorities: a double-edged perception, since there was less than widespread support in 1984 for women, the poor, and minorities.[15]

These two goals created a difficult navigational channel for Mondale. His task was this: Undermine public confidence in Reagan and his programs in a way that (1) appeals to Reagan's supporters and (2) enhances their perceptions of Mondale. If he attacked the president too strongly, the less credible challenger risked galvanizing Reagan's support. If he failed to undermine Reagan's public approval, his subsequent appeals could be easily ignored. If he undermined Reagan without enhancing his own public image, he would find himself still in the 40 percent approval range.

These, then, were the goals of the respective campaigns as they headed into the two-week debate phase of the campaign. But the two debates proved to be two unique rhetorical contests. Barbara Walters of ABC News served as moderator of the first debate as the candidates answered questions about domestic issues from the three acceptable journalists. James G. Wieghart of *Scripps-Howard* newspapers asked about the deficit, changes in American politics, and the problems of the working poor and minorities. Diane Sawyer of CBS News inquired about personal leadership, abortion, and "the most outrageous thing your opponent has said." Fred Barnes of the *Baltimore Sun* asked about religion and federal taxation.

It should be noted that the eight question areas covered only three policy areas susceptible to presidential leadership (economics, programs for the disadvantaged, and taxation). Additionally, the questions dealt with three matters of personal preference or style (religion, leadership, and abortion), and two matters of political strategy (the changing landscape and the "most outrageous" statement). In short, the journalists' questions could scarcely be said to have forced the candidates to confront difficult matters of domestic policy.

THE RHETORICAL STRATEGIES OF WALTER MONDALE: DEBATE 1

If any debater ever carried a burden of proof into a debate, that debater was Walter Mondale on the evening of October 7, 1984, in Louisville, Kentucky. But the Mondale campaign was well-prepared for the first debate, and they caught the president by surprise.

Preparation Strategies

Mondale was prepared for the first debate by lawyer Lewis Kaden and pollster Patrick Caddell. Caddell suggested that Mondale try to catch the usually highly scripted Reagan off guard: "Hit Reagan with a different Mondale, upset expectations, render his scripted responses irrelevant."[16] Where Carter had sought to portray Reagan as a trigger-happy warmonger bent on hurting the disadvantaged, Kaden advised "granting Reagan his sincerely held beliefs and persuasive abilities . . . his optimism, his good intentions, and his beliefs in equality, God, etc." The key tactic was to be an indirect approach to criticism of Reagan with jabs like, "I don't think President Reagan understands that . . . " or "I don't doubt that President Reagan is sincere, but . . . " and with counterpunches like

"I'm sure that's what you want, but your people haven't been going in that direction."[17]

This indirect strategy was an appropriate approach to undermining support for a personally credible incumbent. Its friendly, measured, and generally respectful tone (1) enhanced Mondale's image; (2) granted voters the right to like Reagan as a person; (3) stressed the gap between Reagan's words and his policies; and (4) pressed the point that Reagan was out of touch with reality.

Several observers of the first debate noted Mondale's technical preparation for staged debate. He spent an hour studying camera angles, he watched a mock debate by his aides, and he learned how to maintain eye contact with viewers by looking directly into the camera. [18] He was prepared for presidential mistakes with a one-liner from Will Rogers: "It's not what he doesn't know that bothers me; it's what he knows for sure that just ain't so."[19] And he was ready for the typically scripted Reagan to invoke the wistful "There you go again" that he had used so successfully against President Carter.

Themes

Kaden advised Mondale to demonstrate his sense of fairness, his concern for average people, his visions and plans for the future, and his readiness to "face reality" and make "tough choices."[20] President Reagan was portrayed as insensitive to the disadvantaged and minorities, as one who supported medicare but cut it anyway, and as one who opposed taxes but raised them nonetheless.

Mondale's themes came together in a dramatic exchange when he pounced on one of Reagan's predictable remarks.

Mr. Mondale: Now, Mr. President, you said, "There you go again," right?

The President: Yes.

Mr. Mondale: You remember the last time you said that?

The President: Mm-hmm. [shuffling papers and looking down].

By anticipating Reagan's predictable behavior, by seizing the moment with relish, and by forcing Reagan to answer to him, Mondale had taken center stage away from Reagan who looked like a schoolboy who had forgotten his homework. Although Reagan admitted only that he remembered having said "There you go again" in the Carter debate, Mondale exploited the admission by contextualizing it:

Mr. Mondale: You said it when President Carter said that you were gong to cut medicare, and you said, "Oh, no, there you go again, Mr. President." And what did you do right after the election? You went out and tried to cut $20 billion out of medicare. And so, when I—when you say, "There you go again"—people remember this, you know. [Laughter]

In fact, people remembered nothing of the sort until Mondale constructed the argument. Then, having already put Reagan on the defensive and "established" that Reagan had tried to cut medicare, Mondale moved to Reagan's taxes and the deficit:

Mr. Mondale: And people will remember that you signed the biggest tax increase in the history of California and the biggest tax increase in the history of the United States, and what are you going to do? You've got a $260 billion deficit. You can't wish it away. You won't slow defense spending; you refuse to do that—

Ms. Walters: Mr. Mondale, I'm afraid your time is up.

Through preparation Walter Mondale had climbed into the campaign for the first time since the primaries.

Mondale's two gambits provided good television moments, and they were quickly enshrined in the networks' presidential debates hall of fame. He clearly relished the chance to beat Reagan at his own game, but it was in the end Reagan's game. By using one-liners to advance a cluster of otherwise tenuous arguments, Mondale overshadowed his clearly reasoned answers. In short, Mondale surprised Reagan by playing his game, only to establish Reagan's way as the enduring way for the second debate and for 1988. The era of one-liners had arrived.

Delivery

Mondale's voice, unlike Reagan's, has never been an asset. The *National Review* said that "He looked like Frankenstein's monster and his voice could have unblocked a sink. But, aside from the handicaps God gave him," they conceded, "he was terse, pointed, and aggressive without being disrespectful. Even a joke or two filtered through."[21] He kept his tendency to sound shrill in check by speaking slowly and methodically, choosing his words with care and emphasizing them with pauses rather than passion. Clearly, he enjoyed himself.

Other Characteristics

Mondale fared well in the first debate by presenting himself as reasonable, especially in response to unreasonable questions. For example, when asked if he were a "born-again Christian" Mondale could have bristled about invasion of privacy, railed against the religious right, or preached. But instead he accepted Reagan's affirmation of faith ("I'm sure that we all accept and admire his commitment to his faith, and we are strengthened, all of us, by that fact") and presented his own credentials: "I am a son of a Methodist minister. My wife is the daughter of a Presbyterian minister. And I don't know if I've been born again, but I know I was born into a Christian family. . . . Whether that helps or not, I don't know. I have a deep religious faith." Then, and only then, did he move in measured tones to criticize those who "try to use one's own personal interpretation of faith politically, to question others' faith, and to try to use the instrumentalities of government to impose those views on others. All history tells us that that's a mistake." Mondale's response was perhaps the most reasonable, least doctrinal, discussion of religion yet heard on national television.

Finally, Mondale framed the debate in terms of leadership and vision, two concepts that had been considered Reagan's foremost assets. He did this by advancing an alternative view of leadership in his first answer:

> One of the key tests of leadership is whether one sees clearly the nature of the problems confronted by our nation. . . . I respect the President; I respect the Presidency, and I think he knows that. But the fact of it is, every estimate by this administration about the size of the deficit has been off by billions and billions of dollars . . . I've stood up and told the American people that I think it's a real problem, that it can destroy long-term economic growth, and I've told you what I think should be done. I think this is a test of leadership.

He pressed his point in response to Sawyer's leadership question, saying "There's a difference between being a quarterback and being a cheerleader, and when there's a real problem, a President must confront it." And in his closing statement he said, "I believe that if we ask those questions that bear on the future, not just congratulate ourselves but challenge us to solve those problems, you'll see that we need new leadership."

Mondale fared well in the first debate because (1) he exceeded the low public expectations for his performance; (2) he granted President Reagan credit for his popular personal qualities and concentrated on their political differences; (3) he seemed to be in control of both the terms of the debate and the facts; and (4) he presented himself as a reasonable moderate rather than as a liberal ideologue. But he also had considerable help from the president.

THE RHETORICAL STRATEGIES OF RONALD REAGAN: DEBATE 1

The first debate was perhaps the least impressive moment of Ronald Reagan's illustrious rhetorical career. By all accounts his problems began with preparation.

Preparation Strategies

Facts and figures had long been Reagan's albatross. His critics, and even some of his supporters, would regale one another with his gaffes, inaccuracies, and blunders. But Americans seemed ready to overlook this weakness because he relied primarily upon affective rather than cognitive aspects of persuasion, articulating simple and coherent visions that evoked identification.[22] Especially with his lead, President Reagan need only have reiterated his basic themes, his overarching vision, and his personal warmth.

But Reagan's advisors sought to correct his vulnerability by briefing him—to excess. They prepared him for a debate in which a high-pitched squeaky-voiced Mondale would seek to exploit the president's clumsiness with facts; not one where a deliberate Mondale praised Reagan's personal qualities but challenged his larger sense of vision. Presidential assistant Richard Darman prepared extensive briefing materials, and Budget Director David Stockman played Mondale in twelve hours of practice.

The preparation produced an un-Reaganesque performance. It was studded with such stylistic gems as this on the economy: "In the last 21 months, more than 6 million people have gotten jobs—there have been created new jobs for those people to where there are now 105 million civilians working, where there were only 99 million before; 107, if you count the military." And this on poverty programs: "We are spending now 37 percent more on food for the hungry. . . . We have more people receiving food stamps than were ever receiving them before—2,300,000 more are receiving them—even though we took 850,000 off the food stamp rolls because . . . we found people making 185 percent of the poverty level were getting government benefits. We have set a line at 130 percent." And this from the closing statement wherein President Reagan might have soared above statistics:

> But we have an economy that, for the first time—well, let's put it this way. In the first half of 1980, gross national product was down a minus 3.7 percent. The first half of '84 it's up 8 1/2 percent. Productivity in the first half of 1980 was down a minus 2 percent. Today it is up a plus 4 percent. Personal earnings after taxes per capita have gone up almost $3,000 in these 4 years. In 1980—or 1979, a person with a fixed income of $8,000 would—was $500 above the poverty line, and this maybe explains why there are the numbers still in poverty. By 1980 that same person was $500 below the poverty line.

The usually coherent Reagan had become confusing.

"What happened was that the President got overbriefed," said one aide. "He got so consumed with statistics that he lost his instincts for broad themes."[23] Director of the National Conservative Political Action Committee Terry Dolan lambasted the preparation team after the debate: "They basically think he's stupid and to prove that he's not stupid, he has to mouth off facts and figures."[24] An alternative view, undoubtedly held by Darman and Stockman, was that the president had simply had an off night.

But the preparation problems were not confined to the sacrifices of themes for statistics. By preparing Reagan for a nasty Mondale, Stockman left the president prone to overreaction. Reagan was noticeably stung, for example, by Mondale's allusion to "constantly picking on . . . the most vulnerable in American life" and he responded caustically that, "I don't believe that Mr. Mondale has a plan for balancing the budget; he has a plan for raising taxes." His rejoinder, and the manner of its delivery, suggest a fighter prepared for a bareknuckles brawl who finds himself in need of finesse.

Themes

President Reagan articulated the basic themes of his campaign: that his economic reforms were working and the budget would be balanced by 1989, that he would always do what was morally right for the people regardless of political interests, that the Democratic Party had left people like him during the 1950s, that farmers, minorities, and the disadvantaged were doing better under his administration than under Carter–Mondale, that abortion was murder, and that he would never under any circumstances cut social security. These themes ran throughout his responses, even if they were less clear than usual because of his overpreparation.

The critical point to be made about Reagan's themes is that they were Democratic rather than Republican themes, as writer Scott McConnell noticed:

> Dear Mr. President:
>
> You did less well than one expected in the last debate because you felt obliged to measure your record with yardsticks borrowed from your opponent—liberal Democratic standards that had nothing to do with the reasons you were elected. I hope you won't do that again when you debate Walter F. Mondale the second time, next Sunday night.[25]

But McConnell and many others misunderstood the strategic significance of Reagan's themes.

Predebate polls made it clear that Ronald Reagan was preferred by enough people in states with enough electoral votes to win the election. The key word is "preferred." To lose, Reagan would have had to so alienate the long-decided Republicans and conservatives across the nation that they would come to prefer Walter Mondale to Ronald Reagan. It is hard to imagine a life-long western Republican preferring Mondale over Reagan on the basis of a debate, and it is inconceivable that a majority of such decided voters in half the states would so reverse their preferences. In short, Reagan's electoral base was safe.

In the first debate Reagan went after those who doubted him and, therefore, constituted Mondale's base. He spoke to their concerns in very non-Republican terms:

> I will never stand for a reduction of the social security benefits to the people who are now getting them. I happen to believe in the people and believe that the people are supposed to be dominant in our society. . . . I want to hear only arguments as to whether [a policy] is good or bad for the people—is it morally right. We are today subsidizing housing for more than 10 million people, and we're going to continue along that line. We have preserved the safety net for the people with true need in this country, and it has been pure demagoguery that we have in some way shut off all the charitable programs or many of them for the people who are in real need. And you might find [my] words in a Democratic platform of some years ago—I know because I was a Democrat at that time. And I left the party eventually, because I could no longer follow the turn in Democratic leadership that took us down a path . . . lacking trust in the American people. Many Democrats are seeing the same thing this Democrat saw: The leadership isn't taking us where we want to go. We are spending a third more on all of the—well, all of the programs of human services. Half . . . of the full-time college students in the United States are receiving some form of Federal aid.

Were these the statements of a conservative Republican?

These statements by Reagan were clearly directed at Mondale's Democratic base: traditional Democrats, the elderly, the economically insecure, the populists who mistrust big business and big government. And they worked, as we shall see shortly.

Delivery

President Reagan's usually smooth delivery was interrupted by hesitations and other nonfluencies. Indeed, his performance was so uncertain that his age became an issue overnight. Without minimizing the age factor, the president was tired from the long bouts with Stockman and was working hard to use all of the facts and figures. *The Economist*, for example, observed: "Mr. Reagan's attraction depends to an unusual extent on his skill in communicating, his easy self-confidence and his robust good humour. On Sunday he looked, and sounded, a bit confused. Which he probably was: . . . his head so filled with facts that he was unable to enjoy himself."[26] The "age issue" would hound Reagan until the second debate.

It should also be noted that Reagan suffered, much as Mondale benefitted, from public expectations. "It is the mythology of the strong, warm, faultless performer that carried the Reagan campaign forward so effortlessly" until the first debate, wrote Dudley Clendinen in the *New York Times*. But "the mythology became the third player in that debate, the standard against which Mr. Reagan's performance was judged."[27]

EFFECTS OF THE FIRST DEBATE

The effects of the first debate were mixed. Clearly, it attracted an audience, reinforced some audiences and shifted a limited number of others, and modified the candidates' images.[28] It is less clear, and indeed unlikely, that it helped set the voters' agenda, increased the voters' knowledge of issues (given the panelists' questions), built confidence in American democracy, aroused political interests, enabled interests to be easily acted upon, or facilitated political learning.[29]

But the press overplayed the results of the debate, as can be seen in the *New York Times* reporting of a Louis Harris Poll. According to Harris 61 percent said that Mondale had won, compared with 19 percent for Reagan. So? Did that affect their candidate preferences? President Reagan's support dipped from 54 percent to 53 percent, while Mondale soared from 42 percent to 44 percent. The survey's +/− 3 percent margin for error means that the changes were negligible and that the polls should responsibly have been reported as stable, but the *Times*'s lead sentence was "President Reagan's lead over Walter Mondale has been cut to nine percentage points in the most recent Harris Poll."[30] The important contests were for the electoral votes of states already solidly for Reagan and the story notes that Reagan's lead had been cut from 11 percent to 7 percent after the debate, but they failed to point out that even a 7 percent lead is quite comfortable when the margin for error is but 3 percent.

The first 1984 debate was an experience in dissonance. Already decided pro-Reagan voters saw a confused, facts and figures candidate who sounded like a Democrat contrasted with a respectful, moderate, Christian man of vision and humor who cared deeply about reducing the federal deficit. A scorecard would have been helpful. But in that first debate neither candidate spoke to either conservatives or Republicans. Both candidates tried to persuade Democrats who constituted Mondale's electoral base. In short, despite Reagan's difficulties and Mondale's successes, both candidates accomplished important political objectives.

THE RHETORICAL STRATEGIES OF RONALD REAGAN: DEBATE 2

The second debate was emceed by Edwin Newman and the panelists asked decidedly more demanding questions than had the first panel. Georgia Ann Geyer of the United Press Syndicate asked about the use of force in Central America, differences between conventional and guerilla warfare, and immigration policy. Marvin Kalb of NBC News asked whether we should contain or eliminate Communist influence, which interests were sufficiently vital to warrant the use of American troops, the nature of Soviet influence in Eastern Europe, the Star Wars defense system, and arms limitation. Morton Kondracke of the *New Republic* asked about the use of military force in general and about our actions in Nicaragua and Lebanon in particular, about strategic weapons systems, a nuclear freeze, and about support for our allies. Henry Trewhitt of the *Baltimore Sun* asked about strategic missiles, the doctrine of deterrence, and the "age issue." Unlike the first panel, this group pursued specific policy areas amenable to presidential leadership, and they frequently broke from the question/follow-up format to ask new questions.

In the second debate the advantages swung to Reagan. If he had been overconfident for the first debate, news coverage convinced him that he had a fight on his hands. If he had been overrated as a debater and Mondale underrated, press reaction had now overrated Mondale and dismissed Reagan as marginally in command of his faculties. The first debate had been on domestic issues—Mondale's strength—and the second would be on foreign policy, a Reagan concern and the policy area in which presidents exert the most influence.[31] Despite his effective rational argumentation in the first debate, Mondale had scored with his one-liners and had thereby implicitly agreed to play to Reagan's rules: humor would be admissible. Finally, Reagan was like the grizzled running back who had fumbled on the goal line. He knew that he was still ahead and that his superior skill, experience, preparation, and coaching were likely to produce eventual victory.

Preparation Strategies

The preparation team was changed almost immediately, with Nancy Reagan, Nevada Senator Paul Laxalt, and Stuart K. Spencer taking more important roles.[32] They chose to return to Reagan's characteristic use of themes and images rather than facts and figures, and they relied on two rather than five mock debates.[33]

The change was not only clever because of public reaction to the president's first performance, it was also clever because voters distant from foreign events can interpret them more easily through broad themes and visions. Facts were used, but they were used to support the vision.

"Advice to the pride-wounded champ" came from columnists like Nixon advisor William Safire, who saw "counterpunching" as the key strategy: "The debater who first goes for the jugular will lose his valuable nice-guy image and offend the swing voter. But the debater who listens in ostentatious disbelief to the other guy's opening answer, who then shakes his head more in sorrow than in anger, and only then—with obvious reluctance, all relish concealed—goes for the throat will win."[34] Safire specifically recommended that Reagan be friendly and good-humored because "testiness is seen as a sign of age and anger leads to sputtering."[35] By addressing a rally at the Westin Crown Center Hotel just thirty-nine minutes before airtime Reagan bolstered his confidence, friendliness, and general good humor.[36]

Themes

President Reagan's theme was that he was fully in command of a strengthened America. He emphasized this theme in at least four ways. He relied extensively on personal pronouns, as when discussing the Soviet Union: "*I* have said on a number of occasions exactly what *I* believe about the Soviet Union. *I* retract nothing that *I* have said. *I* believe that many of the things *they* have done are evil in any concept of morality that *we* have. But *I* also recognize that as the two great superpowers in the world *we* have to live with each other. And *I* told Mr. Gromyko that *we* don't like *their* system [emphasis added]."[37]

He stressed it with assertions of personal responsibility: "I have ordered an investigation. I will never send troops anywhere on a mission of that kind [Beirut peace-keeping] without telling them that if somebody shoots at them, they can darn well shoot back. And this is what we did. . . . I have no apologies for us going on a peace mission. It wasn't me that walked out on [the "walk in the woods" argument;] the Soviet Union disavowed it."

He stressed it with humor: "I know it'll come as a surprise to Mr. Mondale, but I am in charge. I know that he has a commercial out where he's appearing on the deck of the *Nimitz* and watching the F–14's take off. And that's an image of strength—except that if he had had his way when the *Nimitz* was being planned, he would have been deep in the water out there because there wouldn't have been any *Nimitz* to stand on—he was against it."

And he stressed it with indignation:

> Well, my rebuttal is that I've heard the national debt blamed for a lot of things, but not for illegal immigration across our border—and it has nothing to do with it.

But I hope that from here on you will no longer be saying that [I said that nuclear missiles could be called back], which is absolutely false. How anyone could think that a sane person would believe you could call back a nuclear missile, I think is as ridiculous as the whole concept has been [*sic*]. So thank you for letting me straighten the record. I'm sure that you appreciate that.

In short, Walter Mondale debated "The President." The transcript is replete with Reagan's self-references and almost devoid of qualifiers.

Delivery

Reagan's delivery was, in the second debate, commanding. His first response seemed to be unleashed, and he spoke more briskly in a deeper voice with few nonfluencies. Because his incoherencies were fluent they proved less worrisome than had his first round coherent nonfluencies: it is better to sound smooth than to make sense. One senses, from the president's manner, that Stockman's facts and figures had been replaced by Nancy Reagan's admonitions not to let Mondale show him up.

Other Characteristics

In addition to stressing his command of the presidency, Reagan turned to his trusty assets of humor and cinematic language. He was ready for the age question, and when Trewhitt lobbed it to him he knocked it out of the ballpark by saying, "I want you to know that also I will not make age an issue of this campaign. I am not going to exploit, for political purposes, my opponent's youth and inexperience." The laughter and applause subsided twenty seconds later. Trewhitt, still smiling, surrendered: "Mr. President I'd like to head for the fence and try to catch that one before it goes over, but I'll go on to another question." In one sentence the slugger had faced the strikeout pitch, hit it over the fence, and eliminated the issue from the campaign.

Secondly, Reagan abandoned his first debate strategy of facts and figures in the closing statement in favor of his familiar cinematic language. After thanking people he began discussing the future, then he digressed to a letter he had once been asked to write for a time capsule, from which he digressed to a ride down the California coast. "I couldn't neglect the beauty around me—the Pacific out there on one side of the highway, shining in the sunlight, the mountains of the coast range rising on the other side. And I found myself wondering what it would be like for someone—wondering if someone 100 years from now would be driving down the highway, and if they would see the same thing." In Reagan's hands the California coast had become the hypnotist's watch. After eighty-five minutes of complicated talk he asked his audience to relax and gaze upon a serene landscape. Then he mused with us about those who might see that image, and then he made those imaginary people, who seemed so similar to us, the object of his closing statement: "I thought to myself, what are they going to say about us, what are those people 100 years from now going to think? Well, what they will say about us 100 years from now depends on how we keep our rendezvous with destiny. Will we do the things that we know must be done [and know that] someone will say, "Thank God for those people back in the 1980s for preserving our freedom, for saying for us this blessed planet called Earth, with all its grandeur and its beauty." It mattered little that Newman had to cut off the president's statement.

In less than four minutes Reagan had ransacked the Democrats' warehouse of cherished symbols and themes—the natural environment, everyday people, the future, the elimination of nuclear weapons, jobs and opportunities, peace and, for the *coup de grace*, Franklin Roosevelt's "rendezvous with destiny"—all while his audience gazed at the scenic California coastline. Moreover, Mondale had no opportunity to respond.

RHETORICAL STRATEGIES OF WALTER MONDALE: DEBATE 2

Preparation Strategies

There is no evidence that the Mondale campaign prepared differently for the second debate. But he had approached the first debate underestimated, far behind, and in possession of a secret strategy. Mondale looked, in the first debate, like the cat that had swallowed the canary.

But early in the second debate Mondale looked more like the cat that chased the canary off the cliff, looked down, and then fell. He may have been surprised by his own success, he might have felt the pressure of a turning tide, or he might have realized that, this time, he held no surprise. He had caught the champ by surprise and knocked him down; could he do it again? Mondale spent the hours before the debate secluded in the Harry Truman Suite of the Radisson Hotel Muehlebach, while Reagan spoke at the rally.[38]

Themes

Mondale's primary theme was that "A President must not only assure that we're tough, but we must also be wise and smart in the exercise of that power." Mondale pounded away on that theme:

> The bottom line of national strength is that the President must be in command, he must lead.

A President is called the Commander in Chief . . . because he's supposed to be in charge of the facts and run our government and strengthen our nation.

A President can't know everything, but a President has to know those things that are essential to his leadership and the enforcement of our laws.

Good intentions, I grant. But it takes more than that. You must be tough and smart.

Mondale used selected case studies to embellish this theme:

In Lebanon, this President exercised American power, all right, but the management of it was such that our marines were killed, we had to leave in humiliation, the Soviet Union became stronger, terrorists became emboldened. And it was because they did not think through how power should be exercised. . . .

The [Middle Eastern] terrorists have won each time. The President told the terrorists he was going to retaliate. He didn't. They called their bluff. And the bottom line is that the United States left [Lebanon] in humiliation, and our enemies are stronger.

As Reagan tried to demonstrate that he was in command, Mondale tried to demonstrate that Reagan lacked the intelligence and managerial qualities to command effectively.

The clash was most apparent in a dramatic exchange about the Star Wars defense system:

The President: But when you keep star-warring it—I never suggested where the weapons should be or what kind; I'm not a scientist. . . . I don't know what it would be, but if we can come up with one, I think the world will be better off.

Mr. Newman: Mr. Mondale, your rebuttal.

Mr. Mondale: Well, that's what a President's supposed to know—where those weapons are going to be. If they're space weapons, I assume they'll be in space. [Laughter] If they're antisatellite weapons, I assume they're going to be aimed against satellites. . . . You haven't just accepted research, Mr. President. You've set up a strategic defense initiative, an agency, you're beginning to test, you're talking about deploying, you're asking for a budget of some $30 billion for this purpose.

Clearly, Mondale's remarks were sufficiently pointed, illustrated, and reiterated to undermine public confidence in Reagan. But they seemed not to do so.

For one thing, Mondale had run afoul of Safire's suggestion to counterpunch thereby jeopardizing his emerging nice-guy image. His breezy use of Will Rogers and "there you go again" in the first debate was replaced in the second debate with one of the weaker Groucho Marx jokes and a demand that Reagan apologize for a rude remark by Vice President George Bush.

Secondly, Mondale failed to pounce on Reagan's oversights in the debate. "Mr. Mondale missed his first chance after the President was asked to name the areas of the world of vital interest to the U.S.," explains Safire: "Mr. Reagan remembered the Middle East and the Pacific Basin, but he forgot Europe . . . [and after] Mr. Reagan had just said that he 'did not order the marines into that barracks. That was a command decision made by the commanders on the spot. . . .' That evasion cried out for sharp rebuttal: did the Commander in Chief not know of the marines vulnerability? Wasn't it his job to know?"[39] In short, Mondale failed to use Reagan's mistakes to advance his own arguments.

Thirdly, Mondale's depiction of Reagan came two weeks later, and the Reagan he faced this night would play his part as neither senile nor stupid. He seemed to recall clearly the decisions he had made, his reasoning, and the results. Perhaps more importantly, Reagan and Mondale both discussed Reagan's decisions, Reagan's reasons, and Reagan's results thereby implicitly affirming Reagan's control.

Delivery

Mondale's delivery and general presentation were above average, clearly superior to those of Nixon, Ford, or Carter. But Mondale faced (1) Ronald Reagan and (2) inflated expectations. For these he was no match. He drew the first question and he seemed not quite ready to begin. His verbal and nonverbal fidgets suggested early that the first performance would not be repeated. By the time Mondale righted himself the first impressions had been formed and the bulk of the electorate had reassured itself of Reagan's command.

Also, Mondale was more strident and intense than he had been earlier. With no secret strategy he seemed less able to grant credit to Reagan and less able to laugh. Where he had earlier granted credit to Reagan, he now demanded credit from Reagan: "Mr. President, I accept your commitment to peace, but I want you to accept my commitment to a strong national defense. I demanded an apology from Vice President Bush. . . . What does the President have to say about taking responsibility for a Vice President who won't apologize for something like that?" The strategy was excessive.

Indeed, by flailing away at Reagan's unfitness for leadership in strident humorless tones, Mondale overplayed his hand. He already had the support of the forty-some percent who disapproved of Reagan and preferred Mondale; he needed to become preferred among those voters whose support for Reagan was soft, and those were people who disliked Reagan's policies but approved of him as a person. Such persons are rarely to be won with strident and repeated attacks on their candidate's intelligence. Rather, Mondale should have (1) retained the moderated and friendly tones of the first debate and (2) criticized Reagan's intelligence and abilities indirectly with more questions for the lukewarm supporters to answer for themselves. He used this technique when criticizing the CIA manual for assassinations and terrorist acts, "How can this happen? How can something this serious occur in an administration and have a President of the United States in a situation like this say he didn't know?" He needed to do more of this.

In short, Mondale's delivery was good, but it was neither as good as it had been in the first encounter nor was it up to the public's inflated expectations.

Other Characteristics

But perhaps Mondale's fatal mistake concerned complication. A foreign policy debate asks citizens to make sense of complicated trends and events, sophisticated weapons technology, and internal politics in faraway lands. Many of us seek shortcuts to understanding. Presidents Reagan and Roosevelt were masters at simplifying complex questions into everyday images, and the public appreciated the premasticated information. Conversely, many had rejected President Carter's tendency to unnecessarily complicate simple matters.

Against this backdrop, Mondale's first sentence, "I believe that the question oversimplifies the difficulties of what we must do in Central America," was almost suicidal. He continued in the follow-up, "It's much more complex." But Reagan quickly saved the audience from considering Mondale's three-pronged approach by saying simply that, "I thought for a moment that instead of a debate I was going to find Mr. Mondale in complete agreement with what we're doing, because the plan that he has outlined is the one we've been following for quite some time."

The nature of the policy and its merits were thus culled from the debate.

EFFECTS OF DEBATE 2

Effects analyses are always tricky, and they are especially so when considering one debate amidst a whirlwind campaign. A *Newsweek* poll found a 43 percent–40 percent advantage to Reagan, but Gallup's weekly poll showed a two-point Reagan slip and a one-point Mondale gain.[40] Most commentators gave the decision to Reagan on points and, of course, with his lead he needed only to avoid a most unlikely knockout punch.

By the second debate the candidates had chosen to focus on Reagan's competence. Mondale tried repeatedly in various ways to establish the perception that Ronald Reagan was too old and too simple to serve effectively as president. Reagan used all of his considerable skills to slip Mondale's characterizations and to reinforce the public's perception of him as a confident, skilled, competent leader. Unlike the first debate, the candidates clashed repeatedly on the same point.

Faced with inflated expectations and an awakened and prepared adversary and armed with no secret weapon Mondale did well, but not well enough. Reagan improved sufficiently to confound Mondale's efforts to portray him as incompetent.

CONCLUSIONS

Gallup concluded that although 81 percent of the nation's registered voters watched all or part of the debates, "The presidential debates apparently did not have a major impact on the election outcome." This seems curious since they also reported a net shift of 13 points toward likely Mondale support and a net loss of 9 points in likely Reagan support.[41] How much of a shift does Gallup require for "major impact"?

Gallup's other polls show that between September 25 and October 27—the period of the debates—Ronald Reagan's approval ratings dropped 34.88 points (from 92.54 to 57.66) among Republicans and climbed 40 points (22.85 to 62.87) among Democrats. Reagan gained more among the poor, the nonwhite, females, and those with less than college education than he did among Republican strongholds.[42] Yet despite this turbulence the preference polls showed Reagan dropping only 2 points to Mondale and maintaining a 17-point lead. Indeed, Reagan won by 18 percent of the popular vote, winning 96 percent of the Republicans, and only 21 percent of the Democrats.[43]

The explanation for these strikingly inconsistent findings lies in three points. First, Reagan used the campaign and the debates to attack successfully Mondale's Democratic base. Second, Republicans did not like to hear Reagan talking about food stamps, poverty programs, and a rendezvous with destiny. Third, no matter how much Democrats liked, and Republicans disliked, Reagan's Democratic rhetoric, they nevertheless voted for their long-term preferences.

The 1984 presidential debates suggest three conclusions. First, presidential debates are as susceptible to strategic manipulation as are political advertising, rallies, bumper stickers, and stump speeches. Perhaps they are more susceptible to manipulation than these other forms of campaign communication because they have an *ethos* of rational deliberation that seduces the voters into relaxing their critical standards. In both debates Reagan emphasized Democratic themes, symbols, and motifs in ways that enabled him to make inroads into Mondale's electoral base. The use of reporters neither guarantees good questions nor precludes strategic answers.

Second, the 1984 presidential debates codified the *expectancy rule*: the candidate expected to excel will fall short of the inflated expectations while the candidate expected to fare poorly will clear the easy hurdle and be perceived as the winner. It happened in both 1984 debates, as it has so often happened in the Iowa caucuses and New Hampshire primaries.

Third, presidential debates and their outcomes are poorly understood because their purposes are so poorly understood. Presidential elections are not held to decide "who won the debate," as reporters like to say. Nor should presidential elections be decided on the basis of staged televised performances in which aspiring leaders are blind-sided by sometimes inappropriate questions that must be answered in three minutes, any more than they should be decided solely on the basis of television spots or speeches.

Presidential debates should inform, educate, and interest citizens in the contest, not just shift them from one candidate to the other. Although Gallup concluded that the 1984 debates had little effect on voter shifts, many other Gallup surveys show tremendous subsurface volatility in voter perceptions.

Clearly, debate polls must begin to move from the superficial directional indexes of attitude change to more sensitive demographic and thematic measures. Further research is needed to determine whether those 1984 changes resulted from the debates or despite the debates, and to ascertain the susceptability of long-term preferences to modification by televised debate.

NOTES

1. Robert V. Friedenberg, " 'We Are Present Here Today for the Purpose of Having a Joint Discussion': The Conditions Requisite for Political Debates," *Journal of the American Forensic Association* 16 (Summer 1979): 1–2.

2. Gallup polls compiled by Gary King and Lyn Ragsdale, *The Elusive Executive: Discovering Statistical Patterns in the Presidency*. (Washington, D.C.: CQ Press, 1988), pp. 306–307, 315, 319.

3. *The Economist* (October 13, 1984): 41.

4. Sidney Kraus, *Televised Presidential Debates and Public Policy* (Hillsdale, N.J.: Lawrence Erlbaum Associates, 1988), pp. 54–55.

5. Gallup Poll cited by Thomas E. Cronin, "The Presidential Election of 1984," in *Election '84: Landslide without a Mandate?*, ed. by Ellis Sandoz and Cecil V. Crabb, Jr., (New York: Mentor Books, New American Library, 1985), p. 51.

6. Kraus, *Televised Debates*, pp. 54–55. Kraus attributes Reagan's decision to debate, in part, to performer's ego.

7. Kraus, *Televised Debates*, pp. 54–55.

8. " 'Tis the Season for Presidential Debates." *U.S. News & World Report*, January 23, 1984, p. 46.
9. Kraus, *Televised Debates*, pp. 56–58; James Reston, "The Press and Debates." *New York Times*, October 17, 1984, p. 27.
10. Kraus, *Televised Debates*, p. 58.
11. Lee Atwater, Campaign Memorandum (November 5, 1983), quoted by Stephen J. Wayne in *The Road to the White House*. 3rd edition (New York: St. Martin's, 1983), p. 192.
12. "The Debate," *National Review*, November 2, 1984, p. 17.
13. New York Times/CBS poll cited in "Reagan and Mondale Debate: Clash on Deficit and Religion," *New York Times*, October 8, 1984, p. B7.
14. *Gallup Reports*, no. 149, 1985, summarized in King and Ragsdale, *Elusive Executive*, p. 464.
15. *Gallup Reports*, nos. 227–228, 1984, summarized in King and Ragsdale, *Elusive Executive*, p. 466.
16. Patrick Caddell, Memorandum (September 30, 1984) quoted by Wayne in *Road*, p. 220.
17. Lewis Kaden, Memorandum (October 1984) quoted by Wayne in *Road*, 221–222.
18. Howell Raines, "Chance of Revival Seen for Mondale After TV Debate," *New York Times*, October 8, 1984, p. A28.
19. "1984 Presidential Debate between the President and former Vice President Walter F. Mondale. October 7, 1984." *Public Papers of the Presidents: Ronald Reagan, 1984* (Washington, D.C.: Government Printing Office, 1984), pp. 1442–1462. All text quotations from the first debate are from this transcript.
20. Kader, quoted by Wayne in *Road*, p. 221.
21. "The Debate," p. 16.
22. Craig Allen Smith, "MisteReagan's Neighborhood: Rhetoric and National Unity," *Southern Speech Communication Journal* 52 (Spring 1987): 219–239; Walter R. Fisher, *Human Communication as Narration: Toward a Philosophy of Reason, Value, and Action* (Columbia: University of South Carolina Press, 1987), pp. 143–157.
23. Steven R. Weisman, "Reagan's Aides to Reassess Tactics and Preparations for Second Debate," *New York Times*, October 10, 1984, p. A20.
24. Raines, "Chance of Revival," p. A28.
25. Scott McConnell, "Memo to Reagan: How to Look Better," *New York Times*, October 15, 1987, p. 19.
26. "Intimations of Mortality," *The Economist*, October 13, 1984, p. 41.
27. Dudley Clendinen, "Reagan and Television: How His Image Leaves Him Vulnerable in Debates," *New York Times*, October 20, 1984, p. 9.
28. Judith S. Trent and Robert V. Friedenberg, *Political Campaign Communications: Principles and Practices* (New York: Praeger Publishers, 1983), pp. 263–272.
29. Sidney Kraus and Dennis K. Davis, "Political Debates," in *The Handbook of Political Communication* ed. by Dan D. Nimmo and Keith R. Sanders (Beverly Hills, Calif.: Sage, 1981), pp. 280–289.
30. "Campaign Notes: Reagan Leads Mondale 53%–44% in Harris Poll," *New York Times*, October 16, 1984, p. 24.
31. Aaron Wildavsky, "The Two Presidencies," *Trans-Action* 4 (December

1966): 7–14; Lance T. LeLoup and Steven A. Shull, "Congress vs. the Executive: The 'Two Presidencies' Reconsidered," *Social Science Quarterly* 59 (March 1979): 707; and George C. Edwards, III, *Presidential Influence in Congress* (San Francisco: W. H. Freeman, 1980), pp. 15–18.

32. Weisman, "Reagan's Aides," p. A20.

33. James Baker, Post-debate interview with Dan Rather, CBS News (October 21, 1984).

34. William Safire, "More Tips for Debaters," *New York Times*, October 18, 1984, p. A27.

35. Safire, "More Tips," p. A27.

36. Bernard Weinraub, "A Bitter Contest in a Lavish Setting," *New York Times*, October 22, 1984), p. B7.

37. "1984 Presidential Debate between the President and Former Vice President Walter F. Mondale. October 21, 1984." *Public Papers of the Presidents: Ronald Reagan, 1984*, (Washington, D.C.: Government Printing Office, 1984), pp. 1591–1610. All text quotations from the second debate are from this transcript. This 10–2 ratio of first- to third-person pronouns came from the president who would later say so impersonally of the Iran-Contra affair, "Mistakes were made."

38. Weinraub, "Bitter Contest," p. B7.

39. William Safire, "Reagan Comes Back," *New York Times*, October 22, 1984, p. A21.

40. "Impact of the 1984 Debates," *The Gallup Report*, November 1984, no. 330, pp. 16, 5.

41. *Gallup*, no. 230, p. 16.

42. King and Ragsdale, *Elusive Executive*, p. 315.

43. *Gallup*, no. 230, p. 32.

SELECT BIBLIOGRAPHY

Drucker, Susan J., and Janice Platt Hunold. "The Debating Game." *Critical Studies in Mass Communication* 4 (June 1987): 202–206. The authors demonstrate that televised debates have the same structural characteristics as television game shows: a similarity deserving of careful empirical analysis. Their disturbingly reasonable essay deserves serious attention by all students of presidential debates.

Morello, John T. "Argument and Visual Structuring in the 1984 Mondale–Reagan Debates." *Western Journal of Speech Communication* 52 (Fall 1988): 277–290. The author argues that visual depictions of the debates foster perceptions different from those warranted by the arguments.

Wall, Victor, James L. Golden, and Herbert James. "Perceptions of the 1984 Presidential Debates and a Select 1988 Presidential Primary Debate." *Presidential Studies Quarterly* 18 (Summer 1988): 541–564. The authors conclude that predebate preference was the most useful predictor of audience reaction and that "strength of argument" was more influential than candidate image.

Debate Transcripts

"1984 Presidential Debate between the President and former Vice President Walter F. Mondale. October 7, 1984." *Public Papers of the Presidents: Ronald Reagan, 1984*. Washington, D.C.: Government Printing Office, 1984, pp. 1442–1462.

"1984 Presidential Debate between President and Former Vice President Walter F. Mondale. October 21, 1984." *Public Papers of the Presidents: Ronald Reagan, 1984*. Washington, D.C.: Government Printing Office, 1984, pp. 1591–1610.

Chapter 6

The 1984 Bush–Ferraro Vice Presidential Debate

Judith S. Trent

As Geraldine Ferraro said of America's first debate between a female and a male candidate competing for a national office, "Once it's done, the question will never rise again, 'Can a woman do it?' So it's much more than me against George Bush. It's much, much bigger."[1]

The postdebate observation of Congresswoman Ferraro, the Democratic Party's candidate for vice president in 1984, was accurate. To a large extent, the very fact that it occurred was far more significant than anything that was said or done by either candidate during the debate. The problem was not that either she or her opponent, the Republican incumbent Vice President George Bush, did anything to disgrace themselves or their runningmates. On the contrary, the overall performance of each was quite good. Nevertheless, the debate took place and may best be remembered primarily because one of the debaters was a woman.[2] Public focus, before and after their confrontation, was heavily centered on questions of whether or not Ferraro had the intellectual capacity and the strength to be "one heart-beat from the presidency," whether she could be"vice presidential" and how Bush should/would/could/did react to the historic occasion of debating a female opponent for the nation's second highest office.[3] Headlines such as "Shoot-Out at Gender Gap" or "She Achieved Another First" were not uncommon.[4] Thus, the spotlight on the debate had less to do with what they said and did than it had with the fact of their gender, a conclusion of little surprise considering the traditional lack of media attention to, or public interest in, whatever charges vice presidential candidates had leveled against each other during previous elections. But with Walter Mondale's selection of Geraldine Ferraro, the Democrats turned the 1984 campaign for vice president into a more intriguing contest than it had ever been.[5] Their debate was a first, and like many such situations, expectations exceeded what might have been possible for even generally acknowledged experts. Neither Vice President George Bush nor Congresswoman Geraldine Ferraro were considered experts. Bush had experienced a disaster in a Nashua, New Hampshire, debate with Ronald Reagan in 1980 and Ferraro had never formally debated a political opponent.

THE GOALS OF THE CANDIDATES

It is no more surprising to learn that the Democratic Party had originally lobbied for a total of nine debates during the 1984 general election campaign (six presidential and three between the vice presidential candidates) than it is to learn that the Republicans wanted as few as possible. The Republican incumbents enjoyed a 16–19 point lead in virtually all public opinion polls as the fall campaign began. Thus it was only the potentially damaging image of appearing to avoid any debate with the Democratic candidates that finally yielded the compromise: two presidential and one vice presidential debate.[6]

While it is doubtful that either the vice president or congresswoman played a dominate role in determining strategy for the fall campaign, there is evidence to suggest that they considered the debate important to their individual goals and wanted it to take place. Ferraro, as part of the overall Democratic plan, challenged the vice president to debate her and then later wrote that not only had the "Mondale–Ferraro campaign considered the outcome of the one and only vice-presidential debate on October 11 to be critical to the election,"[7] but that "the debate would be a pivotal point in my career . . . "[8] Once challenged, Bush was only slightly less enthusiastic in pushing forward the idea of a debate. In August, on a visit to the Reagan ranch in Santa Barbara, he urged the president and their campaign strategists to let the debate occur and to immediately announce arrangements for it. Because the Reagan–Bush election staff had been using the subject of a vice presidential debate as a negotiating factor with the Democrats, following Ferraro's challenge there had been no public Republican response. It was rumored that the vice president felt that his "manhood had been challenged."[9] Thus, when he did not receive what he wanted in Santa Barbara, Bush personally announced to the press that whether or not he would debate was his decision—not the campaign's—and strongly implied that the debate would take place.[10] The vice president's declaration was not only uncharacteristic of the way in which he normally followed the directives of the Reagan staff, it forced the White House to later concede that the question of the debate was "a personal matter for the Vice President to decide."[11]

Geraldine Ferraro talked freely about three of her goals and the media talked just as freely of a fourth. She phrased her debate objectives in terms of their importance to the overall campaign and said there were three considerations: "First, there was the Presidency. When Bush and I would stand together on stage, most people would be evaluating us to see which one of us could best assume the Presidency. . . . Second, there was the race between the two vice-presidential candidates for the few people who were going to vote for the ticket based on the Vice President. And third, there was the uniqueness of my candidacy as a woman."[12]

To some extent the three were one and revolved around the historic nature of her candidacy and the fact that women who have sought political office in this country have been allowed only a narrow range of "acceptable" campaign behaviors. For example, they cannot be too young nor too old. Neither can they be perceived as too sexy nor too severe. Their voices should be well modulated and their clothes well tailored but not fashionable.[13] Female candidates also have to exhibit knowledge in all areas of public affairs to counter the suspicion that women have little competence in understanding complex issues, particularly, economic policies or international relations. Yet they cannot be perceived as talking too much. But above all women should not be too aggressive nor too forceful for fear that they will be considered unfeminine, shrill, vicious, nagging, or a "bitch."[14] In other words, even in 1984, it was difficult for female candidates to create a credible image because "traditional stereotypes about women and conventional expectations about political leaders do not blend together smoothly."[15]

Not surprisingly, the first woman running for the second highest office in the country came to represent the problems faced by all political women. She did not look like a vice president had ever looked or sound like one had ever sounded—two problems impossible to hide. Thus her goal, and the goal shared with all women who watched the debate (no matter their partisan identification), was to prove that Geraldine Ferraro, a woman, had the experience, competence, depth, temperament, leadership, and strength to be vice president. It was, as she said, "as if I am standing in for every woman in this country."[16]

In addition to proving her credibility as a vice-presidential candidate, Ferraro had another objective. It was important that she keep the momentum going that had begun four days earlier when Walter Mondale "defeated" Ronald Reagan in the first presidential debate and thereby began, for the first (and only) time during the campaign, to reduce the gap in the public-opinion polls. Ferraro claimed that the timing of the vice presidential debate made it unusually important to the Democratic effort.[17]

Finally, although Ferraro did not discuss it, the media claimed that one of her goals for the debate was future oriented. When the Democratic ticket lost, so went the assertion, Ferraro would have established her credibility and political presence sufficiently to unseat New York's United States Senator Alfonse D'Amato in 1986. Whether or not this was part of her agenda is largely irrelevant. She did not run for the Senate in 1986 but she did succeed in demonstrating her competence to a national audience and, at least, Democrats believed she was in a position to "project herself to all voters and especially women voters."[18]

George Bush, on the other hand, came to the debate with quite another set of goals. Rather than concentrate on establishing himself, Bush, the incumbent, had to be prepared to defend administration policies, praise the president, recover any momentum lost by Reagan in the debate with Mondale, and rebuild or reformulate his own image as a step toward the realization of his future presidential aspirations. It was a formidable agenda—one made more difficult because he had to do what no other incumbent vice president had ever had to do: debate an opponent who was a woman.

Just as the first vice presidential debate between a woman and a man presented problems for the female, so too did it for the male. Bush had to refute Ferraro's charges against administration policies and practices, attack past and current Democratic arguments and actions, and provide forceful, knowledgeable and convincing positions—all without appearing to attack his opponent. Debates, as political theater, are supposed to be hard-hitting and confrontational. Yet, because of stereotypical attitudes regarding women and the "appropriate" or "proper" treatment of them by men, Bush was prevented from employing those rhetorical behaviors typically associated with political debates. He could not appear to be attacking her. Indeed, prior to their debate he had rarely mentioned her name during campaign appearances because of the risk of voter backlash.[19] His problem was further compounded by Ferraro's normally combative or feisty rhetorical style as well as the fact that she was beginning to establish a far more easy and comfortable rapport with voters than was he. Moreover, once the controversies over her finances and views on abortion had peaked, she began drawing far larger and more enthusiastic audiences.[20] Bush, on the other hand, was reported by the media as being "surprisingly inept as a campaigner." Moreover, his "earnest speeches seldom excite even the smallish Republican crowds he usually addresses, and he sometimes reacts badly to the to-and-fro of daily campaigning."[21] Thus, in preparing to meet the challenges presented to him in debating Geraldine Ferraro, perhaps the vice president himself best articulated his goals when he told reporters, "I will try to be, myself, for better or worse. Not tear her down but let her speak up on her side. You have to be what you are. You gotta hang in there."[22]

Not only, however, was the vice president facing what his staff had come to call "the Ferraro factor," but for the first time in their four-year partnership Ronald Reagan appeared to need him. The president had not turned in a credible performance four days earlier in his first debate with Walter Mondale. In addition to being perceived the loser, the question of Reagan's age became the subject of countless media stories.[23] So, in spite of the fact that the Republicans were still comfortably ahead in the polls, the president would profit from a strong performance from his vice president.

Finally, George Bush brought two separate but related personal goals to the debate with Ferraro: his desire to be president and the necessity to prove his skill in debate and thereby boost his image as a dynamic leader. Although George Bush's loyalty to Ronald Reagan was seldom questioned (it was, in fact, the submersion of his own identity—appearing not to have an opinion of his own—that contributed to the lapdog/wimpish image), neither was his ambition to be president. The debate provided an opportunity to nurture his aspiration by creating a favorable public impression, one that could dispel the negative image of an earlier meeting when Reagan had been his opponent.

The previous confrontation on February 23, 1980, may have determined the results of the New Hampshire Republican primary. Ronald Reagan and George Bush were to face each other in a two-person debate before approximately 2,700 people in a high school auditorium in Nashua. The debate was originally sponsored and planned by the *Nashua Telegraph* and was to be broadcast throughout the state three days before the primary. The *Telegraph* had excluded the other Republican primary candidates because Reagan had initially issued the challenge only to Bush. Reagan and Bush were the front-runners, and all of the contenders had participated in a televised debate three days earlier.

When the program began all six of the candidates were present. The *Telegraph* publisher announced that, nevertheless, the debate would be between only Bush and Reagan with the other candidates permitted to make statements at the end. Reagan tried to interrupt several times and the moderator asked that Reagan's microphone be turned off. When this happened Reagan shouted, "I am paying for this microphone . . . I volunteered to have our campaign pay for this debate. I felt that as a technical sponsor of the debate I had some right. I felt we should make it a debate of all of the candidates."[24] The audience seated in the auditorium cheered and Senator Robert Dole (one of the excluded candidates) requested that the moderator allow them to make their individual statements at that time. This was refused and so the four of them left the stage—after they had shaken hands with Reagan and ignored Bush. Until this point, Bush, who was seated on the stage, appeared oblivious to the situation. Moreover, it appeared that he, like the *Telegraph*, was responsible for excluding his colleagues. He finally asked for permission to speak and when it was granted said he had been challenged by Reagan for a one-on-one debate, that there would be an opportunity next week in South Carolina for all to debate and that he had learned only that afternoon that Reagan wanted to change the rules. He did not, however, do what his staff had planned—say that he had accepted the invitation of the newspaper and would debate in whatever form deemed appropriate. While he was speaking the four excluded candidates were holding a press conference denouncing Bush and calling the debate a raw political act and the "sorriest episode seen in American politics in years."[25] Bush seemed weak, self-serving, indecisive, and wimpish at Nashua. Three days later Reagan won the New Hampshire Republican vote and although Bush remained a candidate through the next series of primaries, the competition for the 1980 Republican nomination was effectively over.[26]

Thus, the confrontation with Geraldine Ferraro, while fraught with the uncertainty of debating a woman, was, nonetheless, an opportunity for the vice president. He could recapture some of the momentum lost as a result of the first Reagan–Mondale debate. He could also dispel the poor impression of his political debating left by the Nashua incident. He, like Ferraro, faced a formidable challenge.

THE RHETORICAL STRATEGIES OF VICE PRESIDENT GEORGE BUSH

To understand more fully the rhetorical strategies used by the vice president in his debate with Congresswoman Ferraro, I have analyzed the event in terms of the tactics apparent in three separate but related stages: predebate; debate; and postdebate.

Predebate Strategies

From the beginning, the Bush campaign did everything it could to create the impression that the vice presidential debate was of very little real importance. The vice president said that the election would be determined by the top of the ticket and his deputy press secretary said there would have been no "clamor for a debate had it not been for the selection of a woman candidate."[27] Moreover, the vice president's staff portrayed him as cooly going about his official business—marching in a Columbus Day parade and conferring with Israeli Prime Minister Shimon Peres. In fact, so much effort was expended to treat the event nonchalantly that downplaying the importance of the debate appeared to be simply another tactic—creating diminished expectations just in case the vice president did not fare well in the confrontation. The debate was too important, the stakes too high for either Bush or his staff to treat the event as casually as they gave the appearance of doing.

There were, in fact, at least five signs that the approaching debate had created unrest and concern in the high command of the Bush campaign. One such signal was the fact that the vice president appeared to be getting depressed with comparisons made by the media of the size crowds he and the congresswoman attracted at their daily campaign stops. In Springfield, Illinois, for example, after a rally at the Republican-controlled statehouse where he had been told to expect 10,000 and only 800 people turned out to greet him, he said he looked forward to returning to the relative "cocoon" of vice presidential obscurity.[28] Another indication of concern was a change in his rhetoric shortly before the debate. For the most part, Bush had rarely mentioned Ferraro or even acknowledged her existence in his campaign speeches. However, in Illinois, before a group of elderly people, he said he was tired of hearing "Mrs. Ferraro invoke her children as a reason she was opposed to the Reagan policy on arms control." He noted that he and his wife, Barbara, had five children and seven grandchildren, suggesting that "Mrs. Ferraro had no right to monopolize the argument as to who is more sensitive about the specter of war."[29]

A third sign of tension in the Bush entourage occurred three days before the debate when Barbara Bush, in complaining to a reporter that Mondale had been unfair in making an issue of her husband's income taxes, called Ferraro "that $4 million . . . I can't say it but it rhymes with rich."[30] In a remarkably similar outburst, another member of the Bush staff, this time the candidate's press secretary, in attempting to forecast what he believed would be the strategies and style of each candidate during the debate, suggested that Ferraro might appear "too bitchy."[31] Finally, although the vice president had consistently denied the importance of the event—even to the point of saying, "We're not talking about a real debate; we're talking about a kind of glorified Sunday news show"[32]—he spent part of the day before in "practice debates" with a Republican member of the House of Representatives, Lynn A. Martin. The Illinois congresswoman was selected as the vice president's sparring partner because of her physical (blond hair) and rhetorical (direct, tough-talking, frequently fiery) similarity to Ferraro. While Bush tried to maintain the appearance of unconcern, Martin was serious about her task—preparing Bush, the "Gentlemen's Gentleman," to respond to a female attacker. The congresswoman said that she had "thrown everything she had at him"[33] and Bush told reporters that Martin had won round one.

Thus the vice president and his staff, despite obviously contrived attempts to appear blasé, were concerned about the debate—concerned that a sense of momentum could be recaptured for the Republican campaign and concerned that a positive impression for future Bush electoral endeavors could be achieved. Adding to these pressures was the matter of finding workable strategies for debating a woman. He needed to find the acceptable "twilight zone" between being perceived as an unacceptably aggressive attacker or an unacceptably passive lap dog. Moreover, his advisers were worried that Ferraro's typically aggressive style, particularly her use of humorous one-liners, might unnerve him and thus reveal the kind of high-strung and nervous manner that had hurt him in other debates—most notably in Nashua.[34] The vice president himself said just before the encounter that he would use the debate to defend the president's record and to "attack Mr. Mondale, rather than Mrs. Ferraro, as much as I can. I don't want my mother mad at me."[35]

Debate Strategies

It is tempting, given the sexist comments of Bush associates before the debate as well as some of the vice president's language and manner during and following the encounter, to analyze his performance from solely a gender perspective. While that would be and has been a legitimate critical focus,[36] to attend only to the vice president's boorish use of sexist language and stories is to miss the larger point: his overwhelmingly successful merger of incumbency and challenger rhetorical styles. Bush's ability and skill in combining significant strategies of incumbency rhetoric with the equally important strategies of challenger rhetoric was a primary factor in the widespread perception that he, rather than Ferraro, won the debate.

Incumbency campaigning has been defined as "a blend of both symbolic and pragmatic communication strategies designed to make any candidate appear as both good enough for the office sought and possessing the office (an assumed incumbency stance)."[37] Among its specific strategies are two (one symbolic and one pragmatic) which the vice president employed in his debate with Congresswoman Ferraro.

The fact that George Bush relied on the use of incumbency strategies is, in one sense, hardly surprising. He was, after all, the sitting vice president—the incumbent—who was debating the challenger. On the other hand, the symbolic strategies of incumbency are typically and successfully employed only by presidential candidates, primarily because there is no other elective office (certainly not the vice presidency) for which Americans have the same kind of idealized vision or elaborated sense of beliefs. In the largest sense, the incumbency rhetorical style "plays on" or reinforces the feelings we possess about the presidency itself, not necessarily the current holder of the office; it takes advantage of the focus of impressions and ideas we have had since childhood of the one institution that stands for "truth, honor, justice, and integrity."[38]

Nowhere are those feelings more pronounced than in the symbolic strategies of incumbency—the tactics that attempt to transfer the power, legitimacy, competence and charisma of the office to the office seeker and thereby contribute a kind of presidential stature or presence.

In spite of a predebate public image as the president's head cheerleader, as opposed to the nation's chief executive, for much of the debate (particularly during the discussion of foreign policy issues), Bush was able to convey a presidential image. His use of symbolic strategies included calling his opponent "Mrs. Ferraro" rather than the previously agreed upon "Congresswoman Ferraro,"[39] although he was referred to by everyone as Vice President Bush. Moreover, much of his nonverbal behavior, including the utilization of large sweeping gestures, frequent signals to the audience warning them not to applaud his comments (extending his arm out as if to halt or stop someone), and a constant smile directed to his opponent as she was speaking were examples of controlling behavior designed to signify that he was in charge. In addition, his use of "we" as in "what we have done," or what "we believe" linked him to the president. Thus, the symbolic strategies of incumbency allowed George Bush to create a presidential aura—a sense of strength, competency, and legitimacy.

Even more obvious than the vice president's use of symbolic strategies was his employment of an important pragmatic one—emphasizing accomplishments—particularly in refutation to, or in defense of, attacks on the Reagan Administration.

One of the strategies important to the incumbency style is emphasizing accomplishments. Incumbents who wish to be reelected must be able to demonstrate tangible achievements as a result of their leadership. When accomplishments are not questioned, the strategy is uncomplicated and straightforward. Complexity occurs if there have been few accomplishments or if major problems overshadow or appear to overshadow positive contributions. When this happens, the strategy becomes more convoluted. Incumbents must either deny that the problem exists, suggest that it is of little importance, or blame someone else—scapegoat. At various times in the debate the vice president used each of the three tactics and even added another: he ignored examples that were given and substituted others. In one instance, in answer to a question from panelist Jack White regarding the perception of some Americans that the Administration was hostile to minorities (White cited the Administration's support of tuition tax credits, the anti-busing amendment, and opposition to the extension of the Voting Rights Act), Bush used all four tactics:

No, Mr. White, I think our record on civil rights is a good record. You mentioned the Voting Rights extension; it was extended for the longest period of time by

President Reagan. But we have some problems in attracting the black vote, and I think our record deserves better. We have done more for black colleges than any other previous administration.

We favor enterprise zones to give—and it's been blocked by Tip O'Neil and that House of Representatives, those liberals in that House blocked a new idea to bring jobs into the black communities across this country. And because it's not an old handout, special Federal spending program, it's blocked there—a good idea. And I'd like to see that tried.

We've brought more civil rights cases in the Justice Department than the previous Administration by far. We believe in trying something new to help these black teenage kids; the minimum wage differential that says, "look," to an employer, "hire these guys. And, yes, they're willing to work for slightly less than the minimum wage. Give 'em a training job in a private sector." We threw out that old CETA that didn't train people for jobs that existed, simply rammed them onto the government payroll, and we put in a thing called the Job Training Partnership Act. Wonderful, new legislation that's helping blacks more and more.[40]

In another example, this time in answer to a question regarding the differences between his ideas and President Reagan's (a subject that always irritated him),[41] he responded by at least partially ignoring the heart of the question, blaming the previous administration (Carter and Mondale), and turning the focus of it into a litany of Administration accomplishments:

Well, I don't think there's a great difference, Mr. Mashek, between my ideas and President Reagan's. One of the reasons I think we're an effective team is that I believe firmly in his leadership. He's really turned this country around. We agree on the economic programs.

When we came into office, why, inflation was 21, 12 1/2 percent interest rates wiping out every single American if you can believe it. Productivity was down. Savings was down. There was despair. In fact, the leadership of the country told the people that there was a malaise out there.

While the vice president's use of incumbency strategies could perhaps have been anticipated, it was the blend with at least two strategies traditionally associated with challenger rhetoric that gave his performance a measure of uniqueness and, I would argue, contributed to the perception that he won. In other words, Bush employed the best of both styles with little regard to his actual position (incumbent or challenger) in the campaign.

The challenger style has been defined "as a series of communication strategies designed to persuade voters that change is needed and that the challenger is the best person to bring about the change."[42] Although the style is hardly new, it has more commonly been employed by those challenging the current officeholder than by incumbents campaigning for reelection. Among its strategies are two that the vice president used to his advantage: attacking the record of opponents and emphasizing optimism for the future.[43] Examples of each are numerous.

Typically we think of the challenger as the attacker. However, almost from the beginning of the debate, Bush made it clear that he also intended to attack, although he concentrated on Mondale, not Ferraro. For example, in concluding his answer to the first question he said: ". . . And why Mr. Mondale can't understand that there's a new enthusiasm in this country, that America is back, there's new strong leadership, I don't know." In addition to leveling charges against the current Democratic presidential candidate, Bush went back four years to attack the Carter–Mondale Administration—blaming them for alleged current problems. For all intents and purposes, it was a replay of the 1980 campaign when Carter and Mondale were the incumbents and Reagan and Bush the challengers. For example, in response to a question regarding why President Reagan, unlike previous presidents, had failed to meet with the Soviet leaders, the Vice President said: ". . . you mentioned the Gromyko meeting, those were broken off under the Carter–Mondale days . . . " At another time, in defending the fact that there had been no further developments in arms control agreements during the Reagan–Bush Administration, Bush asserted that "the Carter–Mondale Administration made an agreement, but the Democratic Senate wouldn't even ratify that agreement. It was flawed, it was unverifiable and it was not good."

Although Bush spent a good deal of time attacking Mondale and other Democrats (who were generally unnamed—except for the generic "liberal Democrat"), his overall message was one of optimism. In fact, the so-called "negativism" of Mondale—his inability, according to the vice president, to understand "silver linings"—was a major theme throughout the debate. In answer to the first question he compared the economic "despair" of the Carter–Mondale years with the economic "recovery" of the Reagan–Bush Administration by saying their programs had "brought America back," and that "America's better off." His closing statement was a virtual litany of optimistic statements for the future. In short, optimism—a strategy more frequently used by challengers who "know" that any future is bound to be better than the status quo—was used effectively by Bush, the incumbent. Because he acknowledged no weaknesses in Reagan policies—the Carter–Mondale Administration was responsible for any and all problems—he could assume the challenger's rhetorical posture and spend much of the time incumbents would normally spend defending decisions and policies, on forecasting a future even more glorious than the present.

Thus, throughout the debate, the vice president, even while wearing the mantle of the incumbent (emphasizing accomplishments of the Reagan Administration), employed elements of the challenger's rhetorical style (attacking liberal Democrats and making clear his abiding and enthusiastic faith in the future). In so doing he convinced at least a majority of those polled immediately following the event that he had won.

The edge in public opinion polls, however, did not mean that Bush had no rhetorical problems. In fact, as one journalist wrote, "he started off the debate like an overwound cuckoo clock—popping off economic statistics and bad jokes ('Whine on, harvest moon') with equal abandon."[44] Democratic media consultant Robert Squier said, "Bush was okay after the drugs wore off."[45] In addition to a frenzied manner during the first part of the debate, Bush made factual errors, one of the most publicized being a denial that the Reagan Administration had cut funding for the poor. He said, "human resource spending is way, way up. Aid for Dependent Children spending is up." Even after Ferraro directly countered the assertion by pointing out that the programs he mentioned had been victims of the Administration's first budget cuts, Bush continued to argue that spending was up for food stamps and for families with dependent children, saying "I am not going to be found wrong on that. I am sure of my facts . . . " He was wrong, however, and as reporters pointed out, he had contradicted statistics from the Office of Management and Budget.

Without question, the most dramatic exchange (and therefore the one that received the most media attention) resulted from another of the vice president's rhetorical problems—his apparent inability to be anything other than condescending or patronizing to his female opponent.

The incident was provoked by questions regarding terrorism and the Administration's reaction to it, particularly in Iran and Lebanon. Bush apparently sought to contrast the problems in dealing with anonymous terrorism as practiced in Lebanon with government-supported terrorism as practiced by Iran during the hostage crisis.[46] He said, "Let me help you with the difference, Mrs. Ferraro, between Iran and Lebanon." His offer of assistance was followed by an equally provocative and mistaken charge in which he accused Mondale and Ferraro of suggesting that United States military casualties in Lebanon had "died in shame."

The congresswoman's response, although controlled, was, nonetheless, the essence from which political theater is created. She said:

> Let me just say, first of all, that I almost resent, Vice President Bush, your patronizing attitude that you have to teach me about foreign policy. I've been a member of Congress for six years. I was there when the Embassy was held hostage in Iran, and I have been there and I've seen what has happened in the past several months of your administration.
>
> Secondly, please don't categorize my answers, either. Leave the interpretation of my answers to the American people who are watching this debate. And let

me say further that no one has ever said that those young men who were killed in the negligence of this Administration and others ever died in shame. No one who has a child 19 or 20 years old, a son, would ever say that at the loss of anybody else's child.

Bush had no response to either point for the remainder of the debate.

There were, I would argue, other instances during the debate when Bush appeared condescending or patronizing. For example, in an early rebuttal he hastened to assure that "I'm not blaming her," and shortly before the closing statements when given the opportunity to "ask the question you'd most like to ask of your opponent," he responded, "I have none I'd like to ask of her, but I'd like to use the time to talk about the World Series or something of that nature." Even ignoring the reference to the Series (whose purpose might have been to appeal to preconceived stereotypes—men have more experience with an affinity for team sports than do women—and thereby remind voters of his "maleness" and her lack of that quality), the remark was another illustration of his patronizing behavior. She had apparently said nothing to this point in the campaign that he considered important enough to warrant further question.

Without doubt, Bush had his share of rhetorical problems. The fact that he was perceived the winner is not to deny their seriousness but to understand the effectiveness of his overall communication posture: a blend of incumbency strategies (highlighting not only his own experience but his association with the president) with the strategies of the challenger (attacking and blaming the opposition for any current problems while projecting a positive vision for the future).

Postdebate Strategies

Although the vice president and his staff and family participated in those events that typically occur following presidential debates (the Bush family came out on the stage and shook hands with the Ferraro–Zaccaro family and the staff immediately announced to all media that Bush had won), one incident for a brief period overshadowed all others.

The morning after the debate Bush was euphoric. The event was over and he said he felt "very, very good" about his performance. During a speech to several hundred longshoremen at a meeting in the port section of Elizabeth, New Jersey, the vice president told them that every poll he had heard of showed him winning the debate. As he left the docks he whispered to one of the union officials, "We tried to kick a little ass last night."[47] Bush had thought that his microphone was off but when he realized that it had picked up his words, he ordered the crew from WNEW-TV in New York to "turn that thing off."[48] The remark was broadcast by the New York station later that day. And at a press conference later in Birmingham, Alabama, the vice president defended his words by saying that it was simply "an old Texas football expression," that he had not intended to be heard publicly, and that his comment was just a way of asserting victory. He declined to apologize to Ferraro and said that "she would understand this. She's a good competitor."[49]

The congresswoman said only that the Bush remark did not reflect proper campaigning. However, Ann F. Lewis, political director of the Democratic National Committee, viewed it within the context of a whole series of comments that Bush, his wife, and his press secretary had recently directed toward Ferraro. Lewis found it "extraordinary and revealing that George Bush and his campaign are incapable of discussing Geraldine Ferraro without being vulgar," and added that Bush's remark showed "a contempt for women that had been implicit in their policy and is now explicit in their rhetoric."[50]

THE RHETORICAL STRATEGIES OF CONGRESSWOMAN GERALDINE FERRARO

To understand more fully the rhetorical strategies used by the congresswoman in her debate with Vice President Bush, I have analyzed the event in terms of the tactics apparent in three stages: predebate; the debate; and postdebate.

Predebate Strategies

It was estimated that 80 million people[51] would watch the vice presidential debate on television, largely because, according to political scientist Nelson Polsby, "Modern debates are the political version of the Indianapolis Speedway. . . . What we're all there for—the journalist, the political pundits, the public—is to see somebody crack up in flames."[52] Thus, with good reason, Geraldine Ferraro later admitted that she "felt a lot of pressure."[53]

For Geraldine Ferraro, typical or traditional trepidations were compounded by the additional variable of gender. Just as her opponent had to find ways in which he could acknowledge, yet not be deterred by debating a woman, so too did she have to explore ways to deal with issues that surfaced only because she was female, and yet not be deterred by them. The debate was, in one sense, a microcosm of the Ferraro campaign: a determined effort to do and say all of those things expected of a vice presidential candidate even while attempting to chart unknown territory.

From the time Walter Mondale announced his choice for a running-mate, issues that had never been considered in the context of a presidential campaign suddenly became relevant. For example, dress size (*Newsweek* began a story on Ferraro's nomination by noting that she wore size 6),[54] an appropriate title to use for the Democratic vice presidential candidate, campaign etiquette for runningmates of the opposite sex (Mondale and Ferraro could not touch or even join hands in the traditional raised-armed salute for fear of suggesting any sexual interaction between them), and flowers given as gifts at appearances were all factors affecting the Ferraro campaign. While it may be possible to view each of these examples as an unimportant form of symbolic communication, cumulatively they help build the idea of gender as an important variable in the debate and in the campaign. In other words, the fact of her "femaleness" influenced how Ferraro was treated, and therefore it influenced the way in which she and her staff had to respond.

Much of Ferraro's predebate strategy was centered around refutation of one of the most damning yet widely believed assertions facing women who seek political office—they are not fit for significant leadership positions because they are not as competent as men. The most important attacks on the congresswoman's competence were that she lacked experience in dealing with matters of national security (particularly in comparison with the extensive experience of her opponent) and the presumed correlation of psychological instability and menstrual cycle. While the first was an argument, the second was a fear appeal.

Thus, the challenges facing Ferraro before the confrontation even began were unique. A major and difficult task for every candidate who debates incumbents is to demonstrate competency and appear to be as knowledgeable and as plausible for the office as the person they hope to replace. For Ferraro, however, the task was even more formidable in that she not only had to persuade the American public of her own abilities and competencies but, by example, the competencies of all women. As Ferraro acknowledged to columnist Ellen Goodman the week before the debate, "it's not just for me. It's for everyone of us to show that we're as good as . . ." Goodman finished the sentence for her, "As good as men."[55]

Unlike George Bush, Ferraro and her staff made no attempt to play down the importance of the debate. In fact, they treated it as a major event for the campaign and for the congresswoman. As Ferraro wrote: "The debate would be a pivotal point in my career and in the campaign. . . . I was secure on the domestic issues, but . . . to counter him, I had to become as knowledgeable about the details of foreign policy as he was."[56]

Long before the debate a separate staff had been assembled to prepare Ferraro for the confrontation. It was headed by Washington attorney, Robert Barnett, who had helped Mondale get ready for his vice presidential debate in 1976 and included experts on domestic policy issues, foreign policy specialists, political consultants and her public speaking coach, Dayle Hardy. Their first task was the compilation of a briefing book. This eight-pound volume that included an analysis of all of Bush's public statements, Ferraro's voting record and major speeches, and the campaign's position on foreign and domestic issues, was given to Ferraro two weeks before the debate. She studied it in all her spare moments, especially while traveling.[57]

The more intense effort to prepare Ferraro began six days before the debate when a hotel suite in New York became, according to the Congresswoman, a "battle zone" where experts would "grill" her on the issues and critique her responses.[58] Two days before, the operation was moved to a rented television studio where a replica of the Philadelphia set had been constructed (including a gently inclining ramp leading to the podium so that she would not look so much shorter than the vice president). With Barnett playing Bush and others on the staff assuming the roles of moderator and questioners, Ferraro was put through four ninety-minute mock debates, each divided into domestic and foreign policy issues. The debates were taped, played back, and critiqued in regard to the substance and style of her responses. The point of the preparation, according to Ferraro, was "to allow the American public to see the other side of me . . . the part of me that was a lawyer, a concerned and caring citizen, an experienced elected official, and now a vice presidential candidate."[59] The other reason for their intense efforts, however, was to make certain that the congresswoman become better informed on foreign policy issues—in part because of the vice president's experience and credentials, but also in response to the stereotype that women are not competent in this area. Later commenting on the stereotype in regard to her preparation for the debate, Ferraro wrote:

> Women were simply not supposed to know as much about foreign policy or be as strong on defense as were men. . . .
>
> Nowhere was the double standard more apparent than over this issue. On the one hand, the perception was that men could speak with more authority than women on foreign affairs. Yet these same men also felt entitled to speak out just as forcefully on abortion. Though they may have been involved in military combat, they had never been pregnant. But their views on abortion were respected and taken seriously, whereas women's attitudes toward national security were not.[60]

Thus, the predebate strategy of the Ferraro campaign not only included study and practice designed to prove that she was competent, but it admitted that the confrontation was important. The stakes were high and the debate was risky for everyone: the Democratic ticket, Ferraro, and for the future of women running for the highest national offices. And neither the staff nor the congresswoman tried to deny it.

As Representative Patricia Shroeder remarked, "if Bush blows it, nobody will say, 'Well, it's all over for men.' "[61]

Debate Strategies

On the 100th anniversary of the birth of Eleanor Roosevelt and as two women astronauts orbited the earth in space, Congresswoman Geraldine Ferraro walked out on the stage and over to the podium prepared for her at the Civic Center in Philadelphia and listened as Dorothy S. Riddings, president of the League of Women Voters, introduced the moderator and panelists for the vice presidential debate. Within minutes, John Mashek, a national correspondent for *U.S. News and World Report*, was asking a question dealing directly with one of the congresswoman's major strategies of the debate: "Congresswoman Ferraro, your opponent has served in the House Representatives, he's been Ambassador to China, Director of the Central Intelligence Agency and now he's been Vice President for four years. How does your three terms in the House of Representatives stack up against experience like that?" She responded by saying:

> Well, let me first say that I wasn't born at the age of 43 when I entered Congress. I did have a life before that as well. I was a prosecutor for almost five years in the District Attorney's office in Queens County and I was a teacher. There's not only what is on your paper resumé that makes you qualified to run for or to hold office, its how you approach problems and what your values are. I think if one is taking a look at my career they'll see that I level with the people; that I approach problems analytically; that I am able to assess the various facts with reference to a problem, and I can make the hard decisions.

Thus, the first question Ferraro was asked provided the opportunity to show that she possessed the experience and qualifications necessary to be a candidate for national office. The strategy, to show the American public that she could "go toe-to-toe with the Vice President of the United States," was necessary because she was the first woman to run on a national ticket and because she had to contend with the experience and credentials of George Bush. There were other instances during the ninety minutes when she returned to this strategy, particularly in the discussion of foreign affairs. For example, when asked how she and Walter Mondale might prevent terrorist attacks such as the bombings in Lebanon, she used the question to expand on her expertise and familiarity with problems by inserting into her answer, "Well, I was at the White House in January, I guess it was, in '81, when those hostages, all 52 of them came home alive . . . " And then later she said, "In April of 1983 I was in Beirut and visited the ambassador at the embassy. Two weeks later the embassy was bombed." And in the debate's most publicized exchange, when she chastised Bush, Ferraro said, "I've been a member of Congress for six years; I was there when the Embassy was held hostage in Iran, and I have been there and I've seen what has happened in the past several months . . . "

Foreign policy issues, of course, were a double-edged sword for Ferraro. Not only a traditional "hook" for gender-based stereotypes, it was, in fact, an area in which she could not match her opponent's experience. She did all that could reasonably be done with the credentials she had. However, resumé building is only one method of creating a credible image. The perception of her competence might well have been enhanced had her delivery been more dynamic and direct and her language more powerful.

Until her closing statement, Ferraro more closely resembled an attorney considering the next line of questioning than an involved, engaged candidate participating in a critical debate. In an effort to appear "presidential," or what her staff called "a stateswoman," Ferraro lowered her voice, spoke softly, slowed down her speaking rate, and looked down at the notes she had taken while Bush was speaking. Only rarely did she look either at Bush or into the camera. A Bush speechwriter said she "looked as if she was on Sominex."[62] Bush said that her demeanor left him "amazed,"[63] and Ellen Goodman called her "subdued, lawyer-like, and cool—too cool for my taste," adding that "only someone who has never seen Ferraro on the campaign trail would think she put in her best performance . . . "[64]

In short, with the exception of her closing statement and the admonishment to Bush that his lessons in foreign policy were unnecessary, Ferraro lost the credibility she might have received had she come across as a strong, dynamic, and forceful speaker. As she later admitted, "no doubt about it, Bush won on style."[65]

In addition to manner of presentation, the congresswoman lost another opportunity to impress the public with her strength and competency. She frequently used hedges such as "let me say" or "I think" and disclaimers such as "let me put it this way" or "from another perspective"—two elements that contribute to powerless speech.[66] As a matter of fact, she not only said, "let me say" twenty times and "I think" twenty-seven times during the debate, she used "let me say" to begin what should have been some of her most powerful statements. For example, in the initial response to the question of how her qualifications could measure up to those of the vice president, she began, "Well, let me say first . . . " And she started the statement rebuking Bush by saying, "Let me just say, first of all . . . " Thus, even as she sought to enhance her image as a competent, experienced, and forceful leader, she used language that created the perception of a tentative and nonauthoritative speaker.

Ferraro's second major strategy was consistent with her position in the campaign as a challenger. She had to use the debate to do what, at minimum, all challengers must do: show that a change is needed because the incumbent's programs and policies have created major problems while simultaneously demonstrating that they, the challengers, are capable of righting those wrongs.

From the beginning of the debate through her closing statement, the congresswoman launched attacks on the policies of the Reagan–Bush Administration and their negative effect on the American people. She talked about the problems of budget and trade deficits, environment, funding for education, social welfare programs, international terrorism and arms control. Attacks such as these, however, lost much of their effectiveness because George Bush did not limit himself to the rhetorical style of the incumbent. When Ferraro cited a problem, Bush responded that the problem had been created by Democrats, either the liberals in the House of Representatives or, more frequently, the Carter–Mondale Administration. So not only did the congresswoman's attack fall short of its mark, she was also unable to establish the idea that Mondale and Ferraro would be able to bring about the changes that were needed because of the Bush charge that Carter and Mondale had created the problem in the first place.

There were two challengers in the debate. Ferraro attacked the current administration; Bush often avoided her challenges by attacking the prior Democratic administration. Perhaps Ferraro's problem could have been blunted had she been specific in her attacks—more carefully documenting her charges so that it would have been difficult for Bush to attribute them to Carter and Mondale. When, for example, she talked about the way in which the Reagan Administration had cut funds for aid for dependent children and for food stamps, had she told specifically how many people lost their funding and how much money had been cut, the vice president might have been forced into a defensive position. With Bush as the incumbent and challenger, the rhetorical responsibilities of the actual challenger were more difficult and may help to explain why Ferraro was not perceived the winner.

POSTDEBATE STRATEGIES

With the congresswoman's closing statement, the debate was over. The candidates shook hands, their families came on stage to join them, Ferraro's staff met with the press to point out the factual errors made by the vice president, and the congresswoman went to a postdebate rally believing she had defeated George Bush.

Not everyone agreed. In fact, the results of early polls, as well as the opinions of political analysts and debate judges, suggested that most viewers thought Bush had done the better job. The *New York Times*/CBS poll, for example, reported 47 percent for Bush/31 percent for Ferraro, the remainder undecided. The ABC poll, which had been taken an hour after the debate, reported 42 percent for Bush, 33 percent for Ferraro and 25 percent who said the debate was a tie. Similarly, after interviewing voters before and after the debate, Walter Mondale's pollster, Peter Hart, said it was 43 percent for Bush and 36 percent for Ferraro, with the remainder undecided. In addition to the polls, four out of seven members of a panel of debate judges assembled by the Associated Press thought Bush had clearly won, two saw it as a tie, and one believed Ferraro had "eked out a victory."[67]

Out of all of the data purporting to explain the results, three important points emerged. First, although the polls gave Bush the victory, Ferraro was generally perceived as having done very well. Hart said that although his overnight poll indicated that viewers thought Bush had done a better job, it also showed that "Ferraro did more to help Mondale than Bush did for Reagan because it added both luster and stature to Ferraro in the eyes of voters, and we needed that. The bottom line is that if you had asked two weeks ago if people could imagine Geraldine Ferraro as Vice President, you would have gotten a lot of questions. More people now see her as a person they can imagine in the office of the Vice Presidency."[68]

Second, the results of the debate revealed a substantial gender gap. In the ABC poll, Bush was the choice of 46 percent of the male viewers to 29 percent for Ferraro, with the remainder undecided. But women gave a slight edge to Ferraro, 38 to 37 percent, with the remainder undecided. In the Gannett poll, 59 percent of the men saw Bush as the winner with 18 percent to Ferraro and the remainder undecided. Among women, however, it was virtually even, 39 percent for Bush, 38 percent for Ferraro, and the remainder calling it a tie.[69]

Finally, and perhaps most important, poll results from the Bush–Ferraro debate confirmed once again that predebate candidate preference is the most important variable in the overall evaluation of debate performance.[70] As Peter Hart said, "I agree that Bush won, but over 70 percent of each side supported their own candidate."[71]

EFFECTS OF THE DEBATE

The 1984 vice presidential debate had few distinctive qualities. No ideas for new programs were discussed, no solutions to old problems were developed and no gaffes significant enough to change the course of the election occurred. Nonetheless, it was important.

One debater had the symbolic advantage of incumbency but the rhetorical obligation of defense. He met the challenge by wrapping himself in the protective blanket of the presidency while simultaneously adopting the posture of a challenger. In so doing, he offered a redefinition, or at least an expansion, of the incumbency rhetorical style. The other debater, the challenger, was unquestionably less unique in the selection and employment of rhetorical strategies but broke all precedence just by her participation. She faced the task of proving, by example, that a woman "could do it." Thus, the Bush–Ferraro debate, while not changing the outcome of the campaign, had some measure of uniqueness.

NOTES

1. Ellen Goodman, "Bush v. Ferraro," *The Washington Post*, October 12, 1984, p. A22.

2. Julia Malone, "Vice Presidential Debate a Political 'Spacewalk,' " *Christian Science Monitor*, October 10, 1984, pp. 1–6.

3. See for example, Phil Gailey, "Bush–Ferraro Debate Today Seen as Altering Campaign Dynamics," *New York Times*, October 11, 1984, pp. 1–11; Rick Atkinson, "Ferraro Practices Hard for Face-Off with Bush," *The Washington Post*, October 10, 1984, pp. A4–5; and Tom Morganthau, "The Veepstakes," *Newsweek*, October 15, 1984, pp. 41–42.

4. Walter Shapiro, "Shoot-Out at Gender Gap," *Newsweek*, October 22, 1984, pp. 29–30; Ellen Goodman, "She Achieved Another First," *The Washington Post*, October 13, 1984, p. A17.

5. Kurt Andersen, "Spotlight on the Seconds," *Time*, October 15, 1984, pp. 25–26.

6. Geraldine A. Ferraro, *Ferraro: My Story* (New York: Bantam Books, 1985), p. 242.

7. Ibid., p. 240.

8. Ibid., p. 243.

9. Tom Morganthau, "Beating His Own Drums?," *Newsweek*, August 20, 1984, p. 36.

10. Ibid.

11. Ibid.

12. Ferraro, *Ferraro: My Story*, pp. 240–241.

13. Jane O'Reilly, "Our Candidate/Ourselves," *Time*, October 29, 1984, p. 33.

14. Judith S. Trent and Robert V. Friedenberg, *Political Campaign Communication* (New York: Praeger Publishers, 1983), p. 115.

15. Ruth B. Mandel cited in Trent and Friedenberg, *Political Campaign Communication*, p. 117.

16. Goodman, "She Achieved," p. A17.

17. Ferraro, *Ferraro: My Story*, p. 240.

18. James R. Dickenson, "Debate Generates Gender Gap," *The Washington Post*, October 13, 1984, p. A7.

19. Morganthau, "The Veepstakes," p. 41.

20. Andersen, "Spotlight on the Seconds," p. 25.

21. Ibid.

22. Ibid., p. 26.

23. See, for example, David S. Broder, "GOP's Hopes Tempered, But Reagan Holds Lead," *The Washington Post*, October 14, 1984, pp. A1–12; Tom Morganthau, "Reagan and the Age Issue," *Newsweek*, October 22, 1984, pp. 26–29; and Charlotte Salkowski, "Presidential Camps Assess Round 1, Plan for Round 2," *Christian Science Monitor*, October 10, 1984, pp. 3–4.

24. For a thorough accounting of the episode, see Myles Martel, *Political Campaign Debates* (New York: Longman, 1983), pp. 165–168.

25. Ibid., p. 168.

26. For eight days prior to the Nashua debate, I was traveling on the Reagan and the Bush press buses in New Hampshire. At that time the media, at least informally, regarded Bush as the leader and I left New Hampshire two days before the debate believing Bush would win the primary. Within hours after the Nashua episode, however, Reagan became the "favorite" and went on to win the primary.

27. Malone, "Vice Presidential Debate a Political 'Spacewalk,' " p. 6.

28. Gailey, "Bush–Ferraro Debate Today," p. B11.

29. Ibid.

30. Juan Williams and Dale Russakoff, "Bush Sticks to Duties as Debate Approaches," *The Washington Post*, October 10, 1984, p. A4.

31. William R. Doerner, "Co-Stars on Center Stage," *Time*, October 22, 1984, p. 31. Both Barbara Bush and Peter Teeley insisted they had meant no "harm"—no "sexual slur." Mrs. Bush said the unspoken word was "witch" and Teeley said he had used the term as a synonym for "crabby."

32. Morganthau, "The Veepstakes," p. 42.

33. Williams and Russakoff, "Bush Sticks to Duties," p. A4.

34. Ibid., p. A5.

35. Gailey, "Bush–Ferraro Debate Today," p. B11.

36. The Ferraro candidacy and this debate produced, at least initially, what Professor Dan Nimmo of the University of Oklahoma once referred to as a "virtual growth industry" in convention papers. While specific points of analysis varied, the general thrust or orientation of these papers was perceived gender differences.

37. Trent and Friedenberg, *Political Campaign Communication*, p. 84.

38. Ibid., p. 85.

39. While I have never found a published explanation for Bush's failure to use Ferraro's title, in introducing the debate Sander Vanocur, the moderator, announced that the candidates had decided the form of address would be "Vice President Bush" and "Congresswoman Ferraro." A day after the debate when Congresswoman Barbara Kennelly was asked whether she believed Bush was disrespectful in addressing Ferraro as "Mrs." rather than "Congresswoman," Kennelly commented, "It's better than what they've been calling her." See Milton Coleman and Rick Atkinson, "Democrats Stump in Wisconsin," *The Washington Post*, October 13, 1984, p. A5.

40. This quotation and all subsequent quotations from the debate are taken from "Transcript of Philadelphia Debate between Bush and Ferraro," *New York Times*, October 12, 1984, pp. B4–6.
41. Anderson, "Spotlight on the Seconds," p. 26.
42. Trent and Friedenberg, *Political Campaign Communication*, p. 105.
43. Ibid., p. 106.
44. Richard Cohen, ". . . But He Won It in the Briar Patch," *The Washington Post*, October 13, 1984, p. A17.
45. Shapiro, "Shoot-Out at Gender Gap," p. 30.
46. Doerner, "Co-Stars on Center Stage," p. 31.
47. Dale Russakoff, "Bush Boasts of Kicking 'A Little Ass' at Debate," *The Washington Post*, October 13, 1984, p. A8.
48. Ibid.
49. Ibid.
50. David E. Rosenbaum, "Rivals' Camps Doubt a Big Shift after 2nd Debate," *New York Times*, October 13, 1984, p. A8.
51. The estimate turned out to be high. Actually fifty million people saw this debate on television.
52. George J. Church, "Debating the Debates," *Time*, October 29, 1984, p. 31.
53. Ferraro, *Ferraro: My Story*, p. 248.
54. There were a few readers so angry at *Newsweek's* mention of Ferraro's dress size that they demanded that suit sizes for Reagan and Bush be published.
55. Ferraro, *Ferraro: My Story*, p. 24.
56. Ibid., pp. 243–244.
57. Ibid., p. 245.
58. Ibid., p. 246.
59. Ibid., pp. 241–242.
60. Ibid., pp. 254–255.
61. Malone, "Vice Presidential Debate a Political 'Spacewalk' " p. 6.
62. Shapiro, "Shoot-Out at Gender Gap," p. 30.
63. Ibid.
64. Goodman, "She Achieved Another First," p. A17.
65. Ferraro, *Ferraro: My Story*, p. 265.
66. See Robin Lakeoff, *Language and Woman's Place* (New York: Harper & Row, 1975), pp. 1–85; Patricia Hayes Bradley, "The Folk Linguistics of Women's Speech: An Empirical Examination," *Communication Monographs* 48 (1981): 73–90; James J. Bradac, Michael R. Hemphill, and Charles H. Tardy, "Language Style on Trial: Effects of 'Powerful' and 'Powerless' Speech upon Judgments of Victims and Villians," *Western Journal of Speech Communication* 45 (1981): 327–341; and James J. Bradac and Anthony Mulac, "A Molecular View of Powerful and Powerless Speech Styles: Attributional Consequences of Specific Language Features and Communication Intentions," *Communication Monographs* 51 (1984): 307–319.
67. Doerner, "Co-Stars on Center Stage," p. 30.
68. Hedrick Smith, "Rivals Doubt a Big Shift After 2d Debate," *New York Times*, October 13, 1984, pp. A1–8.
69. James R. Dickenson, "Debate Generates Gender Gap," *The Washington Post*, October 13, 1984, pp. A1–7.

70. For recent examples confirming the importance of this variable, see Victor Wall, James L. Golden, and Herbert James, "Perceptions of the 1984 Presidential Debates and a Select 1988 Presidential Primary Debate," *Presidential Studies Quarterly* 18 (Summer 1988): 541–563; J. Gregory Payne, James L. Golden, John Marlier, and Scott C. Ratzan, "Perceptions of the 1988 Presidential and Vice Presidential Debates," *American Behavioral Scientist* 32 (1989): 425–435.

71. Dickenson, "Debate Generates Gender Gap," p. 1. Similarly, in a study examining commentary on the Bush–Ferraro debate, researchers found that verbal references to the quantity and quality of emotion differed according to partisanship. For example, left-leaning observers described Ferraro as "in control of herself," "cool," and "calm," while right-leaning observers described her as "inappropriately emotional," "annoyed," and "bitchy." See Stephanie A. Shields and Kathleen A. McDowell, "Appropriate Emotion in Politics: Judgments of a Televised Debate," *Journal of Communication* 37 (1987): 78–89.

SELECT BIBLIOGRAPHY

Ferraro, Geraldine A. *Ferraro: My Story*. New York: Bantam Books, 1985. The chapter on the debate is not only an excellent chronology of Ferraro's preparation for the confrontation with Bush, but it is also helpful in understanding her feelings and thoughts about it.

Jamieson, Kathleen Hall, and David S. Birdsell. *Presidential Debates: The Challenge Of Creating an Informed Electorate*. Helpful glimpses of Ferraro's debate strategy compared to the debate strategies of other national candidates.

Martel, Myles. *Political Campaign Debates: Images, Strategies, and Tactics*. New York: Longmans, 1983. Particularly useful background on Bush's prior campaigning and his 1980 Nashua debate.

Payne, Gregory J., James L. Golden, John Marlier, and Scott C. Ratzan. "Perceptions of the 1988 Presidential and Vice Presidential Debates." *American Behavior Scientist* 32 (1989): 425–435. The results of this study are important as the value of all presidential and vice presidential debates are considered. The authors conclude that debates confirm preexisting attitudes.

Trent, Judith S., and Robert V. Friedenberg. *Political Campaign Communication*. New York: Praeger Publishers, 1983. The chapter on incumbency and challenger rhetorical strategies was the basis for analysis of the combined rhetorical style used by George Bush.

Debate Transcript

"Transcript of Philadelphia Debate between Bush and Ferraro," *New York Times*, October 12, 1984, pp. B4–6.

Chapter 7

The 1988 Bush–Dukakis Presidential Debates

Halford Ross Ryan

Presidential candidates have historically done what their political milieu demanded for election to the White House. From Franklin Roosevelt's mastery of the radio to the televised presidential campaign debates of 1988, one factor remains constant: the media helps the American people elect their presidents. The usual forensic hypothesis is that the candidates shape the issue, mold public opinion, and ultimately persuade the people. This construct unduly emphasizes the candidates' debating and not their argumentative transactions with the audience. The successful debater may be more realistically conceived rhetorically as one who shares, more than shapes, the common concerns of the time; who reads, more than restructures, public sentiment; who reinforces, more than readjusts, the audience's values and beliefs; and who ignores, rather than enervates, pressing political exigencies.

This revision of how the presidential debates of 1988 functioned depends on how one defines *persuasion*. Let us define persuasion as the ability to change an audience's attitudes or actions with delivered language. Thus delineated, Vice President George Bush did not persuade in the debates as much as he reinforced. Is it persuasion in any meaning of the word to claim that Bush convinced Americans not to pay additional taxes or not to be soft on crime or not to short shrift the military?

Bush won the 1988 election because his rhetoric was more reflexive than Governor Michael Dukakis's. This kind of reflexive rhetoric operated in Franklin Roosevelt's presidential campaigns wherein he ran in 1932 against Republicanism and Herbert Hoover, and his stand-ins, Alfred Landon in 1936 and Wendell Willkie in 1940. Adeptly turning the tables on the Democrats four decades later, Ronald Reagan used the same strategy by running against liberalism and Jimmy Carter in 1980, and against that combination whose stand-in was Walter Mondale in 1984. Bush recapitulated his mentor's theme four years later. Since the electorate liked what they saw of themselves in Bush's political portraiture, they voted for the image that best mirrored themselves: George Bush's.

Before addressing the presidential campaign debates of 1988, certain caveats are in order. First, political bias is inherent in deciding debates, so it is fitting to divulge my prejudices.[1]

Second, campaign debates are extraneous to forms of public address that are utilized in the rhetorical presidency. Unlike other indicators, such as campaign speeches and press conferences, the debates add little to the audience's understanding of how the president will be the *vox populi*.

The 1988 debates functioned as a political game show, but they hardly precursed the kind of programmatic rhetoric that the president would deliver in the White House. Assuming the pressure to debate will not abate, Bush will not have to face a formal opponent until the next election. So, from the perspective of the rhetorical presidency, there is no compelling reason for candidates to engage in speaking activities that bear little relationship to actual presidential practices. Rather, equal time should be allowed the candidates to deliver programmatic speeches to the electorate on topics of their choice. It is not unreasonable to give people an opportunity to assess the kind of rhetoric a candidate will employ in the White House.[2]

Third, one utters the usual academic lament that the so-called debates are not really debates. Except for a moderator, there is no reason to have the broadcast media as an intervening variable to ask the questions, shape the issues, and judge by innuendo the candidates' responses. As presently conceived, the debates are at best a kind of a joint press conference, which are not representative of presidential press conferences, and at their worst, according to Sydney Pollock, "not a fair test of which one of them will make a good President."[3] Yet, the media has institutionalized itself in the fray on the assumption that anchors and columnists should make the news they are supposed to report. "The media," the *Nation* editorialized, "deplores the lack of substance but of course encourages it."[4]

The press-conference nature of the debates should be instituted into individual press conferences that would be broadcast nationally. Since any president will engage in significantly more press conferences than debates, the American people could better assess the candidates under fire from the media. Although Jeff Greenfield believed that the debates afforded "the most significant glimpses we have had into the thinking and character of the candidates since the general election began on Labor

Day," I believe these traits can be better observed in press conferences and not under the guise of debates.[5]

Nevertheless, given the likely continuation of debates, the candidates should use the parameters of the Lincoln–Douglas senatorial debates of 1858. The current formats of two-minute responses and one-minute rebuttals cannot present and solve pressing issues. Removed from the restraints that are concocted between the candidates, and concurred with by an all-too-willing media that benefits from making the news as well as reporting it, current candidates, more like Lincoln and Douglas, would be forced to defend their positions and to attack their opponent's proposals. The possibility exists that candidates could covertly agree to handle one another with kid gloves. "But," as the *New York Times* opined, "it's likely that the candidates would provoke even more spontaneity by asking each other questions, with only a skilled moderator and with more time for individual responses."[6]

Nor were the 1988 debates particularly useful in inducing the kind of oratorical encounters the American people evidently desire. For example, there was the silly pretense that the live audience should play dead. Evidently reasoning that the debates were staged enough, the candidates and the media apparently agreed not to compound the problem by airing the debates on an empty sound stage. The planners decided the debates must be ritualistically performed before real people, who figuratively represented voting citizens, but who, unlike their national counterparts, were not supposed to commend the laudable and hiss the lamentable. Thus, when these symbolic Americans reacted to their candidate's occasional parries as real people would, and this was especially so in the second debate, these listeners were solemnly admonished by the moderators and even by the candidates to be quiet. At issue is whether any live audience, which is given tickets by the opposing camps, can be free of partisan shills. It would be honest to remove the ancillary audience on the grounds that it is an impediment to the television audience.

THE DECISION TO DEBATE

The actual debates were preceded by opening gambits. The candidates careened toward debating as the *Titantic* inexorably bore down on the iceberg, the only difference being that the Ice Man, to apply Bush's sideswipe at Dukakis in the first debate, did not sink the Republican ship of state. Robert Friedenberg has determined six variables that predict whether there will be presidential campaign debates, and all six were present to some degree.[7] First, a close race was predicted with more pressure on Dukakis to win because of Bush's lead in the polls and in the Electoral College. But the decision to debate was more conditioned, as *Newsweek* observed, by expectations: "debates became important because the [media] industry believed they were."[8] Second, the candidates perceived advantages in debating, but it would have been to their disadvantage not to debate, which would have disappointed expectations. However, Bush spurned Dukakis's advances, made in the second debate, for an additional encounter because he had a commanding lead and was disinclined to risk losing it. Third, Dukakis reasoned he was a good debater—"he had done 40 in the campaign season alone"—and Bush had considerable forensic experience in his repertoire—the famous encounters with Reagan in New Hampshire in 1980 and with Geraldine Ferraro in 1984—so they were not lopsidedly matched.[9] Fourth, there were only two major candidates running for the office. Fifth, the candidates tried to control the debate situation, so much so that the League of Women Voters declined to sponsor the second debate because it was so co-opted by the candidates.[10] And sixth, the field was clear of incumbents, in the sense that Bush was not president.

Himself a veteran of more presidential campaigns than any American, Richard Nixon opened the dialogue about the 1988 debates. (Notice that Nixon managed to get himself elected in 1968 and 1972 without debating.) Firing the tracer shot that foreshadowed the target of Bush's fusillades in the debates, Nixon trained his party's sights on Dukakis's Achilles' heel: "If Dukakis's record is laid out next to Bush's, Bush stands an excellent chance of capturing the conservative Democrats who have played a decisive role in every election since 1968. If Bush fails to pin Dukakis down, he will lose the election. The owner of the 25-year-old snow blower from Brookline will have pulled off the biggest snow job since the Trojan horse."[11] While not confusing who was snowing whom, Henry Fairlie, uttering the kind of complaints that characterized the cam paign, transcended the contest and focused instead on the losers, the American people: "A vast community of professional and well-fattened advisers and consultants now create their puppets, and what holds the community together is an uninformed media, talking to the speechwriters and not the speech-giver, who direct our attention only to the strings they pull."[12] Although his charge has merit, it nevertheless misses the end of political rhetoric as it has been practiced and mediated in the era of mass communication. Reflexive rhetoric demanded that Roosevelt have his Louis Howe and Samuel Rosenman, that Dukakis have his John Sasso, and that Bush have his Roger Ailes. The Madison Avenue folks are merely an extension of what it takes to win.

Rhetorical Purposes: What is a "Win"?

Given that a verdict might not be clear or that some rhetorical disaster might occur, both candidates' media managers coyly developed fall-back positions from which they could claim victory in the debate.

One of Bush's primary goals was to improve his delivery. James Baker and Lee Atwater, members of Bush's campaign team, "performed major surgery on their candidate's speaking style," and Roger Ailes taught Bush "to speak more slowly and in a deeper voice."[13] Bush's delivery was reasonably effective, especially so in the second debate.

Riding on an impressive lead, some of Bush's goals were defined by negation: do not make a major gaffe and do not appear to lose. Indeed, William Safire opined that "Bush must now stop playing not to lose and start playing to win."[14] In an attempt to carry the debates, Bush maintained the attack that he wisely mounted early in the campaign and sustained throughout the canvass. This strategy demanded that Bush juxtapose his values with Dukakis's. Thus, Bush would spend as much time in defining what he was not, which was Dukakis, as in defining what he was.

Dukakis, although less known than the vice president, apparently had similar goals. Reeling from Bush's offense even before the debates began, Dukakis strove to downplay his image as a liberal and to make Bush defend his perceived weaknesses. The governor's handlers prepared him to achieve two goals. First, Dukakis had "to define himself, conveying an air of energetic, presidential command," an image on which Bush had a slight edge.[15] Second, he had "to unsettle Bush."[16] The governor clearly mastered the first goal—"Dukakis had established in the debate that he was a credible candidate, and he had the nation's attention"—but it is harder to determine whether Dukakis discomforted Bush.[17]

Both candidates prepared for the debates by having mock encounters. By all accounts, the vice president practiced assiduously. He mastered his briefing books, engaged in question-and-answer sessions, and debated Richard G. Darman, a former deputy treasury secretary, who played the governor's role. Dukakis did not want to do a mock debate. He finally agreed to one four days before Winston-Salem, and then rehearsed against Robert Barnett, a Washington lawyer who played the devil's advocate in preparing Geraldine Ferraro for her vice presidential debate in 1984. The result was a "rout" in favor of Barnett.[18]

Finally, the height of the lectern was an issue. It appears to have been a draw: Bush, 6 feet and 1 inch, used a 48-inch-high lectern and Dukakis, 5 feet and 8 inches, spoke behind a 41-inch-tall podium. The missing 2 inches were balanced out by Dukakis's standing on a small riser.

DEBATE 1: WINSTON-SALEM, NORTH CAROLINA, SEPTEMBER 25, 1988

As the affirmative in the debate, Dukakis assumed the *onus probandi*, the risk of advocating change. As a defender of the Reagan Administration, Bush enjoyed the negative's presumption that rested with the status quo. Theoretically, presumption is only descriptive; but Bush's presumption was considerable and favorable. The advantages of the Reagan–Bush status quo, as juxtaposed to Dukakis's policies and untested leadership, were so compelling that the governor had a significant burden of proof. Reduced to a chemical formula, Bush's verbal elements in the debates were P_2C_1: peace and prosperity, and conservatism. Tilting against a popular president who had given his blessing to his heir apparent, Dukakis went for D_2TC_1: drugs and deficit, and tough choices. That Dukakis was unable to make headway against America's apathy to these exigencies, some of which were underwritten by Reagan's deficit spending regimen, is accountable by two factors. (1) Dukakis did not specify the tough choices that he would make to reduce the deficit. (2) Bush successfully dosed the American people with patriotic pabulum. Never mind the outdated patriot who would recoil at the buy-now-pay-later practices of the last eight years that flew in the face of Republican campaign rhetoric from the time of FDR to 1980. Rather than address those ubiquitous choices, which seemed to hover like liberal harpies around Dukakis's head, Bush invited the American people to apply for a greater credit limit with no painful tax increase.[19]

Drug Dealing

If the primacy effect operated in the debates, it surely put Bush at an initial disadvantage with respect to the issue of drug use in the United States. Striving to answer what "drives, or draws, so many Americans to use drugs," Bush responded by stressing a deterioration of values.[20] He invoked one of the "God" terms in his political lexicon by calling for the return of "values in the schools." Sensing Bush's vulnerability on that issue, Dukakis skirted the question and targeted a weakness in the Reagan–Bush Administration. Piously averring that he agreed with Bush on values, Dukakis counter charged that "our leaders demonstrate those values from the top," and he told his audience that as president he would "never again do business with a drug-running Panamanian dictator." Continuing in that vein for his direct question, Dukakis attacked frontally. He bragged about his drug program that was hailed by the Federal Drug Enforcement Administration, and mentioned the irony inherent in squaring with "our kids all over this country" the fact that representatives of the Administration dealt with people "like Noriega."

Bush counterattacked. Asserting that the Reagan–Bush team "brought this man [Noriega] to justice," Bush allowed how there was "no hard evidence" against the general, but that when the evidence was known, the Administration had acted. However, what Bush meant by "justice" was not clear because Noriega remained entrenched in Panama, and Bush did not specify what action the Administration had taken.

Bush's defense was wanting. He, unlike Dukakis, cited no programs that would work to enact his cherished values, and Dukakis raised a doubt about Bush's handling of the Panamanian drug connection. The governor won this issue by focusing his attack on drugs and Noriega—to which the vice president lamely responded—and by pointing to his successful program in Massachusetts. Bush offered only the failure of the status quo.

The Deficit

Arguably more hazardous to the nation's health than drugs, or so Republicans have claimed for federal debt since the days of Herbert Hoover, Dukakis was handed a golden opportunity to discuss the national deficit by delineating "three specific programs that you are willing to cut to bring that deficit down." Dukakis's debater-like one-two-three responses belied his ability to confront the issue directly. Instead, he finessed one program and ignored the other two.

First, after assuring the audience that he had balanced ten budgets, but understandably neglecting to tell his listeners that Massachusetts's law required a balanced budget, he said "there are certain weapons systems which we don't need." What ones and how much he would save, the governor did not say. Second, rather than mentioning another program as requested, he asserted the government must invest in economic growth. Third, he allowed that interest rates must come down "as we come up with a good solid plan." When this might happen and what the plan would be, the governor did not say.

Bush rebutted aggressively. Unleashing his practiced one-liner, to the delight of his fans in the audience, he asserted Dukakis's answer was about as clear as Boston Harbor. Bush turned the tables on Dukakis by mentioning that a liberal senator from Massachusetts said it was dumb to oppose a reduction in capital gains taxation, and then blamed the Democratic Congress for the deficit and reverently repeated Ronald Reagan's Republican rhetoric: "I will not raise taxes," and "we can get it down without going and socking the American taxpayer once again." But on the critical issue of deficit reduction, Bush merely repeated the governor's shell game.

Dukakis, bereft of any specific programs to reduce the deficit, resorted to *argumentum ad hominem* in his rebuttal. Charging Bush with giving $30,000 to people making over $200,000, Dukakis decried: "Why that's more than the average teacher makes. We've had enough of that, ladies and gentlemen." In closing, Dukakis assured the audience he would make "tough choices."

The winner on this issue was Bush, but the real losers were the American people. Bush effectively appealed to Reagan's enviable track record of economic growth. The so-called Reagan Democrats and Republicans would be loath to sacrifice their gains. Bush effectively scored Dukakis with a one-liner, and he blithely asserted that voodoo economics would guide a new witch doctor for four more years. Dukakis was unable to answer the question asked. He appealed to class antagonisms, which was effective in FDR's day when there were so many forgotten men, but not so compelling to the majority of Americans who now fancy themselves as the economic royalists so loathed fifty years ago. Foreign and domestic bond holders won irrespective of what presidential candidate carried the issue.

Health Insurance

Having discussed the fiscal health of the nation, the candidates were invited to address the physical health of poor people. Bush was asked about the "37 million Americans . . . [who] cannot afford any health insurance but earn too much to qualify for Medicaid. What will you do to provide protection for them and how will you pay for it?" The question had two parts, neither of which either candidate would answer.

Bush's non-answer was deftly camouflaged with a metaphor that appealed to the middle class, who would pay the bills rather than to the poor, who would probably not vote for him anyway. Instead of indicating how he would solve the problem, Bush bemoaned: "One thing I would not do is sock every business in the country and thus throw some people out of work." Patricians and employed plebeians were thus reassured.

Evidently reasoning that by now the audience would forget that the poor are supposedly too impecunious to purchase health insurance, Bush sallied forth with an ingenious proposal. He would allow people "to buy into Medicaid," which is comparable to Marie Antoinette's purported remark that the French peasants could eat cake when faced with the rising cost of bread. To cover this faux pas, Bush congratulated himself for passing the first catastrophic health bill, which was laudable, but not responsive to the exigency. As Andrew Rosenthal observed, "It does nothing for the uninsured."[21]

Governor Dukakis retorted in his rebuttal: "Well, George, that's no answer," to which Bush interrupted, "You don't like the answer, but it's an answer," to which Dukakis had the final say—"Well, no, it's no answer to those 37 million people." The governor then narrated a story of an unemployed worker in Houston whose son could not play in the Little League because of fear of injury without insurance. Although Dukakis misstated some of the facts, Charles Strickland, the worker, stated, "Dukakis understood the important point. . . . My children can't play sports because I can't pay for them if they get hurt."[22] However, Dukakis's answer was about as murky as Bush's. Indignantly, Dukakis intoned: "And I think it's time that when you've got a job in this country, it came with health insurance. That's the way we're going to provide basic health security for all of the citizens of this country of ours."

If workers wanted to keep their jobs or entrepreneurs wanted to maintain their profits, which was Bush's basic pitch, then they should not be "socked" for the benefit of 37 million poor. If, on the other hand, one identified with or happened to be one of the 37 million uninsured, then the listener would favor Dukakis's plan. However neither candidate facilitated a reasoned examination of the issue. Neither described even a sketchy plan. Neither indicated how much such a program would cost. To his credit, the vice president did wisely observe that "somebody pays," but both candidates were at a strange loss for words that would enact their proposals.

The American Civil Liberties Union

The ACLU was dragged into the debate by George Bush for apparently no other reason than to reflect conservatives' dislike of that organization and to reinforce general ignorance about its aims and objectives. With overtones of McCarthy era rhetoric, which, when skillfully applied, could malign an opponent's patriotism and character, Bush intoned that Dukakis was "a card-carrying member of the ACLU," which was a shorthand sobriquet for a card-carrying Communist. Taking the bait of what may have been a set-up, a panelist handed Bush a follow-up question that inquired why "you keep repeating the phrase," which inadvertently invited Bush to invigorate his attack.

With an incredible apophysis, wherein an orator affirms a point by ostensibly denying it, Bush coyly observed, "Nothing's wrong with it." Bush affirmed his transparent denial by casting his elaboration in anaphora, or parallel structure, against the ACLU's stands that few Americans held: "I don't want my 10-year-old grandchild to go into an X-rated movie. . . . I don't think they're right to try to take the tax exemption away from the Catholic Church. I don't want to see the kiddie pornographic laws repealed. I don't want to see "under God" come out from our currency. Now, these are all positions of the ACLU, and I don't agree with them." Bush ended his verbal sortie against the governor's liberalism with another apophysis: "And I hope people don't think I'm questioning his patriotism."

Recognizing Bush's rhetorical trick for what it was, Dukakis displayed some emotion for a supposedly passionless technocrat. In the most dramatic exchange of the debate, the governor sharply scolded Bush by turning to address the rhetorical miscreant: "well, I hope this is the first and last time I have to say this. Of course the Vice President is questioning my patriotism. I don't think there is any question about it. And I resent it. I resent it." But the damage was done. Although Dukakis recited his parents' immigrant background and denigrated Bush's making the pledge of allegiance "the acid test of one's patriotism," Bush scored decisively by identifying the ACLU with Dukakis.

The Homeless and Housing

In his second inaugural address, Franklin Roosevelt stated a fundamental problem that inhered in US society fifty years later: "The test of our progress is not whether we add more to the abundance of those who have much; it is whether we provide enough for those who have too little."[23] Bush and Dukakis reflected their parties on this sad fact of the 1980s.

Bush offered his "1,000 points of light," which was his metaphor for community-based action and relief, and the assertion that the federal government should fully fund the McKinney Act as his answer to "What commitment are you willing to make tonight to this voiceless segment of our society [the homeless]?" Bush had no long-range solution and admitted that fully funding the McKinney Act was his "short range answer."

On the attack, Dukakis noted that Bush been a part of the administration that "cut back 90 percent of our commitment" to affordable housing. Consequently, he observed, "we didn't have two and a half million or three million homeless people living on streets and in doorways in this country 10 years ago." Arguing me too, me better, he closed his rebuttal by stating that he also favored the McKinney Act but that it would not suffice—only he could "lead on this issue. . . . And I'm prepared to do so."

On a related issue, Dukakis was asked what promise he would give people who could not afford housing. He vocally stressed "leadership" twice and "lead" once to suggest he would give direction on the issue. Yet, a taxpayer might wonder how much his leadership would cost? Dukakis averred that "we ought to be prepared to provide those funds" but failed to specify how those funds might be found. Obfuscating his weakness with an attack, Dukakis charged that Bush was willing to spend billions on Star Wars, but the audience was left to infer that Dukakis might use these funds to help the homeless and the housing crisis.

Bush clearly stated in his rebuttal that he intended to do very little, if anything, about the problem. Piously claiming that "the Governor is blurring housing and homeless. Let's talk about housing which the question was," Bush implied that he would answer the question. A close reading of the transcript suggests that Dukakis did not blur the homeless with housing, and he did address the question asked. In contrast, Bush did not even obliquely answer the question he professed to address. Leaving the homeless and the housing problem out in the cold, he launched into a self-congratulatory exercise about how when he and Reagan took office the interest rate was 21.5 percent, and then asked "how does that grab you for increasing housing?" Now the rate was half that. And then in one of the clearest passages of the debate, Bush virtually guaranteed he would not solve the problem: "But if we spend and spend and spend, that is going to wrap up the housing market and we'll go right back to the days of the misery index and malaise that President Reagan and I have overcome. Thank God for the United States on that one."

Abortion and Capital Punishment

The nadir of the debate was the discussion of capital punishment for drug traffickers, prison furlough programs, and Willie Horton, the Massachusetts felon who committed murder while on furlough, on all of which Bush won hands down.

Perhaps nowhere in the debate was it clearer that Bush better reflected the views of thinking Americans than on the issue of abortion. If one upholds the sanctity of life, then one must logically ban all abortions because they are murder. However, realizing that voters would not stomach such systematic logic, Bush excepted "rape, incest, or the life of the mother." He went for political expediency over moral consistency. However, he tripped over his logic, for he was unsure about "the penalty side, and of course, there's got to be some penalties to enforce the law, whatever they may be."

Dukakis replied: "I don't think it's enough to come before the American people who are watching us tonight and say, 'Well, I haven't sorted it out.' . . . what he is saying, if I understand him correctly, is that he's prepared to brand a woman a criminal for making this choice." Of course, Dukakis was wrong. It is acceptable to argue hot-button issues.

Appeasing the God of War

Since World War II, Americans have willingly sacrificed a significant portion of their national wealth on Mars's altar. This practice has often been at odds with a people devoted to peace, so presidential candidates, acting as Mars's high priests, have increasingly resorted to verbal entreaties to appease the military-industrial complex. In John Kennedy's day it was a missile gap that did not exist. Ronald Reagan closed the window of vulnerability at the cost of building an entire house. The battle cry had to continue in the 1988 debate, and the issue was which candidate could best serve Mars. Dukakis was asked whether he was "prepared to eliminate weapons systems that will result in the unilateral disarmament of this country."

"Of course not," he replied. Unable to answer an earlier question about what specific weapons systems he would eliminate, Dukakis ducked the question, asserted his competence "to provide leadership," and then counterattacked Bush for dealing arms with the Ayatollah, for being involved with Noriega and drugs, and for supporting Marcos's dictatorship in the Philippines.

When Bush specified what "one system" he would ax, he waxed manly. He was against: "A–6F, for example, DIVAD, and I can go on and on. Minuteman 3, penetration systems, I mean there's plenty of them that I oppose." Borrowing the governor's language, the vice president also allowed how he was prepared to make "some tough choices" on the "Midgetman missile or on the Minuteman, whatever it is." The live audience responded to his verbal gaffe with vocal disapprobation, but he regained his composure and the initiative with a disarming humorous line that concomitantly scored Dukakis: "Wouldn't it be nice to be perfect. Wouldn't it be nice to be the iceman so you never make a mistake."

Dukakis did answer the question asked in his rebuttal by identifying the MX missile system as one "we don't need and can't afford." But rather than supplying warrants for his assertion, he discussed his beloved tough choices again.

Despite the fact, as Andrew Rosenthal observed, that the DIVAD was canceled in 1985, the A–6F bomber was cut by Congress, and the utilization of old Minuteman missiles as decoys was not a major weapons program, Bush appealed to the fear of canceling the MX missile.[24] The fears of forty years of Cold War rhetoric, and Reagan's evil-empire imagery, reinforced the love-hate relationship between the United States and the Soviet Union.

Bush also impaled Dukakis on the horns of a dilemma. Throughout the debate Dukakis berated Bush for spending billions on Star Wars. He also noted that he did not know "of any reputable scientists who believe that this system, at least as originally conceived, could possibly work." Then Dukakis tried to have it both ways: he would continue to fund research at the 1983 level. But Bush was unequivocal: "He's got to get this thing more clear. Why do you spend a billion dollars on something you think is a fantasy and a fraud. I will fully research it, go forward as fast as we can. We've sent up the levels of funding. And when it is deployable, I will deploy it. That's my position on SDI, and it's never wavered a bit."

Enacting Reagan's Lines: Scene One, Take One

Perhaps one of the most disarming lines from the Reagan–Mondale debate in 1984 was the president's retort to Mondale that Reagan would not hold Mondale's inexperience against him if Mondale would not hold the president's age against him.

Bush played this scene especially well when it came his turn. Prompted by a question about American responses to terrorism, Dukakis attacked the administration for trading arms for hostages with Iran. Subtly arguing that he would have made different choices, Dukakis sounded like an ancient Greek tragedian when he used words such as "tragedy," "one of the most tragic . . . foreign policy decisions we've ever made in this country," and "tragic mistake." Although overstated, Dukakis's point against the Reagan Administration, which contradicted itself on never negotiating with terrorists, was compelling.

Bush admitted that "we shouldn't have traded arms for hostages," and then counterattacked Dukakis's patriotism for not supporting Reagan's attack on Moammar Khadafy. Reagan had justified his April 14, 1986, attack on the grounds that he had conclusive evidence that the discotheque bombing in West Berlin, which killed American servicemen, was linked to Khadafy. As a matter of fact, Syrian-backed terrorists were responsible for the bombing, but the nation was ebullient over its first cowboy's standing tall in the saddle by shooting first and asking questions later. Bush's response did not still the controversy because he was next asked "how do we judge your judgment in the Oval Office in the last eight years?"

Bush stressed his strengths and minimized his weaknesses. He asserted that "You judge by the whole record," thus arguing the halo effect by which evil can be made acceptable by association with good. The giveaway to his vulnerability was that he answered a question with a series of seven rhetorical questions that covertly praised the Reagan Administration for positive movement in the Middle East. And then he coalesced his themes of peace and conservatism in a brilliant rhetorical transaction that had served Reagan so well in 1984: "I'll make a deal with you. I will take all the blame for those two incidents, if you give me half the credit for all the good things that have happened in world peace since Ronald Reagan and I took over from the Carter Administration."

Closing Appeals

Bush repeated his P_2C_1 formula in his final speech. For peace, he reiterated his stands on arms control, chemical and biological weapons, and reductions in conventional forces. For prosperity, he favored maintaining the Reagan economic expansion and wisely scored liberalism by announcing he did not "want to go back to malaise and misery index." He stressed his values on the pledge of allegiance, tough sentencing, and the death penalty to identify with conservatives. He ended his speech by appealing to voters to support his candidacy.

It was not an eloquent peroration, but it hammered home the juxtaposition between Bush and Dukakis. If Richard Nixon's recipe for victory had any merit, then surely Bush succeeded in pinning down Dukakis and in laying out his own political, social, and economic values next to Dukakis's for national comparison.

Dukakis eschewed his chemical formula and developed a summary speech that was distinguished by two rhetorical strategies. First, his writers might have read Harold Zullow's work in political rhetoric wherein Zullow predicted that the candidate who was more verbally optimistic should win.[25] The governor used the word "optimistic" once, paraphrased the thought when he stated that he believed in the American dream, was a product of it, and wanted to make the dream come true for all citizens, and sounded more optimistic than Bush: "Yes, it's a tough problem as Mr. Bush says, but it's not an insolvable problem." Second, Dukakis used anaphora to convey an elegant style. The phrase "The best America" initiated five thought groups that also recapitulated his optimism. However, he weakened his recency effect by thanking the people for listening to him, rather than asking, as Bush did, for their support.

Effects of the Debate

In terms of delivery, Dukakis seemed to have an appreciable edge in two areas. First, Bush had trouble with fluently stating his thoughts. He started sentences, changed in midstream, and ended in other areas. If Kathleen Jamieson's observation that "When you want someone to sound competent and decisive, you write short, clear declarative sentences" is true, then Bush suffered by comparison with Dukakis, who delivered his lines smoothly.[26] Second, the governor established eye contact with the camera and hence with the television audience. Bush, however, spent more time addressing either the panelists, who were not there to be persuaded, or the stage audience, which was not a national mediating audience.

Dukakis heavily discomforted Bush on drugs, the deficit, the abortion issue, the selection of Senator Dan Quayle as a running mate, and on the Iran-Contra affair. Indeed, the *New York Times* editorialized: "His [Dukakis's] answers were certainly more pointed, and Mr. Bush often found himself on the defensive."[27] Elizabeth Drew determined that Dukakis "was on the offensive for most of the debate and was clearly the better debater."[28] Charles Madigan believed Dukakis "didn't sound liberal and he didn't look dumb."[29] But at least on two issues that Dukakis seemed to do the better job of debating, mainstream Americans did not agree. A *Newsweek* poll indicated that 64 percent of the respondents were not less likely to vote for Bush because of Iran and Noriega, and 63 percent were not less likely to vote for Bush over the Quayle vice presidency. Bush seems to have better mirrored the American people, leading by 50 percent to 44 percent over Dukakis when *Newsweek* asked who came "closer to reflecting your personal values."[30]

By all accounts, the debate was close. The question seems to be whether the proverbial glass of water was half full or half empty. If Bush did not win by much, neither did he lose by much, which was one of his objectives. Dukakis did not devastate Bush, but E. J. Dionne, Jr., thought the governor "clearly achieved one of his major objectives which was to present himself as a highly plausible President of the United States."[31] Nor were the polls conclusive. A CBS News Poll found Bush over Dukakis by 42 percent to 39 percent and the remainder undecided. A Gallup-*Newsweek* poll revealed a closer reverse: 42 percent for Dukakis versus 41 percent for Bush and the remainder undecided. Thomas Rosenstiel opined that "NBC leaned slightly toward Bush. ABC scored the card for Michael S. Dukakis. CBS bashed both and called it a draw."[32]

DEBATE 2: LOS ANGELES, CALIFORNIA, OCTOBER 13, 1988

As the gun-fight cleared at the O.K. Coral, candidate Bush declared himself Marshall Wyatt Earp. *Time* thought "Bush won the debate largely because he triumphed in the congeniality competition."[33]

Bush entered the second debate in a "buoyant mood" because his polls indicated a forty-five-state landslide, and he enjoyed at least a ten-point lead.[34] He did not, however, take the debate for granted. Bush prepared thoroughly by digesting briefing papers that were assembled for him by his staff. Ailes, his debate coach, worked closely with him on his delivery and poise, and rehearsed him on questions that could arise in the encounter.

Dukakis was not in top mental form. He had slept unusually long on the afternoon of the debate, and met with his coaches, Robert Squier and Thomas Donilon. In the crucial last half hour before the debate, he talked on the telephone to Governor Mario Cuomo for twenty precious minutes. Dukakis's aides claimed this conversation "kept him from gathering his thoughts and focusing on his strategy."[35]

Forensically, the debate was disappointing. Little new argumentative ground was broken as both debaters were content with themes already established in the first encounter. *Time* complained about their "fig leaf" stances: "But the blame rests equally with both candidates, who consciously refrained from raising new issues and arguments before more than 62 million TV viewers."[36] But the media contributed to the disappointment by asking three trite questions.

Trite Questions

1. *Rape and Murder*. Dukakis was criticized in the media for his lackluster answer to the lead question: "Governor, if Kitty Dukakis were raped and murdered, would you favor an irrevocable death penalty for the killer?"[37] Elizabeth Drew characterized the question as "deliberately shocking (and tasteless)."[38] Nevertheless, *Time* opined: "The debate—and perhaps even Dukakis' chance to inspire a late-inning rally to win the election—may have been lost in those opening two minutes."[39] No one noticed that Dukakis answered the question straightforwardly and even supplied a warrant for his claim: "No, I don't Bernard, and I think you know that I've opposed the death penalty during all my life. I don't see any evidence that it's a deterrent and I think there are better and more effective ways to deal with violent crime." Dukakis went to the quick of the question: not even the death penalty's staunchest supporters argue the deterrence effect because it simply does not work. Bush, playing to values his constituents so cherish—whether they are based on any factual evidence is beside the point—sallied forth with a fine rebuttal: "I do believe in the death penalty. And I think it is a deterrent and I believe we need it."

2. *Heroes*. In order to educate prospective voters, the governor was asked "who are the heroes . . . in American life today?" Granted, Dukakis was unable to name any heroes save Jonas Salk and Bush managed to name four figures to which he added "we ought to give a little credit to the President of the United States." Bush thought better on his feet than Dukakis did. But did this question prompt an enlightened answer to a political exigency or did it engage generic answers that one expects at bathing beauty contests in order to make the swim suit competition appear intellectual?

3. *Presidential Likeability*. Was this a debating forum or a Miss America pageant with a third congeniality question: "Governor, you won the first debate on intellect and yet you lost it on heart. . . . Do you think that a President has to be liked to be an effective leader?" He was panned for his "likeable" and "lovable" self-descriptions, but was anybody listening to his answer to the media: "I think the Presidency of the United States is a very serious office. And I think we have to address these issues in a very serious way." Bush evidently agreed when it came his turn: "I don't think it's a question of whether people like you or not to

make you an effective leader. . . . You see, I think it's a question of values, not likeability or lovability." Similarly, a rhetorical critic should pass over the question of whether Bush's father "would see a shocking transformation" in his son. Bush did not deign to dignify such drivel.

The Deficit

"The electorate is disgusted," Michael Kramer advised Dukakis, "by your avoidance of the budget deficit. (Never mind Bush's equal vacuity.)"[40] Bush reiterated he would not kill expansion, offered a flexible freeze, and warned that an army of IRS auditors would invade citizens' homes if Dukakis won. Dukakis attacked by calling the flexible freeze an "economic slurpee," promised to make "tough choices," scored "$200 billion worth of hot checks a year," but offered no ways to address the deficit. Presumption rested with Bush who did not claim he would ameliorate the deficit.

Weapons

When asked to give three weapons he would take from Mars's altar, since in the last debate he "mentioned three that had already been canceled," Bush managed only to drive away a "$850 million" truck. Averring that "the Vice President's mathematics just doesn't add up," in naming only one, Dukakis specified three as asked: Star Wars, the MX missile, and a space plane.

Again, the presumption prevailed. This was also the case in the discussion of nuclear deterrence, the defense budget, and nuclear forces. For each one of these issues, Bush reiterated that the Soviets were forced to negotiate with the United States. Bush's basic pitch is illustrated in the following example: "You just don't make unilateral cuts in the naive hope that the Soviets are going to behave themselves. World peace is important, and we have enhanced the peace. And I'm proud to have been a part of an Administration that has done exactly that—peace through strength works."

Aborting Abortions

Bush was asked: "You have said that you regard abortion as murder, yet you would make exceptions in the case of rape and incest. . . . Why should a woman [whose baby has Tay-Sachs disease] . . . carry a fetus to term?" It was a compound question. Bush wisely skirted the crucial part and answered the second part with a story about his child that lived for six months before dying. The narration was emotional yet tasteful, but it conveniently avoided the crux of the question.

Dukakis reminded the audience that he and his wife had a similar experience as the Bushes had, and then went to the core of the controversy. He answered straightforwardly, but probably not persuasively, to persons who smugly believe that only their position is moral:

> But isn't the real question that we have to answer not how many exceptions we make because the Vice President himself is prepared to make exceptions. It's who makes the decision. . . .
>
> And I think it has to be the woman, in the exercise of her own conscience and religious beliefs, that makes that decision.
>
> Who are we to say, well, under certain circumstances it's all right but under other circumstances it isn't?

Closing Speeches

Bush reiterated the basic themes of the first and second debates in his address. Stressing "enormous differences," he recited his conservative agenda—anticrime and conservative judges, neighborhood control, and the death penalty. To maintain prosperity, he would "hold the lines on taxes and keep this the longest expansion in modern history going until everybody in America benefits." And for peace, he identified with Reagan's achievements in foreign policy. It was not eloquent, but it went straight to his vital differences with Dukakis.

Approximately a third of the governor's short summation was inappropriate. The introduction and the conclusion were too personal. Who cared that he "never dreamed that someday I would . . . be my party's nominee for President" and that he received "the warmth and the hospitality . . . all across this country"? He organized the main body of his speech around the themes that the country should not be satisfied with Reagan's policies and that it could do better. He recited his litany of $150 billion on interest payments, high school dropouts, the homeless, and tax breaks for the rich. Yet, he was unclear in the debates how he would alleviate these exigencies beyond promises of tough choices.

CONCLUSION

Concerning expectations for the first debate, and their observation can be applied to the second one as well, Charles Wilbanks and William Strickland found it easier to advise their readers what the debates were not: "we should not expect great drama. We should not expect an in-depth analysis of the issues, nor should we expect stirring oratory."[41] They were correct.

The debates were media events, and Roger Mudd accurately assayed many of the problem illustated in this study: "For me the basic problem is the conflict between being an honest reporter and being a member of show business. . . . [N]one of us is content to let an event be an event; we have to fix it. . . . We have to take an issue. We won't let the candidate lay out the issue on his own terms; he has to lay it out on our terms."[42]

What did Americans get in the debates? William Schneider wrote that "negative campaigns work. . . . and peace and prosperity work."[43] Americans also glimpsed a man who adeptly ducked questions for which he apparently had no politically viable answers, and saw another man who pressed hot-button issues that "are only marginally presidential concerns."[44]

Inexplicably, Dukakis did not challenge the hypocrisy of hot-button issues, which William Safire opined offered "a silent commentary on the central thrust of this year's political campaign."[45] When the Republicans controlled the Senate and the presidency for four years, why did they not try to enact their campaign rhetoric? They had the chance. To legislate their values would obviate the 1988 campaign, and besides, the issues may still be there to argue in the 1992 debates.

Yet little will change as campaign debates inexorably descend anew to their denouement: "Anchormen read scripts; politicians read scripts. Anchormen talk in bites, politicians talk in bites. . . . Anchormen don't have anything to say, politicians don't have anything to say. . . . They are all, in the end, great communicators, while saying as little as possible."[46]

NOTES

1. I have written kindly on three Democratic presidents, Franklin D. Roosevelt, Harry S. Truman, and Lyndon B. Johnson, and negatively on Senator Richard Nixon's "My Side of the Story" speech in the 1952 presidential campaign.

2. James Caesar, Glen E. Thurow, Jeffrey Tulis, and Joseph Bessette, "The Rise of the Rhetorical Presidency," *Presidential Studies Quarterly* 11 (1981): 158–71.

3. "The Second Debate Gets Hollywood Cast," *New York Times*, September 27, 1988, p. B8.

4. "Sitcom Campaign," *Nation*, October 10, 1988, p. 295.

5. Jeff Greenfield, "There's No Debate: The Format Works," *New York Times*, October 13, 1988, p. A27.

6. Editorial, "Debates Domesticated," *New York Times*, September 27, 1988, p. A34.

7. Robert V. Friedenberg, " 'We Are Present Here Today for the Purpose of Having a Joint Discussion': The Conditions Requisite for Political Debates," *Journal of the American Forensic Association* 16 (1979): 1–3.

8. "Lectern to Lectern," *Newsweek*, November 21, 1988, p. 120.

9. "Lectern to Lectern," p. 123.

10. For why the League of Women Voters did not sponsor the second debate, see "Details about Details," *U.S. News and World Report*, October 17, 1988, p. 18.

11. Richard Nixon, "All the Pressure Will Be on George Bush," *Newsweek*, August 22, 1988, p. 28.

12. Henry Fairlie, "Brief Whining Moments," *New Republic*, October 10, 1988, p. 23.

13. "George Bush's Made-for-TV Makeover," *Newsweek*, September 12, 1988, p. 24.

14. William Safire, "Debate Will Help the Undecideds," *Roanoke Times & World-News*, September 27, 1988, p. A7.

15. "Playing Hardball," *Newsweek*, October 3, 1988, p. 26.

16. "Playing Hardball," p. 26.

17. "Campaign End Games," *Newsweek*, October 10, 1988, p. 44.

18. "Dukakis, Bush Arming for First Debate," *Roanoke Times & World-News*, September 22, 1988, p. A16; "Playing Hardball," p. 26; "Lectern to Lectern," p. 123.

19. George F. Will, "Reaganomics: Transferring Wealth from Labor to Capital," *Roanoke Times & World-News*, September 23, 1988, p. A11.

20. All quotations are taken from "Transcript of the First TV Debate between Bush and Dukakis," *New York Times*, September 26, 1988, pp. A17–19.

21. Andrew Rosenthal, "Like Others before Them, Debaters Stretched the Truth at Times," *New York Times*, September 27, 1988, p. B7.

22. Lisa Belkin, "The Man With No Money to Buy Health Insurance," *New York Times*, September 27, 1988, p. B7.

23. Franklin D. Roosevelt, "Second Inaugural Address," *Public Papers and Addresses of Franklin D. Roosevelt, 1937*, ed. by Samuel I. Rosenman (New York: Macmillan, 1941), p. 5.

24. Rosenthal, "Like Others before Them, Debaters Stretched the Truth at Times," p. B7.

25. "When Optimists Attract," *Newsweek*, October 17, 1988, p. 80.

26. Quoted in Michail Oriskis, "Nominees Battle Tonight to Emerge Most Presidential," *New York Times*, September 25, 1988, p. A24.

27. "Debates Domesticated," p. A34.

28. Elizabeth Drew, *Election Journal: Political Events of 1987–1988* (New York: William Morrow, 1989), pp. 285–86.

29. Charles M. Madigan, "Candidates Define Their Differences," *Chicago Tribune*, September 26, 1988, p. 7.

30. "The Newsweek Poll: Sizing Up the Impact," *Newsweek*, October 3, 1988, p. 25.

31. E. J Dionne, Jr., "Round One Undecisive," *New York Times*, September 27, 1988, p. B6.

32. Thomas B. Rosenstiel, "Ringside Media Give Split Decision," *Los Angeles Times*, September 26, 1988, p. 13.

33. Gerald M. Boyd, "Bush, Fighting Back Glee, Vows Tough Battle to End," *New York Times*, October 15, 1988, p. 8; "Bush Scores a Warm Win," *Time*, October 24, 1988, p. 18.

34. "Bush Bouyant," *U.S. News and World Report*, October 24, 1988, p. 17;

"Anatomy of a Victory," *Newsweek*, November 21, 1988, p. 14; "Nine Key Moments," *Time*, November 21, 1988, p.56.

35. "Nine Key Moments," p 56.
36. "Bush Scores a Warm Win," p. 19.
37. All quotations are taken from "Transcript of the Second Debate between Bush and Dukakis," *New York Times*, October 15, 1988, pp. 10–13.
38. Drew, *Election Journal*, p. 311.
39. "Bush Scores a Warm Win," p. 18.
40. Michael Kramer, "A Memo to Michael Dukakis," *U.S. News and World Report*, October 17, 1988, p. 40.
41. Charles Wilbanks and William Strickland, "Here's What to Look for in the 'Great Debates,' " *Roanoke Times & World-News*, September 23, 1988, p. A11.
42. Quoted in *Television and the Presidential Elections*, Martin Linsky, ed., (Lexington: D.C. Heath and Co., 1983), p. 48.
43. William Schneider, "Solidarity's Not Enough," *National Journal*, November 12, 1988, p. 2855.
44. "The Smear Campaign," *Newsweek*, October 31, 1988, p. 18.
45. William Safire, "Hit My Hot Button," *New York Times Magazine*, November 6, 1988, p. 22.
46. Fairlie, "Brief Whining Moments," p. 22.

SELECT BIBLIOGRAPHY

"Anatomy of a Victory." *Newsweek*, November 21, 1988, pp. 14–15. This article describes the fluctuations of public opinion as the campaign progressed and outlines the reasons why people voted for or against Bush and Dukakis.

Bush, George H. W., with Victor Gold. *Looking Forward*. Garden City: Doubleday, 1987. Although published before the debates, this work is a valuable starting point for assessing the heir apparent's career in terms of his political expectations.

"Bush Scores a Warm Win." *Time*, October 24, 1988, p. 18. This article captures something of the irony of the second debate: why Dukakis did not do as well as expected, and why Bush, although apparently more at ease, did not score a major victory but won by default.

Drew, Elizabeth. *Election Journal: Political Events of 1987–1988*. New York: William Morrow, 1989. In the first book on the 1988 campaign, the author, as in her accounts of past campaigns, treats the entire campaign and explicates the debates *in situ*.

Dukakis, Michael S., and Rosabeth Moss Kanter. *Creating the Future: The Massachusetts Comeback and Its Promise for America*. New York: Summit Books, 1988. A good starting point for biographical details of Dukakis's life in politics, the book is a pastiche of programs of how Dukakis probably would have done it if elected to the White House.

Fairlie, Henry. "Brief Whining Moments." *New Republic*, October 10, 1988, pp. 21–23. Fairlie presents a well argued, although compellingly sardonic analysis of campaign debates, the people who manipulate them, the people who participate in them, and the people who are persuaded by them.

Kenney, Charles, and Robert L. Turner. *Dukakis: An American Odyssey*. Boston: Houghton Mifflin, 1988. Although the book ends just before the first primaries in 1988, it is nevertheless useful for assaying Dukakis's two terms as governor.

"Lectern to Lectern." *Newsweek*, November 21, 1988, pp. 120–40. As a substantial article in *Newsweek's* book-length analysis of the 1988 campaign, this major piece describes the behind-the-scenes transactions of the principles and their advisers, and explicates the rhetorical strategies for both debates, as well as the vice presidential debate. This special election issue is invaluable as a departure point for conducting research on the 1988 presidential debates.

"Nine Key Moments." *Time*, November 21, 1988, pp. 48–56. *Time* magazine also issued an election special. This article is especially useful in criticizing the encounters by suggesting other perspectives on the rhetorical strategies of the debaters, and by giving additional insights concerning the persuasive successes and failures of the candidates.

Rosenthal, Andrew. "Like Others before Them, Debaters Stretched the Truth at Times." *New York Times*, September 27, 1988, p B7. The *New York Times* extensively covered the debates, but Rosenthal provides a needed leaven for the assertions, misstatements, and assorted halftruths with which the candidates obfuscated the issues in the first debate.

Debate Transcripts

"Transcript of the First TV Debate between Bush and Dukakis." *New York Times*, September 26, 1988, pp. A17–19.

"Transcript of the Second Debate between Bush and Dukakis." *New York Times*, October 15, 1988, pp. 10–13.

Videotapes of the Debates are available from C-SPAN, 444 North Capitol Street, N.W., Washington, D.C., 20001.

Commission on Presidential Debates, 09/25/88, Winston-Salem, North Carolina, ID: 4309, Tape: 88–1–09–25–20.

Presidential Debate, Pauley Pavillion, UCLA, 10/13/88, Los Angeles, California, ID: 4256, Tape 88–1–10–14–00.

Chapter 8

The 1988 Quayle–Bentsen Vice Presidential Debate

Warren D. Decker

For the third time since the advent of nationally televised political debates, in 1988 we again had the opportunity to witness a debate between the candidates aspiring to the office of vice president of the United States. The *New York Times* suggested that this debate was, "almost certainly the most important of them,"[1] referring to the vice presidential debates. For the first time there appeared to be a substantial degree of interest generated because of the increased expectation that one of the debaters would perform so unsatisfactorily that it might make interesting television. It is with that mindset that many people sat down to view the October 5, 1988, vice presidential debate between Senators Dan Quayle and Lloyd Bentsen. This essay is an analysis and discussion of what happened in that ninety-minute debate, as well as commentary on the maneuvers that preceded and the effects that followed.

THE DECISION TO DEBATE

Robert Friedenberg outlines a number of criteria that determine whether or not a candidate for the presidency will choose to participate in nationally televised confrontations with their opponents.[2] These criteria, while based upon the presidential debates can be applied to a vice presidential decision to debate. It is informative to examine the decision made by, or perhaps for, Quayle and Bentsen, in light of these criteria. According to Friedenberg, the decision to debate is determined by the answers to several questions.[3]

The first question is whether or not the election is predicted to be close.[4] The closer the election, the more likely it is to produce debates. The Bush–Dukakis debate schedule was decided in early September after Bush had shown a rather strong comeback in August following the significant lead that Dukakis had at the beginning of August.[5] The rather "roller-coaster" character of the race at this time probably contributed to the decision to hold debates.

The second question regards whether advantages are likely to accrue to the candidate because of the debate. The Bush–Quayle campaign handlers were somewhat reluctant to debate, or at least they made it appear that way. They seemed to be concerned about the inability of both Bush and Quayle to perform well in a debate and therefore wanted to deemphasize the potential impact by placing the debates a substantial distance from election day and by downplaying their candidates' abilities as debaters.[6] On the other hand, the Dukakis–Bentsen ticket seemed determined to debate. They felt that both Dukakis and Bentsen could outperform their counterparts, and therefore were quite eager to debate. The issues related to this question were probably based much more on the advantages and disadvantages associated with a Bush–Dukakis meeting than on a Quayle–Bentsen debate. Had the choice been unrelated to the presidential debates, Quayle's handlers may have decided not to debate. They seemed to be very reluctant to put Quayle in situations that created large audiences and called on him to be spontaneous.

This assumes, however, that a primary reason for the selection of Quayle was not motivated by a desire to have someone who would attract more criticism than Bush and therefore act to deflect attention from Bush. Overall the candidates and their handlers decided that the avoidance of debate would be more damaging than the debates themselves.[7]

The question "Am I a good debator?" explains the Dukakis–Bentsen decision to press for debates. Most analysts seemed to agree that in terms of debate talent the two pairs were unevenly matched, and the edge based upon raw talent swung in favor of the Democratic ticket.[8] However, the Bush campaign understood full well the potential negative repercussions that could occur as a result of being perceived as attempting to avoid debates.[9] There was also some evidence that Quayle had handled himself satisfactorily in past debates thereby calming some of the fears of his handlers. Quayle was also much more capable of providing short, brief answers that fit the debate format rather than in-depth responses. Short answers provided Quayle less chance of rambling into areas which could create problems for the ticket. The format, which allowed for less opportunity to give lengthy, rambling answers, probably worked to reduce the discomfort Quayle's handlers had with allowing their man to debate.[10] As Elizabeth Drew notes, "It was widely understood that a great deal rode on Quayle's performance in the Vice-Presidential debate, in Omaha on October 5th. Dukakis had been making an issue of him, but if he performed adequately the issue could be gone, even if that didn't make him any more qualified for the Vice-Presidency."[11] It must also be remembered that the decision to hold a vice presidential debate is largely preordained by the decision to have a presidential encounter.

The fourth question concerns whether the candidates had control over all of the important variables in the debate situation. The fact that several members of the campaign staffs had previous "debate" experience probably reduced the concern in this area. Given the existence of several previous debates, it made it much easier to predict and control the unexpected. The avoidance of the unexpected is the determining factor in many campaign decisions at this level.[12]

The Bush campaign was able to control the timing of the debates when they got the Dukakis campaign to agree to have the debates earlier than Dukakis wanted them. Dukakis had wanted debates considerably closer to the November 8 election.[13] The Bush campaign also reduced the number of debates desired by the Dukakis campaign, from four to two. By sandwiching them between the Summer Olympics and the baseball playoffs and World Series the Bush campaign further defused their impact.[14] Edward Rollins, director of President Reagan's 1984 campaign and now a Republican political consultant, was quoted as saying, "I think in a close election the debates can play a crucial role,"[15] and, "the more debates that are held, the more the likelihood that the Dukakis people can make Bush make a mistake and also give their own man more credibility".[16] The Dukakis camp had recognized that early in September Bush appeared to have the upper hand, and they were forced to agree to fewer debates earlier than they wanted.[17]

The final issue impinging upon the decision to debate was the question of incumbency. The fact that Bush was an incumbent vice president probably contributed to his reluctance to debate. It certainly contributed to his decision to negotiate a reduction in the number of debates.[18] It would seem that an incumbent vice president is in a rather enviable position since he can share in the "unquestioned credibility"[19] of the outgoing president while at the same time being able to distance himself from any unpopular issues. However, vice presidents may well have not had the opportunity "to make their views known to the public."[20] Therefore, they may be a bit more willing to engage in debates. To the extent that incumbency motivated Bush it may have also contributed to the vice presidential debate.

Obviously the decision to debate is a significant one that hinges upon a number of fairly complex issues. The decision was made to have a vice presidential debate and it was scheduled for October 5, 1988, at the Civic Center in Omaha, Nebraska.

GOALS OF THE CANDIDATES

Both Quayle and Bentsen seem to have selected several primary themes, which can serve as a starting point for this analysis. A comparison of these themes is helpful in identifying the goals of the two debaters. One of the more obvious Quayle goals appeared to be a reluctance to confront Bentsen directly. Quayle continually attempted to attack Dukakis rather than Bentsen. In his answer to Judy Woodruff's opening question about his qualifications, we see the first indication of this when he stated, "On each one of those issues I have more experience than does the Governor of Massachusetts."[21] Quayle continued this approach in his response to the second question when he stated:

> As you notice, Senator Bentsen didn't tell you very much about what Governor Dukakis would do—Governor Dukakis, one of the most liberal governors in the United States of America.
>
> The one thing he tried to point out about Governor Dukakis is that he's cut taxes. The fact of the matter is, Senator Bentsen, he's raised taxes five times. He just raised taxes this past year. And that's why a lot of people refer to him as Tax Hike Mike. That's why they refer to the State of Massachusetts as Taxachusetts.

Quayle again returned to the attack-Dukakis theme later in the debate when he addressed U.S. foreign policy in Central America:

> Senator Bentsen talked about the entire Central America. There's another issue that Michael Dukakis is wrong on in Central America, and that's Grenada. He criticized our rescue mission in Grenada, according to a UPI report. Criticized that, yet 85 percent of the American people supported our rescue mission, and we turned a communist country into a noncommunist country.
>
> The Governor of Massachusetts is simply out of step with mainstream America.

The anti-Dukakis remarks confirmed *The Washington Post's* predebate speculation about Quayle's goals for the debate. Before the debate the *Post* wrote, "Quayle, however, is expected to studiously avoid attacking Bentsen. Quayle has said his quarrel is not with Bentsen but with Dukakis."[22]

Bentsen's goal was to focus upon Dan Quayle and his qualifications to be president. In Bentsen's response to Woodruff's opening question he argued, "This debate tonight is not about the qualifications for the Vice Presidency. The debate is whether or not Dan Quayle and Lloyd Bentsen are qualified to be President of the United States." Furthermore, toward the end of the debate Bentsen argued that, "It's a presidential decision that you are facing, and a very important one, because we are talking about who is going to lead this country into its future. And you can't have a more important responsibility than that one." By focusing upon this Bentsen hoped to tap into the significant concern of many voters about the qualifications of Quayle to be president.[23]

Bentsen also wanted to raise the issue of Bush's judgment by attacking the choice of Quayle as his runningmate. The difficulty of accomplishing this goal was addressed by Robert Barnes and R. H. Melton, staff writers for *The Washington Post*, when they reported the feelings of a number of observers that, "Bentsen's avowed goal in the debate—raising the issue of Bush's judgment by attacking the choice of Quayle as a running mate—is also more complicated than Quayle's central objective of holding his own for 1 ½ hours."[24] The *Post* also reported Michael McCurry, Bentsen's campaign press secretary, as saying, "The question for us is how to raise the bar on the high jump high enough for Dan Quayle, so that he has to be more than passably coherent for 90 minutes" and "I don't think we've got the answer."[25]

Closely related to his goal of directly attacking Dukakis, Quayle also wanted to shift the debate away from a Bentsen–Quayle affair to a Bush–Dukakis confrontation. An attempt to do this was made with the statement, "George Bush has more qualifications than Michael Dukakis and Lloyd Bentsen combined."

Making the vice presidential debate into a comparison of the candidates for the presidency was understandable from Quayle's perspective, given the fact that the polls[26] indicated that Bush compared more favorably to Dukakis than Quayle did to Bentsen. This statement also served to deflect some of the concern away from Quayle's lack of qualifications and focus attention on Bush's highly credible qualifications and his incumbency. The deflection of attention away from his qualifications may have been a very significant motive for Quayle. *The Washington Post* highlighted this goal when it reported that, "In addition, Quayle will attempt to use the debate to alleviate fears about his candidacy."[27] It reported that many analysts believed the debate to be a "Quayle versus Quayle" affair.[28]

E. J. Dionne, Jr., writing in the *New York Times* after the debate, reflected in a more general way upon the goals of the Democrats and Republicans in the first two debates:

> The Democrats and the Republicans had clear but distinct goals in the first two debates of the 1988 campaign. If the Democrats needed to use the debates to persuade a wary electorate to give their ticket another hearing, the Republicans had what on its face was a simpler task: to reassure an electorate that seemed on the verge of voting for their "peace and prosperity" ticket that George Bush and Dan Quayle were competent, clear-headed and not gaffe-prone.[29]

ARGUMENTATIVE STRATEGIES

Both candidates utilized a number of notable argumentative strategies during their presentation. Whether it is appropriate to label all of them strategies may be questionable since the nature of a strategy assumes some premeditation and planning on their part and some of these characteristics may have been exhibited spontaneously. This portion of the analysis will be directed toward the identification and discussion of some of those strategies.

Given that a primary function claimed for public political debate is to delineate the positions of the candidates, one can begin this analysis with a discussion as to how well the debate delineated the candidates' positions.[30] The characteristic of a debate that should contribute the most to the clarification of the candidates' respective positions is clash. How well did the candidates initially present their positions so as to promote clash? How well did they respond to the claims made by their opponents?

The answer resulting from an analysis of the issues addressed in the vice presidential debate is that both debaters could have improved significantly. Clash assumes that each debater would be directly responsive to the argumentation of the other and that each would examine in some detail the position presented by the other. However, the primary characteristic of this debate was that charges and countercharges were made with no real attempt to engage in direct refutation. For example, the second question in the debate focused upon whether the Massachusetts state budget had indeed been balanced without increases in taxes. Bentsen made the claim that it had been and Quayle responded, arguing that Dukakis raised taxes five times. Quayle then added a couple of *ad hominem* attacks with his labels of Tax Hike Mike and Taxachusetts. The point to be made is that no resolution to this discrepancy in claims was made.

Perhaps the format was at fault, since the next question directed the attention of the candidates to another issue. However, one could argue that a quick, brief response aimed at that resolution could be made by the next speaker, regardless of the question being asked. Repeatedly issues were never carried beyond the charge-countercharge level.

One noticeable exception occurred when Bentsen took time from responding to the next question to answer Quayle's earlier charges relative to his breakfast club.[31] Bentsen had previously provided an answer related to the acceptance of PAC (Political Action Committee) money, but when Quayle, in his response, mentioned the $10,000 breakfast club, Bentsen did provide a rebuttal during time allocated for another question. He indicated that he could not "leave something on the table he's charged me with." This occurrence was unique, however, and could be explained by the fact that the question preceding Bentsen's rebuttal opportunity related to what Quayle would do if he suddenly became president. Quayle's answer probably didn't necessitate a response, thereby allowing the time for a response to the earlier issue.

As indicated above, if they desire, the format can be altered enough by the candidates during their responses to allow for increased clash. It may also be a question of the candidates' willingness to pursue closure on these issues. Clarity in political communication may not be a highly prized or desired goal.

The debate involved the presentation of positions and counter positions much more than direct clash based upon responses to the claims made by the debaters. Another example of unresolved countercharges flows from the discussion of the votes cast on social security. Bentsen claimed first that Quayle voted eight times to cut social security and secondly that Bush flew back from the West coast just to vote for a cut. Quayle countercharged that Bentsen voted for cuts in social security twice and that Governor Dukakis supported a resolution at a Governors Conference to delay cost of living adjustments to social security. The issue was dropped without any further exploration by either debater. At this level we are left with the assumption that both candidates would vote to cut social security adjustments and the difference between them is merely a question of how often. This does not appear to delineate very well the candidates' positions.

Of the approximately nineteen question-response interchanges few exhibited a substantial degree of clash. The primary way to characterize these interchanges is as charges and countercharges rather than as substantive analysis of one another's positions, i.e., clash. It would seem if the candidates truly wanted to clarify and delineate their positions to the electorate, they could do better by being somewhat more responsive to their opponents.

At the end of a debate the audience should have some idea of what each candidate thinks is wrong with the other person's position, not just the rival position. Perhaps modifications of the format would allow the candidate to dwell on a particular issue and improve the delineation of positions. Modifications in the format might also allow the debaters to follow up a second and third time on the same issue and promote clarification of positions. Finally, clash might also serve to add a bit more life to the debates. Of course the added life might introduce new risks, which would again prompt the very avoidance behavior Quayle and Bentsen often exhibited.

An argumentative strategy Bentsen appeared to use a number of times was to focus his attack upon the Reagan–Bush Administration. Early in the debate he argued, "It was this administration, their administration, that cut out the money early on to be able to clean up water." Later while addressing a question related to safety in the workplace he stated, "And then you've seen an administration that came in and really didn't have it's heart in that kind of an enforcement." Later Bentsen argued, "We've seen an administration that has lost much of our market abroad." He continually leveled charges against the administration, which one must remember was only partially associated with the Bush–Quayle ticket. It would have been somewhat more effective to try to attack the Bush–Quayle ticket more directly.

Similarly Bentsen also repeatedly defended generic Democratic party programs as opposed to Dukakis–Bentsen programs. He made statements like, "the people that are going to protect it are the Democrats that brought forth that program," and "We are the authors, the Democratic Party, of Clean Air, of Clean Water, of the superfund." A primary goal for Bentsen was to respond to worries about a policy split between himself and Dukakis. The fact that he continued to focus upon the generic policies of the Democratic Party, as opposed to what he and Dukakis would do, did not seem to be an effective way to defend the Dukakis–Bentsen ticket directly.

ASSERTIONS

As with much political rhetoric the debates appear to be overflowing with assertions, or statements not supported with either evidence or reason. Some of the examples in this debate were statements such as, "I have more experience than others that have sought the office of Vice President" and "George Bush has more qualifications than Michael Dukakis and Lloyd Bentsen combined." Perceptive observers such as Elizabeth Drew noted Quayle's assertions.[32]

Bentsen also contributed his fair share of assertions with statements like, "And it was this administration, their administration, that cut out the money early on to be able to clean up water, and made it impossible to move ahead at that time on Boston Harbor" and "the way I would accomplish that—was with a tough policy, opening up those markets, getting those prices back up to market prices." A bit more explanation attached to these statements might have elevated them above the level of assertion. As with the charges and countercharges discussed above, a certain amount of refutation addressed to these assertions might help to eliminate them and increase the quality of the argumentation in the debates.

Assertion appears to be a prominent characteristic of this debate. It could be argued that members of the audience can fill in the missing reasoning and/or evidence and, therefore, the assertions function fairly well for the debaters. This point would be well taken if the sole purpose of the debate was to persuade and not delineate the candidate positions.

FIT BETWEEN QUESTIONS AND ANSWERS

Another characteristic of the interchanges in the vice presidential debate was a noticeable lack of fit between the questions and the answers. For example, when Senator Quayle was responding to a question from Jon Margolis regarding the subsidy payment to large farmers, the senator did not mention the subsidy program, but rather he began his response with a generic attack on Carter's grain embargo and ended the answer with an attack on Dukakis and his Harvard associates wanting farmers to grow Belgium endive. This had no direct relationship to the question asked.

Bentsen also had some misfits between questions asked and answers given. Specifically, when he responded to another lengthy Margolis question related to the Occupational Safety and Health Administration (OSHA), the senator managed to spend more time talking about the "Bonnie and Clyde of environmental protection" Ann Gorsuch and James Watt than the mishandling of OSHA regulations.

Another distinguishing characteristic in this debate appeared to be the amount of detail each debater used while providing their answers. Most critics seemed to agree that Senator Bentsen did a much better job than Quayle with regard to providing detailed responses to questions. For example, midway in the debate Bentsen, responding to a question on farm subsidies, stated:

> I was in January visiting Mr. Takeshita, the new Prime Minister of Japan. I said, "You're paying five times as much for beef as we pay for in our country—pay for it in our country, six times as much for rice. You have a $60 billion trade surplus with us. You could improve the standard of living of your people. You're spending 27 percent of your disposable income on food. We spend 14 or 15 percent." "Where you have that kind of barrier up against us, that's not free trade and we don't believe that should continue."

Senator Quayle's response provided a bit less detail when he stated, "Senator Bentsen talks about recapturing the foreign markets. Well, I'll tell you one way that we're not going to recapture the foreign markets and that is if, in fact, we have another Jimmy Carter grain embargo." This interchange demonstrates the difference in the level of detail in responses. It remains to be seen which is the most effective. One could argue that simplicity has significant rewards in a televised debate. One could also argue that talking about hiking and fishing with children on a question regarding the environment might be overly simplistic.

LANGUAGE USAGE

Elizabeth Drew, in her book, *Election Journal: Political Events of 1987–1988*, suggested that then Vice President "Bush's mangling of thoughts or words when on his own bespeaks a certain sloppiness of thought processes, or some sort of short-circuiting that goes on in his head."[33] This same comment could probably be made about Senator Quayle in the debate. Like Bush, Quayle had a number of "manglings" to his credit by the end of the debate. Examples of this are, "Believe me, we have a commit to preserving the environment," and, "But let me tell you something, what we have done for the poor. What we have done for the poor is that we in fact—the homeless bill, the McKinney Act, which is the major piece of legislation that deals with the homeless—the Congress has cut the funding that the administration has recommended." Later in that same answer, Quayle states, "the poor and the poverty—the biggest thing that we have done for poverty in America is the Tax Simplification Act of 1986: six million working poor families got off the payroll." And finally, "Jimmy Carter—Jimmy Carter grain embargo set the American farmer back. You know what the farmer's interested in? Net farm income. Every one percent of increase in interest rates, a billion dollars out of the farmer's pocket. Net farm income, increased inflation, another billion dollars." Quayle's utilization of oral language was weak. He obviously meant to say commitment and not commit, he left out words that should have been a part of intelligible oral speech, and he used the wrong words such as taking six million people off the payrolls rather than taking them off the taxrolls.

Bentsen also had his moments when he mangled language. In his response to Quayle's response to Brit Hume's question regarding what Quayle would do if he had to assume the presidency, Bentsen stated, "Once again I think what we are looking at here is someone that can step in at the presidency level at the moment, if that tragedy would occur." This is not a particularly strong or compelling statement. Bentsen did occasionally show flashes of brilliance and one of those flashes came during the interchange with Quayle regarding his comparison of himself to John Kennedy. Quayle reacted to Bentsen's initial response with, "That was really uncalled for, Senator." As one observer noted, Bentsen responded "with elegant phrasing" claiming "You're the one that was making the comparison, Senator. . . . I did not think the comparison was well taken."[34]

Another notable aspect of language concerns the choice of certain labels used by Senator Quayle to identify groups of Americans to which he referred during the debate. Quayle made two poor choices when he said "old people" in reference to the elderly and "those people" in reference to the poor. The first denoted a certain degree of insensitivity and the second suggested that the candidate selected to dissociate himself from the poor. Neither choice appeared to enhance Quayle's relationship with the electorate.

Bentsen's selection of language was much better during most of the debate. It seemed like he had adopted the language style of the Senate, which was a bit more diplomatic and less harsh. Phrases such as, "I don't understand that," or "I find that very interesting," were used rather than using more combative language. This lack of abruptness toned down the debate and probably worked to reduce the conflict between the debaters.

It would appear that both debaters could stand to work on their oral language skills, particularly Quayle, who needed to fill in the missing words. Such gaps seemed dangerously equatable to gaps in thinking.

EMOTIONAL APPEALS AND REAGANISMS

One rhetorical tactic that Bentsen seemed to use rather effectively early in the debate was a veiled fear appeal. When responding to the first question of the debate, posited by Judy Woodruff, Bentsen stated,

> This debate tonight is not about the qualifications for the Vice Presidency. The debate is whether or not Dan Quayle and Lloyd Bentsen are qualified to be President of the United States.
>
> Because Judy, just as you have said, that [the death of a President] has happened too often in the past. And if that tragedy should occur, we have to step in there without any margin for error, without time for preparation, to take over the responsibility for the biggest job in the world, that of running this great country of ours; to take over the awesome responsibility for commanding the nuclear weaponry that this country has.
>
> No, the debate tonight is a debate about the presidency itself, and a presidential decision that has to be made by you. The stakes could not be higher.

Later in the debate, Bentsen states, "I think he's arrived at a very dangerous judgment in the question of war and peace and it concerns me very much." He continued with, "He's listening once again to the winds of the radical right." Clearly, Bentsen was attempting to take advantage of the concern people had about Quayle's ability to run the country and make sound judgments on significant issues.

In contrast to the fear appeals used by Bentsen, it appears that Quayle wanted the viewers to "feel good" about America and about themselves. This appeal seemed vaguely familiar since it had been used in the Reagan campaigns. Examples of these attempts were, "But we believe in the market, we believe in the people . . . " and "Well, I can tell you, the American people think the United States of America is the envy of the world." Obviously, these appeals had worked fairly well four years earlier.

DELIVERY

Some might argue that delivery should not play a critical role in deliberations of this magnitude. However, Senator Quayle's hesitations at certain critical junctures in his responses may have provided the most decisive moments of the debate. The most obvious hesitations, and perhaps the most counterproductive from Quayle's standpoint, came when he was asked about what he would do if he suddenly became president. He responded, "First—first, I'd say a prayer for myself and for the country that I'm about to lead." This statement, coupled with the hesitations during delivery, seemed to do much to deny Quayle's claim that he could decisively lead the country if called upon to do so. The hesitations were critical for the viewer, whereas, a reader of the debate would not get the same impact out of his statement. The nonverbal behaviors were critical to the outcome of the statement.

It is possible that Quayle had planned some hesitation to appear thoughtful, if so, it was counterproductive. A quick and decisive response to this particular question would have been much more desirable. Given the fact that one of Quayle's primary goals was to convince the American public that he was not a "slow student" and dispel doubts about his general capability, he probably should have tried to eliminate as many hesitations or faltering answers as possible. Particularly on questions as central to the role of the vice presidency as what would he do if, "the President is incapacitated for one reason or another, and you have to take reins of power."

The effect of these hesitations were excerbated when in response to a later question on the same subject Quayle again provided what appeared to be a faltering answer. Tom Brokaw asked for the third time what Senator Quayle would do in the event he had to assume the presidency. Quayle responded in part by saying, "I would [hesitation] make sure [hesitation] that the people in the cabinet [hesitation] and the people that are advisors to the president are called in, and I would talk to them, and I will work with them." He was given yet another opportunity to rectify his early impressions and failed again. One could argue that Quayle's reponses to these two question did much to help prove Bentsen's claim that Quayle was not ready to assume the presidency.

In contrast, Bentsen handled the delivery aspects of his responses quite well. He appeared as the reasoned, self-assured, experienced person in the debate who was fully capable of being president. His utilization of pauses contributed to this image. The best example of this came during the most discussed and studied interchange in the debate.

Quayle stated, "I have as much experience in the Congress as Jack Kennedy did when he sought the presidency." And Bentsen responded,

"Senator, I served with Jack Kennedy, [pause] I knew Jack Kennedy, [pause] Jack Kennedy was a friend of mine. [pause] Senator, you are no Jack Kennedy." Here the slow, self-assured, deliberate nature of the pauses appeared carefully crafted to produce the effect Bentsen wanted.

Elizabeth Drew provides a detailed analysis of this moment in the debate.

"As soon as Bentsen gave his withering response, one knew that this would be the most memorable moment of the debate, the one that would be replayed often, and Bentsen delivered his lines with perfect timing. The effectiveness was in the way it was done: Bentsen's saying, more in sorrow, slowly, 'Senator, I served with Jack Kennedy.' (Pause.) 'I knew Jack Kennedy.' (Pause.) 'Jack Kennedy was a friend of mine.' (Longer pause.) 'Senator, you're no Jack Kennedy.' As Bentsen started to go ahead with what he would do if he had to take over as President, an obviously wounded Quayle said stiffly, and with what seemed more petulance than anger, 'That was really uncalled for, Senator.' So Bentsen leveled him again, with elegant phrasing: 'You're the one that was making the comparison, Senator. . . . I did not think the comparison was well taken.' "[35]

In addition to her impressions of this particular interchange, Drew comments more generally about Bentsen's behavior during the debate. She notes that Bentsen seemed commanding, assured, and at ease. Like many, Drew concluded that Bentsen was the best of the 1988 political debaters.[36] Bentsen seemed more natural and wiser than the other candidates.[37] Drew summarizes by suggesting, "He [Bentsen] came across as a man we could feel comfortable with in a crisis—which is, of course, the whole point in thinking about potential Vice-Presidents."[38]

In contrast, Drew's impressions of Quayle's performance were very different. She writes that Quayle looked "wooden and frightened—like a young man hesitantly reciting his lessons and knowing little else."[39] She relates further that the pressure of debating or his staff's overcoaching contributed to his tense, unnatural appearance.[40]

On one of the more obvious aspects of public political debating, it appeared that Bentsen had won the day. As noted earlier, one could argue that Quayle's delivery problems alone did much to deny the attainment of his main goal in the debate: convincing the American people that he was capable of being president.

HUMOR

Humor has long been a powerful tool in the hands of those who know how to utilize it. Both debaters made several successful attempts at using humor. The first instance occurred during Bentsen's response to the answer provided by Quayle relative to Quayle's record on the environment. The fact that it was a response made it a bit more effective since the audience had already reacted with laughter to Quayle's claim that he had a "strong record on the environment." Bentsen's relatively sarcastic response was, "This late conversion is interesting to me" to which the audience reacted with both laughter and applause. Quayle's first humorous comment came in the context of his charges about Bentsen's $10,000 Breakfast Club." Quayle stated that, "I'm sure they weren't paying to have cornflakes." The audience, given the fact that this line was delivered midway through an answer, did not react as raucously as they could have, given the nature of the line. Timing is worth a lot when using humor.

The next line came from Bentsen and was a mix of humor and sarcasm. It was a response to Brokaw's laundry-list question about how good things are under the current administration: "Let me offer you an inventory if I may: Lower interest rates, lower unemployment, lower inflation and an arms control deal with the Soviet Union." Bentsen responded quickly with, "You know, if you let me write $200 billion worth of hot checks every year, I could give you an illusion of prosperity, too." This comment was followed by both laughter and applause. Obviously, there was not a dearth of humor in the debate, and those interchanges utilizing humor were memorable.

AUDIENCE

The behavior of the audience assembled at the vice presidential debate warrants at least a passing comment. It seemed that audience members played a much more active role than in previous debates. They seemed to be ready to react in a partisan way much more quickly than in the past. In an editorial following the debate *The Washington Post* commented that all aspects of the debate seemed to be highly programmed, "So, for that matter, did the jeering audience, poised to come in relentlessly at the end of an answer."[41] Tom Shales, commenting on the behavior of the crowd, wrote: "She [Woodruff] spent a lot of time shushing the crowd and warning them not to make loud displays of approval or disapproval." He reacted further by asking, "why don't the dunderheads who put on these debates either banish the audience altogether or just let them yell?"[42] He suggested further that, "there was no audience for the first presidential debate, between John F. Kennedy and Richard Nixon. It was held in a TV studio, where such television events ought to be held."[43] Given the role played by the audience in this debate, the existence of an audience in future debates may well be reconsidered.

EFFECTS

The Washington Post reported that the "vice-presidential debate drew an estimated audience of about 60 million, according to one network estimate."[44] This figure represents a substantial decrease when compared to the size of former debate audiences. On October 10, *The Washington Post* in an editorial elaborated upon the decrease in viewership over the past debates.

> Preliminary ratings of the vice-presidential debates confirm what the ratings of the presidential debates showed already this year: the number of viewers is sharply down. Nielsen reported that 71 percent of television households were watching the single Carter–Reagan debate at the end of the 1980 campaign, and in 1984, 45 to 48 percent were tuned in to the three debates. This year Nielsen estimates that 38 percent were tuned in Sept. 25 to Michael Dukakis and George Bush, and that in the top 17 percent of the markets (which have 40 percent of the nation's population) only 32 percent were watching the debate between Lloyd Bentsen and Dan Quayle.[45]

These figures reveal that while political debates continue to draw very large audiences, the size of those audiences appears to be decreasing significantly. Obviously, comparing vice presidential debates to presidential debates does account for some of that decrease. There are other explanations. Some attributed the decline to the general dissatisfaction of the electorate to the style of the 1988 campaign. As the *Post* commented, "no one can know the extent to which the turn-off has been not the general subject of politics and the presidential election but rather the manipulative, patronizing imagery by which the campaigns have sought to achieve their goals in this election."[46] It is also important to realize that network viewership is down across the board as a result of the increased availability of non-network programming. This factor was explained by the *Post*. "Once upon a time, scheduling a broadcast on ABC, CBS and NBC was called a 'roadblock': viewers had to watch it. But now the proliferation of independent stations and cable channels and the wide use of videotape recorders (in 56 percent of households now) has reduced the networks' audience."[47] Therefore, "much of the decline in the number of viewers of the debates may just mean that people who don't vote anyway are deciding to watch something else."[48] They concluded their analysis by speculating that an additional reason might be that some "people are not being fooled by the cooked-up, unspontaneous, totally scripted presentations they are being offered."[49] As Trent and Friedenberg suggest, one of the reasons people watch is that, "Debates create conflict, the essence of drama,"[50] but highly scripted presentations that avoid clash may do much to deny this reason for tuning in.

A strong case can be made for increased interest being a function of increased conflict when one considers the amount of attention paid to the one interchange during the debate that exhibited the most clash. The "Senator, you're no John Kennedy" comment received by far the most attention after the debate. Indeed, the comment even drew a reaction from the president of the United States when he stated, "I thought that remark was a cheap shot and unbecoming to a Senator of the United States."[51]

Debate analysts also claim that the debates usually reinforce the predispositions of voters rather than changing large numbers of votes.[52] Given the early postdebate reactions, it appeared that the public's reaction to the Bentsen–Quayle debate might be different. The *New York Times* reported that, "The public, which was divided in its view of the Bush–Dukakis debate, seemed to have few doubts about this one. In a CBS News Poll of debate watchers conducted Wednesday night, the popular verdict was overwhelming: 50 percent said Mr. Bentsen had done better or won; only 27 percent said Mr. Quayle had won."[53] Among those with predispositions toward the Bush–Quayle ticket they reported that, "Even among Mr. Bush's supporters before the debate, only 44 percent rated Mr. Quayle the winner."[54] However, it is obvious, given the outcome of the election, that many of these immediate effects did not translate to actual votes. Tracing the actual relationship between debate effects and voting is an extremely precarious business.

Both Quayle and Bentsen benefited by improvements in their images.[55] According to the poll data reported by the *New York Times*, "before the debate, only 37 percent of those who watched the debate said Mr. Quayle was qualified to serve as President; afterword 47 percent said so."[56] Further, the *Times* reported that "before the debate, 42 percent said Mr. Quayle 'understands the complicated problems a President has to deal with'; afterward 54 percent said this."[57] Bentsen improved his image even more, "before the debate, 64 percent of those who watched the encounter thought Mr. Bentsen was qualified for the Presidency; afterward, 78 percent did. Before the debate 78 percent thought Mr. Bentsen understood the complicated problems that confront a President; afterward, 84 percent said this."[58] Both candidates appeared to benefit from the debate in terms of building their images.

One claim made numerous times by the Bush campaign, both before and after the debate was that "the Vice-Presidency is important to only a minority of voters in helping them to decide which ticket to vote for. It is even less likely that a single Vice-Presidential debate will loom as important on Election Day."[59] Given the fact that the main effect of the vice presidential debate was to establish Bentsen as the clear winner, one could easily agree with the Bush campaign that the debate had insignificant overall effects.

NOTES

1. B. Drummond Ayres, Jr., "Flash of Lightning Ignites a Long-Becalmed Debate," *New York Times*, October 6, 1988, p. B19.
2. Robert V. Friedenberg," 'We Are Present Here Today for the Purpose of Having a Joint Discussion': The Conditions Requisite for Political Debates," *Journal of the American Forensic Association* 16 (1979): 1–9.
3. Ibid.
4. Ibid., pp. 1–2.
5. Lloyd Grove, "Dukakis Accepts Bush's Limit of 2 Debates," *The Washington Post*, September 7, 1988, p. A6.
6. Ibid.
7. Friedenberg, "Conditions Requisite for Political Debates," p. 2.
8. See Elizabeth Drew, *Election Journal: Political Events of 1987–1988* (New York: William Morrow, 1989).
9. For a discussion of potential repercussions from refusing to debate see Robert V. Friedenberg," 'Selfish Interests,' or the Prerequisites for Political Debate: An Analysis of the 1980 Presidential Debate and Its Implications for Future Campaigns," *Journal of the American Forensic Association* 18 (1981) p. 93.
10. Drew, *Election Journal*, p. 298.
11. Ibid.
12. Friedenberg, "Conditions Requisite for Political Debaters," p. 2.
13. Lloyd Grove, "Dukakis Accepts Bush's Limit of 2 Debates," *Washington Post*, September 7, 1988, p. A6.
14. Ibid.
15. Ibid.
16. Ibid.
17. Ibid.
10. Ibid.
19. Friedenberg, "Conditions Requisite for Political Debates," p. 2.
20. Ibid.
21. *"Transcripts of the 1988 Presidential and Vice Presidential Debates"* (Washington, D.C.: Commission on Presidential Debates, 1988), 70. All subsequent references to and quotations from the debate are to this version.
22. Robert Barnes and R. H. Melton, "In Vice Presidential Debate, the Main Question May Be Quayle," *Washington Post*, October, 5, 1988, p. A17.
23. See E. J. Dionne, Jr., "The Debates: Revival for Democrats," *New York Times*, October 7, 1988, p. B6.
24. Robert Barnes and R. H. Melton, *The Washington Post*, October 5, 1988.
25. Ibid.
26. See E. J. Dionne, Jr., *New York Times*, October 7, 1988.
27. Robert Barnes and R. H. Melton, *The Washington Post*, October 5, 1988.
28. Ibid.
29. E. J. Dionne, Jr., *New York Times*, October 7, 1988.

30. See Sidney Kraus, *Televised Presidential Debates and Public Policy* (Hillsdale, N.J.: Lawrence Erlbaum Associates, 1988).

31. Bentsen had organized a fundraising scheme wherein lobbyists could attend morning sessions with the senator in return for substantial donations. This fundraising effort came to be named the $10,000 Breakfast Club. Given poor publicity Bentsen quickly dismantled and attempted to distance himself from the group.

32. Drew, *Election Journal*, p. 299.

33. Drew, *Election Journal*, p. 263–264.

34. Drew, *Election Journal*, p. 300.

35. Drew, *Election Journal*, p. 300.

36. Drew, *Election Journal*, p. 298.

37. Ibid.

38. Ibid.

39. Ibid.

40. Ibid.

41. "The Vice-Presidential Debate," *The Washington Post*, October 7, 1988, p. A22.

42. Tom Shales, "Bentsen and Quayle: A Single Point of Light," *The Washington Post*, October 6, 1988, p. C1.

43. Ibid.

44. "Vice-Presidential Debate," *The Washington Post*, October 7, 1988.

45. "Who's Watching," *The Washington Post*, October 10, 1988.

46. Ibid.

47. Ibid.

48. Ibid.

49. Ibid.

50. Judith S. Trent and Robert B. Friedenberg, *Political Campaign Communication Principles and Practices* (New York: Praeger Publishers, 1983), p. 264.

51. E. J. Dionne, Jr., *New York Times*, October 7, 1988.

52. Trent and Friedenberg, *Political Campaign Communication*, pp. 265–267.

53. E. J. Dionne, Jr., *New York Times*, October 7, 1988.

54. Ibid.

55. Trent and Friedenberg, *Political Campaign Communication*, p. 270.

56. E. J. Dionne, Jr., *New York Times*, October 7, 1988.

57. Ibid.

58. Ibid.

59. Ibid.

SELECT BIBLIOGRAPHY

Ayres, B. Drummond, Jr. "Flash of Lightning Ignites Long-Becalmed Debate." *New York Times*, p. B19. Brief analysis of the vice presidential debate focusing primarily on Quayle's comment that he was similar to John Kennedy.

Barnes, Robert, and R. H. Melton. "In Vice Presidential Debate, the Main Question May Be Quayle." *The Washington Post*, October 5, 1988, p. A17. Predebate speculation about who would outperform whom during the debate. Includes the expected predictions of a number of prominent republicans and democrats.

Dionne, E. J., Jr. "The Debate: Revival for Democrats," *New York Times*, October 7, 1988, p. B6. Reports a number of reasons why the Democrats benefitted from the vice presidential debate. Provides poll data to back many of his claims as to who won the debate.

Drew, Elizabeth. *Election Journal: Political Events of 1987–1988*. New York: William Morrow, 1989. A detailed account of the 1987–1988 campaign complete with commentary about the impact of many of the events on the outcome of the election.

Grove, Lloyd. "Dukakis Accepts Bush's Limit of 2 Debates." *The Washington Post*, September 7, 1988, p. A6. A report and discussion related to the negotiations that yielded the decision to hold two presidential and one vice presidential debate.

Ifill, Gwen, and Paul Taylor. "Sampling of Viewers Shows Debate Reinforced Doubts on Quayle." *The Washington Post*, October 7, 1988, pp. A14–15. Reports the reactions of a group of voters assembled in New Jersey to view and provide reactions to the vice presidential debate.

Shales, Tom. "Bentsen and Quayle: A Single Point of Light." *The Washington Post*, October 6, 1988, p. C1. Shales provides his analysis of the vice presidential debate complete with an explanation of who he thought won and why. He also includes commentary related to the format and panel of questioners.

The Washington Post. "The Vice-Presidential Debate," October 7, 1988, p. A22. Addresses the inconsistent reactions to the debate and comments on the role played by the audience.

Washington Post. "Who's Watching." October 10, 1988. An analysis of the television debate ratings during the 1988 presidential campaign. Provides some explanation for the audience decline from that of past debates.

Debate Transcript

Janscripts and News Transcripts, Inc. *Transcripts of the 1988 Presidential and Vice Presidential Debates*. Washington, D.C.: Commission on Presidential Debates, 1988.

Chapter 9

Patterns and Trends in National Political Debates: 1960–1988

Robert V. Friedenberg

Each of the preceding chapters has focused on one of the major national political debates held in the United States since 1960. Each chapter addressed such questions as:

1. What factors motivated the candidates to debate?
2. What were the goals of each candidate in debating?
3. What were the rhetorical strategies utilized by each candidate?
4. What were the effects of the debates?

This chapter will also address these and related questions, examining the patterns and trends that have evolved in national political debates since 1960.

CANDIDATE MOTIVATION TO DEBATE

In 1960 the circumstances described by Theodore Windt caused both Senator John F. Kennedy and Vice President Richard Nixon to desire political debates. That combination of circumstances did not materialize again until 1976. As has been discussed in several chapters, a variety of factors contribute to causing candidates to seek political debates. In the years between 1960 and 1976, one or more significant factors were absent.

Although debates were not held in 1964, 1968, and 1972, speculation about them took place, caused no doubt by both the memories of the 1960 presidential debates and the proliferation of political debates in campaigns for lesser offices. In 1976, as illustrated elsewhere in this volume, President Ford and Governor Carter agreed not only to a series of debates, but to allow their vice presidential candidates to debate also. In retrospect, this election seems pivotal in institutionalizing political debates.

The 1976 election was pivotal in the institutionalization of political debates for three reasons. First, it marks the first time that an incumbent president engaged in political debates. Although Ford was an unelected president who was not in the normal defensive posture of an incumbent, defending his own record, he was nevertheless an incumbent. At the conclusion of the 1976 campaign, much of the conventional wisdom concerning an incumbent president debating no longer seemed quite so valid. In the course of his series of debates with Governor Carter, Ford had neither given away state secrets nor been at a handicap by virtue of his knowledge of such secrets. The oft voiced concerns, that an incumbent debating foreign policy might put the nation at risk, seemed far less valid after 1976.

As Goodwin Berquist has illustrated earlier in this volume, Ford issued his challenge to debate Carter when he trailed the Georgia Governor by approximately 30 points in most public opinion polls. Moreover, as Berquist has illustrated, it was the challenger candidate, Carter, whose credibility to serve as president was enhanced as a consequence of these debates. It is this very problem, that by the very act of debating a challenger the incumbent enhances the credibility of the challenger, that traditionally contributed to the reluctance of incumbents to debate. Nevertheless, Ford closed Carter's 30-point lead during the period of time when the debates were being held, eventually losing by only 2 percent of the vote.[1] While the increased credibility that Carter may have gained from the debates no doubt worked to his advantage, clearly it could not have been decisive in the election. For, at the very time that Carter may have been gaining credibility from the debates, Ford was closing the gap between the two men. Hence, the oft voiced concern that incumbents will suffer because the very act of debating their challengers vests those challengers with credibility was diminished by the 1976 campaign. Though Carter's credibility was enhanced by the debates, the importance of that increased credibility seems to have been minimal.

Thus, the first reason that 1976 was a pivotal year in the institutionalization of political debates is that it forced a rethinking about the nature of incumbency and political debates. Two of the principle reasons incumbents avoided political debates did not seem as valid in the wake of the 1976 experience as they had previously. In 1976 an incumbent president debated without any appreciable harm being done to American foreign policy. In 1976 an incumbent president debated and thereby perhaps contributed to his opponent's growth in credibility during the campaign. Nevertheless, Carter's increased credibility did not seem to translate into an increase in his popularity vis-à-vis Ford.

The second reason that 1976 was a pivotal year in the institutionalization of political debates was that a candidate who had debated would seek reelection four years later. In 1960 Kennedy had debated, but his assassination meant that in 1964 Lyndon Johnson was the incumbent. In 1980 Jimmy Carter sought reelection. Kurt Ritter and David Henry have illustrated elsewhere in this volume that having chosen to debate in 1976 made it extremely awkward for Carter to avoid debating in 1980.

As we have seen, several of the reasons typically offered by incumbents to avoid debating became subject to question after Ford's participation in the 1976 debates. Moreover, Carter had himself favored debates when he perceived them to be advantageous in 1976. Consequently, he might well have expected a highly negative public reaction had he avoided debates in 1980. This was especially true in light of his failure to debate during the Democratic primaries, in contrast to challenger Ronald Reagan's willingness to debate both in the Republican primaries and early in the general election against third-party candidate John Anderson. Had Carter failed to debate Ronald Reagan, the public might well have perceived Carter as a weak president unable to defend the poor policies of his administration.

His participation in the 1976 debates contributed to placing Carter under considerable pressure to debate in the 1980 general election. When Carter acquiesced to that pressure, the nation for the first time experienced political debates in two successive presidential elections. Public expectations were being conditioned to expect presidential debates. That conditioning began in earnest in 1976, and by 1980 it had seemingly made it impossible for a man to debate in one election and avoid debating in the next without suffering badly in the public's mind.

The final reason that 1976 was a pivotal year in the institutionalization of political debates is that it marked the introduction of vice presidential debates. In their enthusiasm to aggressively challenge Jimmy Carter who was well ahead of President Ford, the Ford–Dole campaign arranged, shortly after Ford had challenged Carter to debate, for Senator Robert Dole to challenge his counterpart, Senator Walter Mondale, to a debate. As Kevin Sauter has ably illustrated elsewhere in this volume, that decision seems to have been made without fully considering the position in which it placed Senator Dole.

As Ritter and Henry have illustrated, it was not until very late in the 1980 campaign that the two principles, Carter and Reagan, debated, largely due to Carter's reluctance. Hence, it is not surprising that no arrangements were made that year for a vice presidential debate. However, as we have seen elsewhere in this volume, vice presidential debates were important parts of the 1984 and 1988 campaigns. The presence of

Geraldine Ferraro on the Democratic ticket in 1984, as Judith Trent has illustrated, made the 1984 vice presidential debate unique in a variety of ways. As Warren Decker has illustrated in his study of the 1988 vice presidential debate, the many controversies surrounding Senator Danforth Quayle in 1988 made his debate with Senator Lloyd Bentsen one of the most dramatic moments of the 1988 campaign. The precedent for vice presidential debates set in 1976 had been followed in three of our last four national elections.

Thus, because 1976 witnessed an incumbent president breaking with tradition to debate a candidate who debated and who would run again four years later, and the first vice presidential debates, it is a pivotal year in the institutionalization of national political debates.

In 1980 a reluctant Jimmy Carter debated Ronald Reagan. Carter's strategists, particularly Patrick Caddell, felt that debating was not in his best interests. On October 14, as Ritter and Henry note, they considered attempting to sabotage debate negotiations by delivering an ultimatum to Reagan that they felt would force him to reject debating. Yet, ultimately Carter debated Reagan. No doubt public opinion played a major role in the Carter campaign deliberations. October polls showed the public increasingly desirous of a debate and by significant majorities expressing their disapproval of Carter's reluctance to debate. By 1980, the public's expectations that presidential candidates would debate emerged as a significant factor candidates had to consider when determining whether or not to debate.

As Craig Smith and Kathy Smith ably illustrate, in 1984 an incumbent president with an overwhelming lead in both the public opinion polls and the electoral college chose to debate. As early as 1960, Richard Nixon's decision to debate had been based in part on his concern for the negative public reaction that he perceived would result from refusing to debate. That Ronald Reagan debated Walter Mondale in 1984 suggests a shift in the nature of public expectations regarding presidential candidates in the years since 1960. It is entirely fair to suggest, as Smith and Smith do, that by 1984 even an incumbent president with a commanding lead "could not withstand" public pressure to debate. Though, as Smith and Smith also acknowledge, Reagan's "actor-ego" and other factors may have also contributed to his decision to debate; nevertheless the role of public opinion cannot be minimized.

It seems fair to conclude that ever since 1980, public expectations that major contenders for national office will debate have been so great as to constitute a compelling reason for candidates to debate. In 1980 Jimmy Carter recognized that he might well pay a costly political price if he failed to debate. By 1984, that price had become so heavy that, as Smith and Smith have illustrated, incumbent Ronald Reagan by all measures overwhelmingly on his way to reelection never thought seriously about not debating his challenger, Walter Mondale. By 1988 debates had become a part of national campaigns because the public expected them. The candidate who declined to debate could expect to endure intense criticism not only from his opponent but, more importantly, from the public. Neither Bush nor Dukakis was willing to risk that criticism in 1988. Indeed, in 1988, prior to either party officially identifying its nominee, arrangements for debates were being put into place by the Republican and Democratic National Committees. It would appear that the 1988 claim made by the editors of *Time*, that political debates are now inevitable, seems well warranted.[2]

Thus by 1984, if not as early as 1980, the decision to debate was largely out of the candidates' hands. Today public expectations have grown so strong, that it is difficult to imagine candidates for national office refusing to debate. Windt's study reminds us that public expectations were a factor as early as 1960, when they contributed to Nixon's decision to debate. In 1960, 1976, and perhaps in 1980, the decision to debate was largely in the hands of the candidates. By 1984 the public was growing to expect debates of their national candidates. In that year, even though Reagan had few of the self-interests that tend to motivate candidates considering debates, he nevertheless agreed to debate. To do otherwise might have generated enormous negative opinion. It would appear that by 1984 the decision to debate was no longer exclusively in the hands of the two presidential candidates. Rather, debates had become an expected feature of our presidential elections, and the risks involved in rejecting debates had outgrown the risks involved in debating poorly.

In 1988, as Halford Ryan illustrates, though George Bush may not have wanted to debate, public expectations largely took that decision out of his hands. Part of an incumbent administration, Bush held a commanding lead in both the polls and the Electoral College. His motivation to debate was minimal. Though perhaps not possessing the zest for debate that Reagan may have had in 1984, like his predecessor, Bush no doubt felt that the risks involved in rejecting debates exceeded the risks of debating poorly.

Today, as we look toward the 1992 elections, it is difficult to imagine national candidates refusing to debate. The public's expectations that national candidates will debate, which became a significant factor in determining candidate debate participation in 1980 has grown to the point where today it is a compelling factor. Primarily because of public expectations, presidential debates, and to large extent vice presidential debates, have became an institutionalized feature of America's national political campaigns.

CANDIDATE GOALS IN DEBATING

Since no two elections are identical, the candidates goals in political debates necessarily differ. However, since 1960 some have consistently surfaced as candidates and their strategists think about political debates. Those goals can be understood when we realized that they are of two distinct types. Candidates develop issue goals and image goals for debates.

Issue Goals

Issues vary from debate to debate. Today Americans under the age of forty could scarcely identify the islands of Quemoy and Matsu, much less attach significance to them. Yet, in 1960, as Windt illustrates, they were of vital concern not only to Kennedy and Nixon but to the entire nation. Similarly, it is likely that within a few years the few Americans who recognize the name Willie Horton will more likely identify him as the power-hitting Detroit Tiger outfielder of the 1960's than as the convicted murderer of the same name who left jail under the Massachusetts prisoner furlough program, committed heinous crimes in Maryland, and became notorious throughout the nation in 1988 when that furlough program was used by George Bush as an example of Michael Dukakis's soft stand on crime. Nevertheless, though issues vary from debate to debate, most candidates develop similar issue-oriented goals for their debates.

As Myles Martel has observed, "in high level, heavily-financed campaigns involving potentially decisive debates, specific goals designated for targeted audience segments are, naturally, more likely to be well formulated than in lower level campaigns."[3] That is, candidates will target audience segments that are vital for their success, and treat specific issues that are designed to appeal to these targeted audiences. For example, as Windt illustrates, at the time of the first debate, Kennedy realized that he needed far greater support from the black community if he was to win. Moreover, as Windt also illustrated, Kennedy had targeted other constituent groups to whom he wished to appeal during the debate. Similarly as Ritter and Henry observed, in 1980 Carter and his strategist developed a list of three major voting blocs and two secondary voting blocs to whom the president was to aim his remarks. Targeting audiences and treating issues in the debate so as to have maximum impact among targeted audiences is the first issue goal consistently used in national political debates.

The second issue goal commonly used in national political debates is to develop a broad, inclusive, overall theme with which most voters can identify. For example, Smith and Smith illustrated that Ronald Reagan entered his second 1984 debate with Walter Mondale seeking to develop one basic theme: affirming that he was a strong and able president fully in command of a great nation. Americans want and can identify with such leaders. Similarly, as Ryan has illustrated, George Bush's principle goal in the 1988 debates was to juxtapose his values with Dukakis' values, thereby developing his overall theme that he was far more conservative than the liberal Massachusetts governor and hence much more attuned to the goals and aspirations of most Americans. John Kennedy first evidenced this goal in 1960 when he developed his overall theme that though the country was doing well, it was not doing well enough.

A third issue goal that has been used frequently in national political debates is debating not to lose. As Berquist has illustrated in his study of the 1976 debates, Jimmy Carter adhered to abstract statements of principle that voters could interpret according to their own predispositions. Many voters could find satisfaction in Carter's remarks. Few could disagree with his abstract statements of principle. Carter might not have aroused passionate support or won large numbers of converts because his positions were rarely specific. But because voters could see what they wanted to see in his treatment of specific issues, he was equally unlikely to lose large numbers of voters because of his treatment of specific issues.

As many of these essays have illustrated, playing safe, playing not to lose, is a goal common to many national political debaters. Jimmy Carter exemplified that strategy in 1976. Playing not to lose was a Reagan goal in both 1980 and 1984, as well as a Bush goal in 1988. At first glance, this goal seems appropriate only to the candidate who enjoys a comfortable lead. Such a candidate could, understandably, seek to avoid the major controversies that fresh new specific policy proposals might entail.

But why would candidates running behind in the campaign also choose this goal? They too often run not to lose. The answer is a function of the nature of national political debates. These debates have become potentially the most significant sixty to ninety minutes in political campaigns that have become marathon efforts of several years duration. Speaking to the largest audiences they will ever address, in a situation that creates far more drama than virtually any other speaking situation they will ever face, few candidates, even those that are behind, are inclined to take risks. Risks, even for candidates who trail in the election, are simply too great to take in the high-stakes arena of national political debates.

This fear of failure seems to have intensified in the wake of the intense press coverage of President Ford's Eastern European gaffe. As Goodwin Berquist's study illustrates, most Americans might have totally ignored Ford's remark without the intensive press attention it received. Yet such press coverage is a routine aspect of contemporary national political debating. With the entire country watching, in a dramatic situation subject to intensive press coverage, candidates today feel that they simply cannot afford to take risks in national political debates. Their goal is frequently to play safe, to avoid losing.

Image Goals

The second group of candidate goals in national political debates are related to the images that candidates seek to project to the voters.

Through the use of semantic differentials and similar polling instruments, which can be crosstabulated among a wide variety of demographic groups, contemporary political campaigns typically develop an understanding of the images projected by both their candidate and their opponent. National political debates offer candidates an excellent opportunity to effect those images. Debates attract viewers who may have never before observed the candidate seriously. Such viewers have images of the candidates that are often not well formed and are amenable to change. Hence, it is only natural that candidates develop image goals for national political debates. Typically, the image goals of candidates include: (1) creating a more positive image of themselves; (2) creating a more negative image of their opponent; (3) positively modifying existing images of themselves; and (4) negatively modifying existing images of their opponents.

One or more of these four image goals has been among the goals of virtually every contemporary national political debater. Because they are normally less well known and hence have less of a public image, vice presidential candidates tend to place great emphasis on image goals. In his insightful study of the first vice presidential debates, Kevin Sauter observes that in 1976 both Walter Mondale and Robert Dole shared a goal central to their vice presidential debate: impressing the voters with their presidential potential. Because they are often comparatively unknown, vice presidential candidates often have vague or ambiguous images with the public. Hence, they tend to focus their image goals on building a positive image of themselves. This was certainly a major goal of both Mondale and Dole, and as the essays in this volume illustrate, this was perhaps the principle goal of all four subsequent vice presidential debaters.

By the time they engage in presidential debates, most presidential candidates are reasonably well known and already have firmly established images with the public. Consequently, presidential image goals often involve modifying existing images. In 1960 Richard Nixon sought to modify his image as a political hatchetman, or assassin. John Kennedy sought to modify his image as an inexperienced leader. In 1980 Ronald Reagan sought to modify his image as an overly aggressive war-prone hawk. By the second debate in 1984 Reagan had to modify the growing public image of him as a weakened older man not up to the demands of the presidency.

Political observers have been virtually unanimous in noting the growth in negative campaigning, which culminated with the 1988 election.[4] Hence, it should not surprise us to find that recent debates have witnessed more attempts at creating negative opponent images and negatively modifying opponent images than earlier ones.

Recognizing that few people vote for vice presidents, most vice presidential candidates have focused their negative image goals on the opposing presidential candidate. As Sauter illustrates, Dole attempted to portray Carter as vague and indecisive, with three positions on every issue, rather than the decisive leader America needed. As Trent illustrates, Ferraro attempted to portray Reagan as cold and unsympathetic to the poor, rather than the warm-hearted even-handed leader America needed.

Even when vice presidential candidates have focused on the image of their counterparts, they have done so as a means of questioning the wisdom of the opposing presidential candidate. As Trent has observed, Bush's attacks on Ferraro, attempting to portray her as poorly qualified and inexperienced not only serve to contribute to her image but, if accepted by the voter, also negatively modify the image of the man who selected her, Walter Mondale. As Smith and Smith observed, Mondale had trouble shaking the image of being little more than a tool of labor, feminists, and other special interests within the Democratic party. That negative image of Mondale is reinforced if Bush is successful in his goal of portraying Ferraro as inexperienced and ill qualified. In like manner, as Decker has observed in his study of the 1988 vice presidential debate, to the extent that Bentsen could portray Quayle as too shallow to serve as president, he not only helped create a negative image of the Indiana senator, but he negatively modified Bush's image as an experienced reliable leader.

Robert Weiss has argued that in political debates images and issues "intertwine in all manner of convolutions and mutually affect one another in countless ways."[5] Weiss's observation is undeniable, as candidates frequently respond to issues in ways designed to advance one or more of the four image-related goals that characterize contemporary political debates.

RHETORICAL STRATEGIES IN NATIONAL POLITICAL DEBATES

The results of political debates are ultimately a function of what the public perceives. Consequently, national campaigns typically attempt to condition public perceptions of an upcoming debate prior to the event itself. Moreover, they attempt to shape the interpretation of the debate once the event is over. Consequently, any discussion of rhetorical strategies must consider not only those strategies utilized by the debaters during the debate, but also those that are utilized on their behalf both before and after the debate.

Predebate Strategies

Candidates in national political debates have typically engaged in three predebate strategies. The first two involve the candidate. The third is primarily a function of the candidate's staff.

First, the candidate prepares. Just as different individuals prepare differently for speaking situations, so too do candidates prepare differently for debate situations. Nevertheless, it would appear that the most effective political debaters invariably include as part of the preparation process an oral rehearsal of the questions they anticipate. As Windt observed in his study of the 1960 debates, and on the basis of his own experience coaching political debaters, mental rehearsal by candidates is rarely as useful as oral rehearsal. It is probably more than coincidence that candidates who have done well in debates—such as Kennedy in 1960, Reagan in 1980 and Bush in 1988—spent considerable time in oral rehearsals and mock debates. Moreover, it is probably more than coincidence that many of the debaters who had considerable difficulty in their encounters, Nixon in the first 1960 debate, Dole in the 1976 vice presidential debate, and Dukakis in 1988, were all either unable or reluctant to engage in extensive oral rehearsals and mock debates.

Second, candidates recognize that they are debating on television and not simply in an auditorium; those who prepare accordingly, typically fare better. Such preparation consists of considering the many variables involved in a television appearance, and calmly making reasoned decisions to best handle each variable. Those variables include such things as: (1) the type of dress; (2) the type of makeup: (3) when to maintain eye contact with the opponent, the panel, or the camera: (4) whether to sit or stand at the lectern; and (5) how to use what Martel calls "stage tactics" when walking on stage, greeting the opponent, or waiting for the debate to open.[6] National political debates gain their significance from the fact that they are televised. The candidate who ignores that fact does so at his or her own risk. Those candidates who consider the television-related variables of the situation, such as Kennedy in 1960, Mondale in 1976, and Reagan in 1980, are typically at an advantage. Ronald Reagan, who was enormously successful in televised debates, is often perceived to have had the advantage of a first career before the cameras prior to his second political career. While that experience no doubt was an advantage, what is often overlooked or overshadowed by Reagan's prior career is the meticulous concern for the variables of television that characterized his preparation for televised debates.[7]

The final predebate strategy engaged in by many candidates and their staffs is attempting to lower public expectations of their performance. If prior expectations are low, it may not require a strong effort by the candidate to appear to have done well in the debate. Moreover, if the candidate is expected to do poorly, and does in fact do well, it may resound as a major victory whose very unexpectedness gives the entire campaign a big lift. Consequently, because the candidate who is perceived to have won the debate is in part a function of what people expect, many candidates seek to lower public expectations of their debate performance.[8]

The impact of John Kennedy's 1960 first debate "victory" was magnified by the expectation that he would have difficulty in holding his own with Richard Nixon, whose reputation was based in no small part on his television and debating skills, evidenced in his 1952 "Checkers" address and his 1959 "kitchen debates" with Soviet Premier Nikita Khrushchev. Significantly, Kennedy's campaign did not publicly boast of their candidate's highly successful debate in his first successful bid for the Senate. Though key Kennedy strategists were highly sensitive to the many analogies between 1952 and 1960, they did not make a point of publicizing the fact that in 1952 Kennedy had more than held his own while debating another far more experienced Republican, well known for his mastery of foreign affairs, who in 1960 ironically found himself again running against Kennedy, this time as Richard Nixon's vice presidential nominee, Henry Cabot Lodge.[9] In 1960 Kennedy won the expectations game and with it perhaps the debates and the election.

In 1980 President Carter, who had been successful in his 1976 encounter with Gerald Ford, was expected to do well when he debated Ronald Reagan. Many suspected that Reagan was somewhat shallow and might lack the background and knowledge necessary to do well in a political debate. Indeed, as Ritter and Henry point out, the Carter strategy was partially based upon the expectation that Ronald Reagan would make mistakes. Reagan made no serious mistakes, and the impressiveness of his performance was no doubt magnified by his ability to exceed expectations.

Similarly, as Smith and Smith have observed, in 1984 expectations for Walter Mondale in his first debate with Ronald Reagan were low. However, his very success in that debate increased expectations for him in the second debate, while lowering the expectations placed on President Reagan. Mondale's failure to meet those higher expectations in the second debate, coupled with Reagan's ability to meet or exceed the lowered expectations placed on him, tended to magnify both the weaknesses of Mondale's shortcomings and the strengths of Reagan's successes. In sum, from 1960 forward, it has been a common predebate strategy to downplay expectations.

Strategies for the Debate

The strategies used by candidates during the debate itself are largely a function of the specific goals each candidate has set. Consequently, this section will examine debate strategies by suggesting the common strategies utilized by candidates to implement the principle debate goals discussed earlier. Because goals can be well understood by thinking of them as issue goals and image goals, strategies will be treated in a like manner.

Issue-Oriented Debate Strategies

As mentioned earlier, the first common goal of national political debaters is to target specific audiences and then to treat issues that will have maximum impact on the targeted audiences. Typically, this is accomplished through the utilization of several strategies. First, it can be accomplished through the opening and closing statements. The only time during the entire debate over which candidates have complete control are those few moments when they are given the opportunity to make opening and closing remarks. Consequently, these remarks are often planned to appeal directly to targeted audiences. Windt's analysis of the 1960 opening statement of John Kennedy clearly illustrates Kennedy's targeting of blacks, and how he directed much of his opening statement directly to blacks. In 1988, targeting conservative Republicans, especially in the West and South, as well as blue-collar conservative Democrats in the South and Midwest, George Bush chose as the subjects for his concluding remarks in his last debate the issues of crime, conservative judges, the death penalty, taxes, and Reagan's foreign policy initiatives.

A second common strategy utilized to facilitate appeals to target audiences is well illustrated in Decker's analysis of the Quayle–Bentsen debates. Decker found what he characterized as a poor fit between the questions and the answers. In effect, as his study illustrates, Quayle and Bentsen, like many candidates before them, were forcing the questions to fit their answers, rather than fitting their answer to the questions. In this manner, they could treat the issues they wished to treat.

When Quayle was asked about subsidy payments to farmers, he responded by discussing Carter's grain embargo and Dukakis's admiration for Belgium endives as the crop of the future. When Bentsen was asked about the Occupational Safety and Health Administration, he responded by discussing James Watt and the environmental protection practices of the Reagan–Bush Administration. Quayle and Bentsen are simply among the most recent in the long line of candidates who realize that panelists may not ask questions that enable them to address the audiences they had targeted. One approach is to answer the question, addressing the panelists. The other, widely practiced, is to make the question fit the prepared answer, thus addressing the concerns of a targeted constituency. A question about subsidy payments to large farmers and agro-businessmen, a relatively small constituency, thus elicits an answer that relates to small farmers and small-farm-related businessmen, a large targeted constituency for Quayle. A question that addresses concerns of the business community, a largely Republican constituency, thus elicits an answer that relates to environmentalists, a targeted Democratic constituency whose concerns Bentsen wishes to address in the debate.

In like manner in 1980 President Carter's strategists even developed a standard pattern for answering debate questions that facilitated fitting the question to the answers. As Ritter and Henry illustrate, Carter first determined which targeted audience he wished to address with the answer and often began his answer with a preamble announcing his targeted audience. This preamble was his effort to fit the question to his answer. He then provided his prepared answer which was aimed at a specific, targeted audience. In attempting to fit the questions to his answers, as Ritter and Henry note, Carter avoided answering over 40 percent of the questions asked him, though he clearly addressed his principle targeted audiences.

Thus, political debaters attain their goal of treating issues related to specifically targeted audiences first by utilizing the blocks of time over which they have complete control, their opening and closing addresses. Second, they often make the questions fit their answers by ignoring, twisting, or broadly interpreting questions in a manner that enables them to present an answer that strikes the concerns of their targeted audiences.

As has also been discussed earlier, the second issue-oriented goal of many candidates is to develop an overall theme. Two strategies have been frequently utilized to achieve this goal. First, candidates use their opening and closing remarks to express this theme and reaffirm it. Second, candidates consistently use their answers to each specific issue to reinforce this theme.

In 1976, as the essays by Berquist and Sauter point out, Jimmy Carter made leadership the central theme of his campaign and frequently spoke in abstract terms of the high principles of leadership he would bring to office. His vice presidential candidate, Walter Mondale, was portrayed during the campaign as the insider who knew his way around Washington and could get things done. Carter would set the tone and principles upon which the new administration would operate, providing the leadership the nation needed. Mondale would be the nuts-and-bolts man, securing the legislation and programs needed to implement Carter's high-principled leadership. Thus the overall theme of the Democratic candidates was that they would provide new leadership.

Walter Mondale's performance in the 1976 vice presidential debate well illustrates how candidates develop an overall theme. First, Mondale used his opening statement to discuss a variety of problems confronting America, concluding that to solve these problems America "desperately needs new leadership." Like Carter, without providing answers to the problems he cited, he asserted that the Carter–Mondale administration would provide a new generation of leaders to solve America's problems. Thus, Mondale used his opening statement to present a broad and inclusive overall theme that might appeal to most Americans.

Second, Mondale used many of the specific issues raised in the debate to develop and reinforce his leadership theme. Virtually every attack he made on specific Republican policy was accompanied by a reminder of failed Republican leadership on the issue and/or a promise of better Democratic leadership on this issue. Better leadership, Mondale asserted, would handle such problems as high unemployment, the housing crisis, the health crisis, the problem of seniors, and a variety of other difficulties facing the nation. Each issue was utilized as a means of reminding the audience of his overall theme.

Similarly, in 1984, as Smith and Smith illustrate, Reagan encountered difficulty in his first debate when, perhaps in part because of over preparation, he seemed so concerned to provide specific detailed information in response to questions that his principal themes did not come through well. In the second debate Reagan's theme was that he was fully in command of a strengthened America. He emphasized this theme in a variety of ways. He utilized answer after answer to indicate that he was a competent and able chief executive. One might well not agree with the specifics of many of Reagan's responses in the second debate, but, as Smith and Smith have illustrated, one could hardly question that he was fully in command. Response after response served to reinforce this basic overall theme that Reagan sought to convey to the American people.

In like manner, George Bush used his opening statements in the 1988 debates, as well as his closing statements, to develop his basic overall theme: that he was far more conservative than Governor Dukakis and that as a consequence of his conservative bent he was much more understanding of what Americans wanted. Bush strove to illustrate this theme throughout his set speeches, concluding the second debate by observing that there were what he termed "enormous differences" between himself and Michael Dukakis.

Moreover, on answer after answer throughout both debates, Bush strove to reinforce the public perception of those differences. Bush's effort to distinguish his conservative values from Dukakis's liberal values was perhaps at no time more evident than during the first debate when Bush was asked about his constant labeling of Dukakis as "a card-carrying member of the ACLU." Though this exchange prompted one of the rare bursts of emotion Dukakis evidenced in the debates, as Ryan concludes, "Bush scored decisively," for in identifying the ACLU with Dukakis, while simultaneously distancing himself from that organization, Bush dramatically positioned his conservative values against Dukakis's more liberal values.

Thus, the second issue-oriented goal of developing a broad, inclusive, overall theme with which most voters can identify, is typically accomplished by national political debaters through the use of two strategies. First they use their opening and closing remarks to present and reiterate their theme without interruptions or distractions from their opponents or the panel. Second, they consistently return to that theme with many of the specific answers they provide. Specific answers are used throughout the debate to constantly reinforce the overall theme presented in the opening speech.

Again, the third issue-oriented goal of national political debaters is debating not to lose. The fear of failure which is the motivation behind this goal is a pervasive one among national political debaters. Consequently, the three strategies commonly used to avoid a fatal mistake are evident in virtually every national political debate.

The first strategy has already been examined. Debaters will ignore, twist, or broadly interpret questions to facilitate providing the answers they want to provide. This strategy, fitting the question to the answer, has already been discussed as a means of allowing candidates to address targeted audiences. In addition, it also serves to enable the candidate to fall back on frequently delivered past messages that have proven safe and uncontroversial. By fitting the dangerous question to the safe answer, the danger is removed and the candidate escapes the possibility of making a serious error.

The second strategy frequently used when debating not to lose is to avoid specifics. The candidate avoids indicting or praising any specific program or action and speaks in generalities. Berquist characterized Jimmy Carter's overall strategy in 1976 as one of "issue avoidance," observing that Carter adhered to abstract statements of principles which generated little controversy. Carter's overall strategy in 1976 is a common one in the context of political debates, where candidates frequently avoid speaking in specifics, which might offend some voters, and deliberately speak in generalities, which are unlikely to offend.

This tactic was particularly evident in the 1988 Bush–Dukakis debates, as Ryan elucidates throughout his study. Both men, for example, had difficulty in naming three weapons systems they would cut from the military budget. To do so would invite criticism and provoke controversy. No doubt the weapons systems so named would immediately be thoroughly investigated by both the press and their opponents. Perhaps those systems would be found to have value, and their elimination would be viewed as a grave mistake; but both men could safely indict our weapons-procurement procedures. Both could also claim that they were well qualified to make the "tough choices" the next president would confront when the Pentagon budget came under review. Such indictments and claims were vague enough to be safe.

In like fashion, with millions of Americans homeless, neither candidate ventured to provide a specific remedy. To do so would immediately invite a close inspection of their recommendations. How much would the new programs cost? Could the federal government afford it? Would it create a new federal bureaucracy? Would it be yet another income transfer program from the middle class taxpayer to the poor? On and on the questions would no doubt go. So rather than prepare a specific proposal to address a grievous national ill, both men played safe. They both lamented the plight of the homeless. Certainly that was a safe approach. Dukakis did blame the problem primarily on Reagan Administration policies. Bush tried to blame the problem on the high inflation of the Carter years. Given their respective constituencies, such were surely safe approaches.

Bush did suggest that local government and private agencies might help provide a solution, here using his "1,000 points of light" metaphor. This too was a safe response, for certainly few would dispute that local and private groups have a role to play in resolving this problem. But thus far such organizations have clearly been unable to cope with the problem. Bush offered no real proposal. To do so would not be safe.

Dukakis claimed that "we ought to be prepared" to provide funds for the homeless. This too was a safe response for certainly few would dispute the humanitarian and charitable motives of such a claim. But Dukakis was ill prepared to offer a real proposal. He could not indicate how much he wanted to provide. Nor could he indicate the means of providing it. He offered no means of determining who should receive it. His "solution" was a relatively safe compassionate statement of purpose, not a specific policy proposal. Like Bush, Dukakis chose to play safe, to avoid specifics. The avoidance of specifics, which characterized Bush and Dukakis's approach to these two topics, exemplifies the second strategy commonly used by political candidates debating not to lose.

The final strategy widely utilized by candidates who are debating not to lose is to fall back on the stock responses they have utilized throughout the campaign. Because they have been used repeatedly in the past, such responses are safe. They involve no serious risk or gamble. It is impossible to calculate how often a response in a national political debate has been little more than a digest, often an exact repetition, of the candidate's stock response on an issue. The frequent press criticism of debates, that little new information was offered by the candidates, attests to the widespread reliance candidates place on stock responses. Occasionally, as when Quayle repeated his comparison of himself to John Kennedy, stock responses may backfire. The opponent may be ready for them, as was Bentsen. Or they may not work as well with a national audience as they have worked in front of largely sympathetic audiences in the primaries, at the convention, and elsewhere. Nevertheless, for the most part, candidates who are debating not to lose will rely heavily on the tried and true responses of the past. Rarely will they venture forth with new and novel ideas.

As these essays have illustrated, national political debates are high-stakes games. Candidates and their staffs typically fear failure and a principal goal frequently becomes not to lose. This goal frequently prompts the use of three strategies. The first is to fit the question to the answer, enabling candidates to treat the topics they wish to treat, rather than those upon which they are questioned. The second is to avoid specifics. Inherent in responding to questions specifically is the possibility of making a mistake, of committing an error, which in the glare of a national political debate might result in losing the election. Finally, candidates rarely offer ideas in national political debates. Rather, they repeat stock responses that have been frequently used on the campaign trail. When debating not to lose, such responses are particularly inviting.

Image-Oriented Strategies

As indicated earlier, national political debaters typically have one or more of four image-related goals. To attain the two positive goals—creating a positive image of themselves or positively modifying their existing image—or to attain the two negative goals—creating a negative image of their opponent or negatively modifying their opponent's existing image—candidates utilize a variety of strategies.

Many scholars and practitioners have commented upon image-oriented strategies.[10] The essays in this volume illustrate virtually all of the more common image strategies. Positive image goals are commonly implemented by utilizing four strategies. Candidates seeking to create or enhance their own image in a positive fashion typically try to (1) present themselves as vigorous active leaders; (2) foster identification of themselves with national aspirations; (3) foster identification of themselves with the dominant political party/philsosphy; and (4) personify themselves as exemplifying a desirable characteristic.

First, most candidates seek to create an image of themselves as experienced, activist leaders, who take charge of events, rather than as passive leaders who respond to events. In 1980 both Carter and Reagan attempted to portray themselves as activist leaders. Carter constantly reminded the audience of his many actions as president, claiming "I've made thousands of decisions. . . . We initiated. . . . We are now planning." Likewise, Reagan reminded the audience that he was an activist leader, claiming "I have submitted. . . . I have opposed. . . . I stood. . . . As Governor when I. . . . " In 1984, as Smith and Smith note, Reagan utilized language such as that he used in 1980, assumed personal responsibility, and made use of both humor and indignation all in the attempt to portray himself as a competent and commanding leader. In 1988 the relatively unknown Dan Quayle attempted to do this by citing his background in government, claiming that he had more experience than others who had sought the vice presidency, and likened himself to John Kennedy.

Often, as with the cases of Kennedy in 1960, Reagan in 1980, Bush and Ferraro in 1984, and Quayle in 1988, efforts of the candidates to project their leadership qualities may well be the most important aspect of the debate. Kennedy and Reagan had great success in this regard in 1960 and 1980, making themselves dramatically more acceptable to the public as potential presidents. As all three of the studies of vice presidential debates have noted, an important consideration of virtually all of the vice presidential debaters was to portray themselves as strong leaders, able to assume the mantle of the presidency if that occasion arose. In his 1984 vice presidential debate, Bush's use of incumbent strategies, stressing his experience and the accomplishments of the administration in which he served, as well as his use of what Trent characterizes as "controlling" nonverbal behavior facilitated the perception that he was a leader.

In contrast, Quayle had difficulty in projecting leadership. As Decker has observed, Quayle's delivery was marked by repeated hesitancies which did much to deny his claims to be a decisive leader. Moreover, his repeated inabilities to indicate how he would first respond if he had to assume the presidency also worked to undermine claims that he was prepared to lead. Similarly, though she did not suffer from some of the content-associated problems that marked Qualye's efforts at establishing his credentials as a leader, in 1984 Congresswomen Ferraro's attempts to establish herself as a leader were hindered by her subdued, cool delivery and her use of what Trent characterizes as elements of "powerless" speech.

A second strategy candidates commonly use to create a positive image is to identify themselves with the principal aspirations of their audience. As Ritter and Henry have illustrated, Reagan was exceptionally effective at this in 1980, particularly in his closing remarks when he presented himself as the candidate who could best improve the nation's economy. During his closing remarks in the second 1984 debate, with an economy much improved over that of 1980, or at least not as vulnerable to attack since he had been the major player in shaping economic policy for the preceding four years, Reagan chose to identify with our national aspirations to maintain peace and the natural environment.

A third strategy candidates commonly use to create a positive image is to identify themselves with a party or philosophy. Because nationally the Democratic party is far larger than the Republican party, Democratic candidates have consistently attempted to identify themselves with their party. In 1960 Kennedy went out of his way, as Windt illustrates, to mention the major constituent groups of the party in his opening remarks. Throughout the debates he repeatedly identified himself as the heir to the Democratic Party tradition. Both as a vice presidential and a presidential candidate, Mondale stressed his Democratic heritage, as did Carter in both 1976 and 1980. Similarly, Ferraro and Dukakis were not bashful in reminding voters that they were the Democratic Party candidates.

Clearly this strategy is not available to Republican candidates. As Windt notes, in 1960 Richard Nixon actively avoided identifying himself with the Republican party. However, by 1980 Ronald Reagan had coopted the Democratic strategy of identifying with the party by instead identifying with a philosophy. Reagan identified himself with the majority conservative philosophy that encompassed Republicans and disaffected Democrats. In 1988 George Bush similarly identified himself with the majority conservative philosophy. Thus, whether it be identification with party or philosophy, national political debaters commonly will attempt to shape their image through identification.

Finally, debaters will attempt to positively influence their images by suggesting that they personify characteristics or roles that the public seeks in the president. As Berquist notes, Jimmy Carter built his entire 1976 campaign around personifying honesty, trustworthiness, and managerial competency. In 1980, recognizing that many Americans were fearful of his hawkish record and statements, Reagan used his debate with Carter to personify the image of a reasonable, trustworthy, religious, family man. Thus, through the development of leadership styles, identification with party or philosophy, and personification, national political candidates seek to build positive images of themselves.

The principal negative-image strategy is to attack the opponent, attempting to tarnish his or her image. Typically, the attacks focus around the same strategies as the positive-image-building strategies. John Kennedy attacked the leadership of the Eisenhower–Nixon Administration by claiming that America could accomplish more. Jimmy Cater attacked the leadership of the Nixon–Ford Administration by claiming that America deserved more ethical leadership. Ronald Reagan attacked the Carter Administration's ability to lead us out of our of our economic difficulties and to lead the free world.

John Kennedy, and virtually every national Democratic candidate since, has sought to identify his or her opponent as a Republican, presumably a candidate from the party of wealth, who consequently could have no sympathy for the middle and lower classes. By 1976 Robert Dole was indicting Walter Mondale as the "most liberal member of the United States Senate," thereby attacking philosophy rather than party. Ronald Reagan and George Bush continued this Republican assault on their respective opponents by seeking to identify them not as Democrats but as liberals.

Finally, in 1976 Carter attempted to use Watergate and Ford's pardon of Nixon to personify Ford as untrustworthy, and of dubious character. In 1980 Carter sought to personify Reagan as untested and overly hawkish. In 1988 Dukakis sought to personify Bush as a man with a long resume but little accomplishment. His runningmate Bentsen portrayed Quayle as inept, having neither resumé nor accomplishment. Hence, negative attempts to tarnish an opponent's image reflect the same basic strategies as positive attempts to build one's own. Rather than focus constructively on one's self, negative strategies consist primarily of attacking the leadership style, identification, and reputation, of one's opponent.

Postdebate Strategies

National political debaters seemed to have learned much from the second 1976 debate, best remembered because President Ford seemed to be unaware of the Soviet domination of Eastern Europe. Importantly, as Berquist points out, Ford was not perceived to have erred when he first made that remark. It was not until the next day, by which time the media had focused on the remark, that the public began to perceive it as a serious mistake. Consequently, postdebate strategy today focuses on providing a massive and well-coordinated surrogate effort. Prominent spokespersons for the candidate are made readily accessible to the media. Not only do they suggest that their candidate won, but often they have been alerted in advance to stress key themes in their analysis.

Research suggests that audience members often do not make their judgment on the outcome of the debate until they have talked with others and observed media reaction.[11] It is during this crucial period of time, shortly after the debate and through the next few news cycles, that the campaign attempts to effect audience perceptions. Typically this is done by presenting a variety of respected figures each offering a cogent analysis of why the candidate did so well.

DEBATE EFFECTS

Perhaps no other aspect of political debating has been subject to as much study as the effects of political debates. As each of these studies has indicated, after each debate public opinion polls attempt to measure the impact of the debate on voter attitudes. Columnists and political commentators utilize polls and anecdotal evidence to speculate about the consequences of the debate. And, of course, scholars from a variety of disciplines including political science, journalism, and communication utilize a wide variety of methodologies to examine the effects of political debates. That material is widely available and it would serve little point to review it here.[12] Suffice to say that these essays confirm the findings of prior studies that the principal effect of political debates is to reinforce, rather than shift, voter attitudes. Debates do shift some voters. The studies in this volume suggest that they did so most notably in 1960 and 1980. Nevertheless, the principal effect of debates upon voting behavior seems to be to reinforce the existing attitudes of voters.

However, it should be remembered that debates do have a variety of effects in addition to simply helping voters make up their mind. National political debates help to educate our citizens. National political debates help to reinforce our open Democratic heritage. National political debates help to socialize our young people. National political debates help to legitimize the transference of power from one administration to another. All of these positive effects that national political debates have on our society clearly justify the continuation of some from of national political debates.[13]

FORMATS AND JOURNALISTS

Throughout the preceding chapters comments often disparaging have been made about either the format of a particular debate or the questions asked by the journalists. A variety of formats have been used in national political debates. A variety of means have been used in selecting the panelists.[14] Most criticism of debate formats claims they impede the public's learning. Most criticism of the journalists' questions suggest they too impede the public's learning by virtue of their focus on trite or inappropriate issues.

While such criticism has merit, it frequently seems to be offered without consideration of the rhetorical situation that governs political debates. From the standpoint of the two participants, the motivating exigency is not the desire to educate the public. It is the desire to win the election. From the standpoint of panel journalists, the motivating exigency is not the desire to educate the public. It is the desire to create a newsworthy event. Hence, none of the participants in national political debates are highly motivated to provide an educational experience for the viewer.

Given that the basic motivation of each candidate is incompatible with the basic motivation of the opponent, and given that debating not to lose—a major strategy of most national political debaters—is clearly incompatible with the desires of the panelists, it should certainly not surprise us that decisions about formats and panels, as well as a variety of other factors, are made through negotiation.

No one at the negotiating table clearly represents the public. Even sponsoring agencies have motivations and agendas that do not necessarily reflect the public. Moreover, the strongest hands at the bargaining table are held by the candidates, for without them, there is no debate. In recent years, as we have seen, public pressure for debate has largely eliminated the once viable option that national candidates had of refusing to seriously consider debating. However, the details of format and panel selection, as well as a host of other variables such as the number and length of debates, the topics to be covered, and the presence and role of a live audience are all subject to negotiation. Consequently, we must expect that the decisions made on subjects such as these will be compromise decisions, reflecting the best interests of no one, least of all an amorphous public that is poorly represented at the bargaining table. It is unlikely that this situation is liable to change in the foreseeable future.

Moreover, perhaps it should not. Few would argue that the public has been ill served by the eight national political debates chronicled in this study. Democracies are nothing if they are not compromise. Indeed, the virtue of Democracy is that each voice counts. When voices offset one another with opposing attitudes and interests, negotiation and compromise ensues. The results typically do not satisfy everyone perfectly. Rather they reflect the constraints of the situation, typically enabling all participants to derive at least some benefit. To the extent that political debates are a uniquely Democratic experience, why should we expect them to differ?

NOTES

1. See appendix 4 of Martin Schram, *Running for President: A Journal of the Carter Campaign* (New York: Pocket Books, 1977), p. 436.

2. Donald Morrison, ed., *The Winning of the White House: 1988* (New York: Time Books, 1988), p. 258.

3. Myles Martel, *Political Campaign Debates: Images, Strategies, and Tactics* (New York: Longmans, 1983), p. 58.

4. Virtually all accounts stress the unprecedented degree of negative campaigning used in 1988. See for example Morrisson, *The Winning of the White House*, pp. 10–12, 208–209, 215–225, and 260–261.

5. Robert O. Weiss, "The Presidential Debates in Their Political Context: The Issue-Image Interface in the 1980 Campaign," *Speaker and Gavel* 18 (Winter 1981): p. 22.

6. Myles Martel, *Political Campaign Debates: Images, Strategies, and Tactics*, p. 78.

7. See Martel, *Political Campaign Debates*, pp. 78–83, for an exceptionally informed description of Reagan's preparation in this regard.

8. See Goodwin F. Berquist and James L. Golden, "Media Rhetoric, Criticism, and the Public Perception of the 1980 Presidential Debates," *Quarterly Journal of Speech* 67 (May 1981): 125–137, for an insightful analysis of the dynamics among the candidates, their staffs and the media that helps to create public expectations.

9. Kennedy intimates such as his brother Robert and long-time aid Kenneth O'Donnell felt that the 1960 debates were, in many respects, a "rerun" of Kennedy's 1952 debate with Lodge. See Kenneth P. O'Donnell and David F. Powers, *Johnny, We Hardly Knew Ye* (New York: Pocket Books, 1973), pp. 103–104, 243–244. Inexplicably, I am aware of no evidence that Lodge forewarned Nixon about Kennedy's debating skills.

10. Two of the better such discussions are those of Dan Nimmo, *Popular Images of Politics* (Englewood Cliffs, N.J.: Prentice Hall, 1974), pp. 102–104; and Martel, *Political Campaign Debates*, pp. 62–75.

11. Frederick T. Steeper, "Public Response to Gerald Ford's Statements on Eastern Europe in the Second Debate," in *The Presidential Debates: Media, Electoral, and Policy Perspectives*, eds. George F. Bishop, Robert G. Meadow, and Marilyn Jackson-Beeck (New York: Praeger Publishers, 1978), p. 101. Roger Desmond and Thomas Donohue, "The Role of the 1976 Televised Presidential Debates in the Political Socialization of Adolescents," *Communication Quarterly* 29 (Summer, 1981): 306–308; and George A. Barnett, "A Multidimensional Analysis of the 1976 Presidential Campaign," *Communication Quarterly* 29 (Summer 1981): 156–165.

12. Many of the books and articles cited in the individual chapter bibliographies discuss the effects of a specific debate. For overviews of the effects of political debating, see Judith S. Trent and Robert V. Friedenberg, *Political Campaign Communication: Principles and Practices* (New York: Praeger Publishers, 1983), pp. 263–273; and Sidney Kraus, *Televised Presidential Debates and Public Policy* (Hillsdale, N.J.: Lawrence Erlbaum Associates, 1988), pp. 103–134.

13. This is not to suggest that the flaws currently associated with national political debate cannot be corrected. For cogent suggestions about improving future debates, see Kathleen Hall Jamieson and David S. Birdsell, *Presidential Debates: The Challenge of Creating an Informed Electorate* (New York: Oxford University Press, 1988), pp. 194–221. Also see Kraus, *Televised Presidential Debates and Public Policy*, pp. 135–160.

14. See Martel, *Political Campaign Debates*, pp. 126–132 for a discussion of the selection process and the role of panelists in political debates. Additionally, see pp. 116–150 of Martel for an exceedingly thorough discussion of debate formats. Kraus also presents highly informed discussions of debate formats, as well as the selection and role of panelists. See Kraus, *Televised Presidential Debates and Public Policy*, pp. 29–72 and 135–160.

Select Bibliography on Political Campaign Debating

At the conclusion of each chapter of this volume the reader can find a select annotated bibliography that focuses on the specific debate examined in that chapter. Additionally, the chapter bibliographies provide the reader with sources for debate transcripts and audio/video recordings. Thus, this bibliography excludes all works that focus exclusively or heavily on one debate or a highly limited number of debates. Rather it presents works that treat the genre of political debating, particularly at the presidential level. Hence this bibliography focuses on works treating questions and themes applicable to a wide variety of political debates rather than a single debate or series of debates.

BOOKS

Jamieson, Kathleen Hall, and David S. Birdsell. *Presidential Debates: The Challenge of Creating an Informed Electorate*. New York: Oxford University Press, 1988. The first three chapters constitute the best short history of American political debating prior to the broadcast age. The remainder of this excellent study focuses on the impact of broadcasting on political debates, the problems broadcasting has created, and suggestions for future political debates.

Kraus, Sidney. *Televised Presidential Debates and Public Policy*. Hillsdale, N.J.: Lawrence Erlbaum Associates Publishers, 1988. An excellent study treating such topics as the role of television in presidential elections, formats for televised debates, media coverage of debates, and the impact of televised debates. Concludes with a discussion of policy options for future presidential debates.

Martel, Myles. *Political Campaign Debates: Images, Strategies, and Tactics*. New York: Longmans, 1983. The best examination of political debate strategies available. Martel's study is based heavily on his own experiences as a political debate coach to a variety of candidates and his interviews with over one hundred candidates, advisors, network officials, journalists, and others.

Mitchell, Lee D. *With the Nation Watching*. Lexington, Mass: Lexington Books, 1979. This report of the Twentieth Century Fund Task Force on Presidential Debates presents specific policy recommendations to institutionalize presidential debates. The recommendations are placed in perspective by an extensive background paper in which Mitchell treats such topics as the history, impact, formats, and financing of debates.

Ranney, Austin, ed. *The Past and Future of Presidential Debates*. Washington D.C.: American Enterprise Institute for Public Policy Research, 1979. A scholarly study that attempts to place political debates in the context of a democratic society.

Swerdlow, Joel L. *Beyond Debate: A Paper on Televised Presidential Debates*. New York: Twentieth Century Fund, 1984. Arguing that debates should become an institutionalized feature of American campaigning, Swerdlow addresses such topics as debate formats, the role of non-major-party candidates, and candidate willingness to debate.

Swerdlow, Joel L., ed. *Presidential Debates: 1988 and Beyond*. Washington D.C.: Congressional Quarterly Press, 1988. The editor's history of political debates as well as survey and other data on political debates dating back to 1948 makes this a valuable reference work for those interested in political debates. Sponsored by the League of Women Voters, this volume also features a selection of six essays treating the sponsorship of political debates.

ARTICLES AND CHAPTERS

Chaffee, Steven H. "Approaches of U.S. Scholars to the Study of Televised Political Debates." *Political Communication Review* 4 (1979): 19–33. Examines research questions and methods used in the academic study of political debates.

Drucker, Susan J., and Janice Platt Hunold. "The Debating Game." *Critical Studies in Mass Communication* 4 (1987): 202–207 A disturbing and thought-provoking critique that argues that in substance, style, and audience perception, political debates are already highly analogous to television game shows and likely to move even more toward entertaining television rather than bona fide news events.

Friedenberg, Robert V. " 'Selfish Interests,' Or the Prerequisites for Political Debate: An Analysis of the 1980 Presidential Debate and Its Implications for Future Campaigns." *Journal of the American Forensics Association* 18 (1981): 91–98. Extends the author's prior examination of candidate motivation to debate and suggests that the institutionalization of presidential debates is near at hand.

Friedenberg, Robert V. " 'We Are Present Here Today for the Purpose of Having a Joint Discussion': The Conditions Requisite for Political Debates." *Journal of the American Forensics Association* 16 (1979): 1–9. Claims that candidates agree to debate out of self-interest and posits six conditions necessary for candidates to agree to debate.

Lang, Gladys Engel. "Still Seeking Answers." *Critical Studies in Mass Communication* 4 (1987): 211–213. Finds that in addition to their potential effect on voting decisions, political debates may have positive effects on the conduct of political campaigns, the ease presidents have in governing, and the public image of politics. Lang also notes that debates may foster citizens to behave as spectators of, rather than participants in, political events.

Meadow, Robert G. "A Speech by Any Other Name." *Critical Studies in Mass Communication* 4 (1987): 207–210. Argues that debates do not contribute to the election dialogue and claims that the pressure for political debates comes from the very group that benefits from debates: journalists.

Ritter, Kurt, and Susan A. Hellweg. "Televised Presidential Primary Debates: A New National Forum for Political Debating." *Journal of the American Forensic Association* 23 (1986): 1–14. An insightful examination of the history and growth in importance of televised presidential primary debates 1956–1984.

Trent, Judith S., and Robert V. Friedenberg. "Debates in Political Campaigns," chapter 6 of *Political Campaign Communication*. New York: Praeger Publishers, 1983, pp. 233–273. An overview of the history, strategies, and effects of political debates.

Vancil, David L., and Sue D. Pendell. "Winning Presidential Debates: An Analysis of Criteria Influencing Audience Response." *The Western Journal of Speech Communication* 48 (Winter 1984): pp. 62–74. The authors argue that at least six criteria exist that audiences use to determine who won a presidential debate. This is an excellent short analysis of the complexity involved in determining political debate winners.

DEBATE TRANSCRIPTS AND VIDEOTAPES

Each of the individual chapter bibliographies includes sources for the transcripts of the debates and in some instance sources for videotapes of the debates. Additionally, it should be noted that the best single depository for videotapes of national political debates is the Vanderbilt Television News Archive, Vanderbilt University Library, Vanderbilt University, Nashville, Tennessee, 37240.

Index

About the Contributors

GOODWIN BERQUIST (Ph.D., Pennsylvania State University) is Professor Emeritus of Communication and Journalism at the Ohio State University. He pursues his continuing interests in communication, politics, and history from his home at Washington Island, Wisconsin.

WARREN D. DECKER (Ph.D., Temple University) is Associate Professor of Communication and Director of Debate at George Mason University. He has been actively involved in the study and evaluation of presidential and vice presidential campaign debating for several years.

ROBERT V. FRIEDENBERG (Ph.D., Temple University) is Professor of Communications at Miami (Ohio) University. He has approximately seventy publications in a wide variety of scholarly and popular journals. He is a former communications consultant with the Republican National Committee and has coached a variety of candidates for political debates. He is coauthor with Judith S. Trent of *Political Campaign Communication: Principles and Practices* (Praeger, 1983). His most recent book is *Hear O Israel: The History of American Jewish Preaching, 1654–1970*. He is currently combining his interests in political and religious rhetoric in a rhetorical biography, *Theodore Roosevelt: Spokesman for Militant Decency*, for Greenwood Press.

DAVID HENRY (Ph.D., Indiana University) is a Professor of Speech Communication at California Polytechnic State University, San Luis Obispo, California, where he teaches rhetorical theory and criticism, public discourse, and persuasion. His essays and reviews on political communication, social movements, criticism, and public address have appeared in the *Quarterly Journal of Speech, Communication Education, Southern Speech Communication Journal*, and several anthologies. He is coauthoring, with Kurt Ritter, a book on Ronald Reagan for Greenwood Press's series on Great American Orators. Current projects include a book on science, technology, and political advocacy during the Cold War, and the critical study of selected texts from the 1960s student movement. He has been appointed an associate editor of the *Quarterly Journal of Speech* for 1990–1993.

KURT RITTER (Ph.D., Indiana University) is Associate Professor and Department Head in the Department of Speech Communication and Theatre Arts at Texas A&M University. His research, which focuses on political communication, has been recognized with the Karl R. Wallace Memorial Award, the Winans-Wichelns Award for Distinguished Scholarship in Rhetoric and Public Address, and the B. Aubrey Fisher Memorial Award. Ritter and David Henry are currently writing a book with the tentative title, *Ronald Reagan: The Great Communicator*, which is under contract with Greenwood Press for its series on Great American Orators.

HALFORD ROSS RYAN (Ph.D., University of Illinois) is Professor of Public Speaking and Director of Forensics at Washington and Lee University. He teaches courses in argumentation and debate, American public address, and the rhetorical presidency. He has authored or edited seven books, two of which are *Oratorical Encounters: Selected Studies and Sources of Twentieth-Century Political Accusations and Apologias* and *Franklin D. Roosevelt's Rhetorical Presidency*.

KEVIN SAUTER (Ph.D., Pennsylvania State University) is an Associate Professor in the Department of Communication, Telecommunications and Theater at the College of St. Thomas, in St. Paul, Minnesota. His research interests include the rhetoric of Hubert H. Humphrey and the qualitative analysis of media. He teaches courses in persuasion, media criticism, and video production.

CRAIG ALLEN SMITH (Ph.D., Purdue University) is Associate Professor and Director of Graduate Studies in the Department of Speech Communication at the University of North Carolina at Chapel Hill. His books include *Political Communication, Persuasion and Social Movements* with Charles J. Stewart and Robert E. Denton, and *The President and the Public: Rhetoric and National Leadership* with Kathy B. Smith. Other works have appeared in the second edition of *The Handbook of Political Communication* edited by Dan Nimmo and David Swanson; *Oratorical Encounters* edited by Halford Ross Ryan; *American Orators of the Twentieth Century* edited by Bernard Duffy and Halford Ross Ryan; *Essays in Pres-*

idential Rhetoric, second edition, edited by Theodore Otto Windt and Beth Ingold; *Presidential Studies Quarterly; Communication Quarterly; Southern Speech Communication;* and the *Central States Speech Journal.*

KATHY B. SMITH (Ph.D., Purdue University) is Associate Professor in the Department of Politics at Wake Forest University. Her publications include *The President and the Public: Rhetoric and National Leadership* with Craig Allen Smith; a chapter in the second edition of *The Handbook of Political Communication* edited by Dan Nimmo and David Swanson; and a chapter in *The Presidency in Transition,* edited by James Pfiffner and R. Gordon Hoxie. Other works have appeared in *Presidential Studies Quarterly; Communication Quarterly; News for Teachers of Political Science;* and the *Southeastern Political Review;* with reviews in *American Political Science Review; Journal of Politics;* and *The Quarterly Journal of Speech.*

JUDITH S. TRENT (Ph.D., University of Michigan) is Professor of Communication and Associate Vice President for Graduate Studies and Research at the University of Cincinnati. She has published widely in communication journals and is coauthor with Robert V. Friedenberg of *Political Campaign Communication: Principles and Practices.* In addition to her study of presidential campaign communication, she has frequently examined the role and strategies of women in elective politics.

THEODORE OTTO WINDT, JR. (Ph.D., Ohio State University) is Associate Professor of Political Rhetoric at the University of Pittsburgh. He teaches courses in presidential rhetoric from Kennedy to Nixon and from Nixon to Reagan. He is one of the Chancellor's Distinguished Teachers. He has edited two books on Presidential rhetoric and is the author of the forthcoming book *Presidents and Protestors: Political Rhetoric in the Nineteen Sixties.* In addition to his academic duties, Dr. Windt is a political commentator on television station KDKA-TV, and a professional political and public affairs consultant.